A Quick Index to Twenty Essential Questio...

Gr...

CALLISON

LONDON RESEARCH CENTER
T 44-0-203-008-4985   www.callison.com

BUILDING TYPE BASICS FOR

office buildings

BUILDING TYPE BASICS FOR

office buildings

Stephen A. Kliment, Series Founder and Editor

A. EUGENE KOHN AND PAUL KATZ

Kohn Pedersen Fox

With chapters by LESLIE ROBERTSON and SAW-TEEN SEE,
NORMAN KURTZ, JOHN VAN DEUSEN, DEBRA LEHMAN-SMITH,
JOSEPH KHOURY, JOHN McCORMICK, and FRANKLIN BECKER

JOHN WILEY & SONS, INC.

Wiley also publishes its books in a variety of electronic formats. Some content that appears in print may not be available in electronic books. For more information about Wiley products, visit our web site at www.wiley.com.

Interior design and layout: Thumb Print and Jeff Baker.

Library of Congress Cataloging-in-Publication Data:

Kohn, A. Eugene, 1930-
  Building type basics for office buildings / by A. Eugene Kohn and Paul Katz.
    p. cm.
  ISBN 0-471-38923-4 (alk. paper)
  1. Office buildings—Design and construction. 2. Office buildings—Planning. I. Katz, Paul.
II. Title.
  NA6230 .K64 2002
  725'.23--dc21

                                            2002004755

Printed in the United States of America.

10 9 8 7 6 5 4 3

CONTENTS

CONTENTS

PREFACE

STEPHEN A. KLIMENT *Series Founder and Editor*

Despite the apparent simplicity suggested by its standardized floor areas, the modern office is one of the most complex of building types to finance, plan, program, and design. More than most other building types, it must not only accommodate the rapidly evolving demands of workers, it has to combine in a single building the often conflicting demands of structure; heating, ventilation, and air-conditioning (HVAC); communications; electrical systems; plumbing; space division; and safety and security.

Other concerns unique to offices are the building's prominence in the landscape or cityscape and the image it presents to occupants and the public. And before a line is even drawn, an owner or developer must see eye to eye with legions of lawyers, accountants, real estate consultants, bankers, and city officials on the feasibility of the project. Once the office building is occupied, it is subject to a continuous pattern of alteration and renovation, the ease or difficulty of which often depends on the caliber of flexibility the architect incorporated into the design.

This volume in the Wiley "Building Type Basics" series provides answers, guidelines, and cautionary advice, as well as lessons to be learned from actual completed buildings, in order to steer architects and their specialty consultants, developers, members of corporate boards, and financial institutions toward making sound decisions early in the planning cycle. *Office Buildings* is, like the other volumes published in the Wiley series to date, not a lavish coffee-table book heavy on color photography and weak on usable content. Rather, it contains practical information that architects, their clients, and consultants require in their work, especially in the crucial early phases of a project.

Like the other volumes in the series, *Office Buildings* is tightly organized for ease of use. The template for the volume is a set of twenty questions most commonly asked about a building type in the early phases of its design. A complete listing of these questions is printed on the inside of the front and back covers of this volume. The list also serves as an index to the pages that provide answers to each question. The fact-filled text is supplemented by diagrams, drawings, lists, and illustrations.

Students at architecture schools will also find the volume useful, as a kind of Cliffs Notes, to get a head start on an assigned studio problem.

Office Buildings is made up of three parts.

Part I comprises an introductory essay by A. Eugene Kohn, partner of Kohn Pedersen Fox (KPF), in which Kohn provides a historical perspective for the office building that extends to this day. Paul Katz, also a KPF partner, then defines the planning and architectural basics of office building design, including such issues as floor area measurement (categories), core configuration, module selection, floor-to-floor height, and coordination of design, structure, HVAC, space division, and other systems. Part I also discusses such intangible influences as building location, markets, "exit strategies" (a corporate ownership concept that anticipates an eventual move out of a building), adaptability, and long-term value of an investment.

Part II offers contributions from key members of a consultant team — Leslie Robertson and Saw-Teen See on structural systems, Norman Kurtz on MEP systems, Debra Lehman-Smith on interiors, Joseph Khoury on curtain wall design, and John van Deusen on vertical transportation. Franklin Becker contributes an essay on the workplace as idea, addressing such matters as workplace attitudes, organizational ecology, options, and values.

Part III is a detailed casebook of nine completed office projects. The buildings featured as case studies were chosen to cover a total range of office building configurations, types of ownership, and locations. High-rise, mid-rise, and low-rise structures are included, as well as owner-occupied and investment buildings, domestic and overseas locations, and offices as part of multiple-use complexes. Each case study includes photographs, floor plans, sections, details, and an explanatory, analytical text.

This volume was to go into production during the momentous and tragic week when the World Trade Center was destroyed and the Pentagon damaged. Although the manuscript contained material on safety and security, the authors decided that the subject called for more detailed treatment. Accordingly, the chapter on structures was revised. In addition, John McCormick, a code expert and authority on building security, has written a chapter on this crucial topic. Along with a review of fire protection and detection issues and life safety concepts, especially as they bear on high-density occupancy venues such as high-rise buildings, John McCormick takes up the critical issue of penetration of fire-rated construction.

I hope you find this volume both helpful and inspiring.

ACKNOWLEDGMENTS

The book is based on a course, "The Design of Office Buildings," taught at the Harvard Graduate School of Design as part of the school's professional development courses in spring and summer.

For a book of such broad scope, there are necessarily many who make essential contributions—of their time, ideas, writing, editing, and administrative skills.

I would therefore like to thank all the authors, whose chapters together provide a complete understanding of the design of an office building.

John Morris Dixon deserves tremendous gratitude for his editing, for his contributions to the organization and the graphic content of the book, for writing the case studies, for keeping all the authors on track, and for keeping the book concise.

The idea for this book originated with Stephen Kliment, in his role as editor of Wiley's "Building Type Basics" series. He participated in our strategy sessions for the book, reviewed all materials, was an important critic, and deserves a great deal of thanks and credit.

We would also like to recognize — for their many efforts in relation to preparing drawings, organizing photographs, making valuable suggestions, and performing many other tasks — from the New York office of KPF, Tomas Alvarez, Eric Howeler, Doug Hocking, Duncan Reid, Roger Robison, Rob Whitlock, Ian Luna, Thomas Tsang, and, from KPF London, our partner Lee Polisano and Marjorie Rodney-Goodin.

We are grateful as well for the efforts of Kelly Dougherty and Denise De Lorey of LSM, Diane Peck of Flack & Kurtz, and Chato Loanzon of Joe Khoury's office.

The case study project examined in the course and featured in this book is the Headquarters of Gannett/USA Today, designed by KPF. We had an exceptional client throughout the design and construction. In addition, during the course and for the book, we were fortunate to have the enthusiasm and input of Nancy Hauser of Gannett.

The Gerald Hines office of Washington, D.C., was the development manager for this wonderful project, and we recognize Greg Spivey of Hines for his key contributions to the project's success, to the course, and to the case study.

Administrative support from Delva Cameron and Nicola Barry was invaluable in so many ways, and we thank them.

Thanks are also due to the editorial and production staff at John Wiley & Sons, above all Amanda Miller, executive editor, David Sassian, associate managing editor, and Nyshie Perkinson, editorial program assistant, for their commitment to quality.

Finally, Harvard University's Graduate School of Design made the course possible and is very supportive of this book. We recognize Corlette McCoy, director, executive education, and Margaret Moore de Chicojay, program manager.

Thank you.

A. Eugene Kohn

PART I

ARCHITECTURAL ISSUES

© Barbara Karant.

CHAPTER 1
INTRODUCTION

A. EUGENE KOHN *Kohn Pedersen Fox*

When we say "office building," we are talking about a great variety of structures. We may mean anything from a two-story suburban building to a 100-story urban high-rise. The building we have in mind may be constructed purely on speculation, to house whatever tenants choose to locate in it, or it may be built to suit the specific needs of a corporate headquarters.

Whatever its size or type, the office building is a complex building type and is affected by many forces. Its most important role is as a home for the people who work there—not for all of them eight hours a day, but perhaps four or possibly twelve hours—and its design greatly affects their performance.

The number of individuals and firms involved in the design of a speculative or corporate office building is significant. Obviously, there are the architects and their many consultants: the structural, mechanical, electrical, plumbing, civil, acoustical, special lighting, parking, and food service consultants, to name a few. Preservationists are added to the team when historic buildings are affected by or incorporated into the design. Building owners rely on real estate brokers (for tenants), financial advisers, and the bankers and investors who provide the money for the project. They also have their consultants, who may include construction managers, real estate attorneys, accountants, public relations advisers, and others. These people influence the design in various ways, many of them dealing with the community and the approval process and—of utmost importance for investment buildings—attracting tenants.

To arrive at a superior design, it is essential to work with the client organization and its consultants. It is crucial not to settle too quickly on a scheme. The most effective way to gain the client's confidence is to listen. When the client team is convinced that the architect has listened and grasped its objectives, there is a much greater likelihood that the architect can raise the sights for the project by generating alternatives, overcoming caution, improving design quality, and, in some cases, even increasing the budget.

◀ DG Bank Headquarters, Frankfurt, Germany, 1993, by Kohn Pedersen Fox Associates. A mix of uses that includes offices, apartments, and a winter garden is expressed in a variety of volumes related in scale to the varied neighborhoods around the building. Photo © Dennis Gibert/KPF.

▼ JR Central Towers, Nagoya, Japan, 1999, by Kohn Pedersen Fox Associates. A mixed-use complex at a high-speed railroad station includes offices and a hotel in complementary towers rising from a retail podium, all of the parts linked by a fifteenth-floor "sky street." Courtesy Taisei Corporation/KPF.

LOCATION AND DESIGN

Office building design is affected in many ways by location—by whether its site is in a rural, suburban, or urban area and by local zoning and building codes. In terms of geographic distinctions, there are relatively minor differences within the United States and Canada due to local codes and cultures. The principal differences are in mechanical design, responding to North America's sharp variations in climate.

Differences in design criteria for other countries can be dramatic. In the last ten years of office development, it seems that the United States has been concerned with workplace efficiency, productivity, and communication technology; Europe with energy conservation, environmental concerns, and employee access to natural light and air; and Asia with filling a great demand for space, as well as the symbolic importance of tall buildings.

In Germany, Holland, and Belgium, for example, every worker must be near a window, so the maximum allowable distance from the core to the exterior wall is 25 ft (8 m). In the United States office floor areas began expanding after World War II, as air-conditioning and improved artificial lighting became the norm. Today American and Asian office floors often have dimensions of 55 ft (17 m) from core to exterior wall, with even greater dimensions for trading floors.

In Europe natural ventilation is not only desired but required. The cost of energy is approximately six times the cost in the United States and has a significant impact on the design of mechanical systems, exterior walls (double walls, for instance), and other components, justifying higher first costs through subsequent savings in operating costs.

While U.S. office buildings have become increasingly dependent on air-conditioning and artificial lighting systems, these systems have been improved in their performance world-wide. Other significant technical advances have occurred in recent decades, such as the greater strength of structural steel and concrete, new high-performance glass, and improved curtain wall design. We now have high-speed elevators capable of traveling 1600 ft per minute and sophisticated control systems that provide superior service. The most recent system, whereby passengers select their floors before entering the cab, makes the most efficient use yet of the elevator cabs and the space they take up in a building, such as Miconic X.

INTERIOR LAYOUTS

Floor layouts within the typical North American office building have also been evolving. In the 1960s the typical office building was composed primarily of private offices. The status of the individual occupying an office was reflected by the size of the room (number of window modules wide) and its furnishings. Today most U.S. companies—and to varying extents those all over the world—use predominantly an open plan. In IBM's new Armonk headquarters (see pages 18–19) only 20 percent of the employees are in private offices.

Today conventional open-office layouts are giving way to innovative concepts such as *hoteling*, whereby staff members have personal lockers and may be assigned to a different workstation each day. This "nonterritorial" concept allows for some staff to be working in lounges or even in cafeterias. And there is a
(continued on page 8)

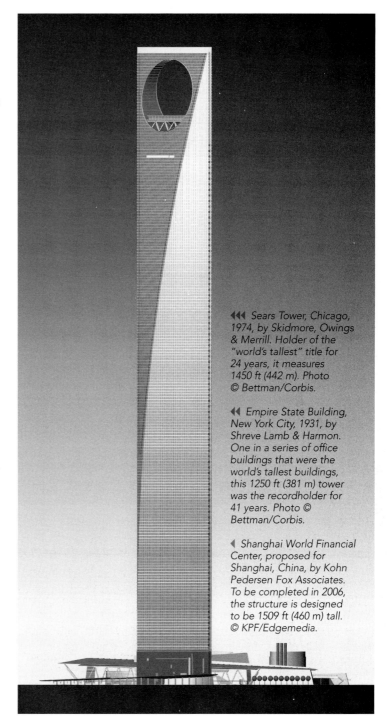

◀◀◀ *Sears Tower, Chicago, 1974, by Skidmore, Owings & Merrill. Holder of the "world's tallest" title for 24 years, it measures 1450 ft (442 m). Photo © Bettman/Corbis.*

◀◀ *Empire State Building, New York City, 1931, by Shreve Lamb & Harmon. One in a series of office buildings that were the world's tallest buildings, this 1250 ft (381 m) tower was the recordholder for 41 years. Photo © Bettman/Corbis.*

◀ *Shanghai World Financial Center, proposed for Shanghai, China, by Kohn Pedersen Fox Associates. To be completed in 2006, the structure is designed to be 1509 ft (460 m) tall. © KPF/Edgemedia.*

AAL Headquarters

In the early 1970s, Bill Pedersen as senior designer and I as partner in charge for John Carl Warnecke designed the Aid Association for Lutherans (AAL) headquarters in Appleton, Wisconsin. The client, with Ware Travelstead acting as its programmer and representative, inspired a unique building. An entirely open-plan office landscape, featuring unique workstations designed by George Nelson, is interspersed with trees and landscape in the numerous atrium courtyards. Raised floors used throughout serve the interior distribution of communication and power lines, enhancing a very flexible scheme.

The design features a roof of more than 250,000 sq ft that is totally skylighted, providing daylight to all the workers in the partially one-story double-height space, partially two-story structure. This lighting concept is democratic, not limiting the enjoyment of natural light to those located along the window wall.

The building is planned for growth by extending the work space, like the branches of a tree, at the end of each linear module. The work space and amenities of AAL are gathered around a circular landscaped garden that gives a sense of place and of community. Amenities include a choice of several eating experiences and menus, and recreation areas including pool and card tables, movies, and other features, as well as physical workout areas.

Since the completion of this building, many corporate headquarters have been built, but except for more advanced communications technology and possible mechanical systems, there have been few advances beyond it. In fact, many companies and architects are now discovering the virtues of high ceilings, atriums, daylight, and the introduction of landscaping in interiors, all found in the 1970s at AAL. –A.E.K.

▲ Aid Association for Lutherans. Office spaces are punctuated by garden courts and illuminated with daylight dispersed by cylindrical diffusers. Photo © KPF/Elliot Fine.

◀ Aid Association for Lutherans, Appleton, Wisconsin, 1974, by John Carl Warnecke & Associates. The circular geometry of the cafeteria, seen in the central court as well, suggests the unity of the workforce in an extensive low-rise building. Photo © KPF/Elliot Fine.

▶ Aid Association for Lutherans. The floor plan shows work spaces under linear skylights, surrounding a central court, with shared facilities, including the half-circular cafeteria, at one corner. Courtesy KPF.

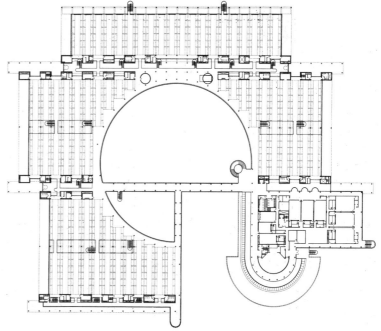

World Trade Center, New York City, 1972–2001, by Minoru Yamasaki and Emery Roth & Sons. The world's tallest for two years, one of these towers measured 1368 ft (417 m), and its "twin" was 6 ft (2 m) shorter. Photo © Jeremy Horner/Corbis.

(continued from page 5)
current move, led by many of the high-tech firms, to create more democratic, loftlike, technologically advanced work environments, typically with ceiling heights of 12–14 ft.

The most significant current development in the United States is the increased emphasis on the employee's environment, accompanied by and partly in response to advancing computer and communications technology. There has been a realization that the work environment is critical to the performance of companies, how they communicate ideas, and how they can attract the best talent. As salaries become more competitive, the type and quality of the workspace becomes a more important part of recruiting and retaining an excellent staff.

Increasingly, a corporation or user can decide what kind of environment it wants to create for its culture. Low-rise buildings are normally adapted better to corporate headquarters. In such buildings there is a possibility of visually interconnecting floors through the use of atriums and the potential to have high ceilings without the significant cost penalty imposed by increasing the height of many floors in a high-rise.

All sorts of amenities, including child care, fitness centers, convenience retail stores, a variety of coffee bars and dining facilities, and even concierge services, can be program components of a corporate office building. The building can become a small city with a number of neighborhoods, indoor "streets" with amenities, and a major enclosed or exterior space creating a sense of place—a focal point.

IMPACT OF MARKET FORCES

One of the strongest forces in the design of an office building is the real estate market. The effect is most apparent on investment buildings, but the market strongly affects corporations as well, in their decisions to move, consolidate dispersed offices, renovate, build anew, sell, and so forth. Any proposal for an office building is driven by a user type, such as investment banks, professional firms, or high-tech companies. The needs of these users normally dictate the floor size and the marketable location of the building.

Real estate developers respond to market demand, and they are vulnerable when the supply coming on the market exceeds the demand or follows after the demand has weakened. This is what happened in most large American cities in the late 1980s, when many of the buildings constructed were delayed responses to demand that was fading. It took about ten years, until the late 1990s, before demand for office space rose enough to justify construction of new office buildings in our major cities.

The first wave of investment buildings built after a deep and long recession is usually conservative in approach, with cost the key concern, because of the uncertainty of the real estate market and the caution of lenders. If the economy stays strong, developers will increasingly want to build something special to compete in an active and competitive marketplace. In such circumstances, the real estate broker can be the architect's ally in persuading the client to upgrade the building's quality. The downside of a lively office market is that developers will want their buildings designed and completed "yesterday."

The highs and lows of demand affect not only the quantity of office building space constructed, but also its evolution. While office building construction languished for a decade in the United States, construction of many office buildings in Europe and Asia incorporated technical advances such as energy-efficient glazing and more

efficient elevator systems. And because many of these overseas buildings were shaped by U.S. design teams, the expertise of these designers has been enhanced so that they are now introducing to the U.S. market advances proven abroad.

▼ Petronas Towers, Kuala Lumpur, Malaysia, 1998, by Cesar Pelli & Associates. Twin towers, both measuring 1483 ft (452 m), were the current record holders in 2002 and represent the transfer of the "world's tallest" title to East Asia, where even taller office buildings are planned. Photo © John Dakers/Corbis.

Procter & Gamble

Working with Procter & Gamble (P & G) officers and their team in the 1980s afforded Kohn Pedersen Fox (KPF) a chance to see one of the great American corporations at work. Before P & G decides to market any product, it researches every detail, testing three times or more to make sure it will achieve the company's goals of excellence. This was certainly true with the selection of the architect and the design process for its expanded headquarters in Cincinnati. Key P & G executives worked along with KPF, analyzing numerous alternatives, to solve the challenging problem of adding a new, larger structure to an existing building from the 1950s. The scheme developed through this painstaking process created an expanded P & G campus in the heart of its home city. The new building was able to establish its identity on the skyline, while the dignity of the old building was not diminished, allowing those who remained there to feel proud of their location.

One way the new and old P & G structures were made to be equal parts of a larger whole was by creating an important and welcoming open space around which these buildings are situated. Interaction between employees working in the old and new parts of the headquarters was accomplished by a bridge connection and the location of alternative dining experiences in both buildings. The development of a signature architectural presence on the city skyline was the subject of extensive study and review, finally leading to the distinctive twin tower scheme.

An internal goal of management, one that was very difficult for the staff and a number of vice presidents to accept, was to create an all-open office plan, instead of giving vice presidents private offices as in the existing buildings. An internal atrium helped to make the new large floor plates more successful, but it took more than one year of presentations and selling before the open plan was accepted, and even then not whole-heartedly. Placing the vice presidents in open offices along the atrium gave them some status and more privacy. There was resistance, but eventually the staff came to enjoy the open plan with its flexibility, and they began to fully appreciate the qualities of the new building.

The design process was made more effective and enjoyable by the hands-on approach of P & G's president/CEO John G. Smale and board chairman Brad Butler, who met with us once a month during the design phase for review and approval, and by the outstanding day-to-day leadership of the company's project manager, John Lehigh.

My partner, Robert Cioppa, and I visited the P & G campus in mid-1999, and it looked as good then as it did when it was just finished. The mature gardens make the public open space look even better. With the exception of carpet replacements and some new paint, there have been no changes to the building. It is beautifully maintained. –A.E.K.

◀ *Procter & Gamble Headquarters, Cincinnati, Ohio, 1985, by Kohn Pedersen Fox Associates. An extension of the earlier headquarters, left in photo, forms an L around an urban garden, with twin towers marking the complex on the skyline. Photo © Timothy Hursley.*

EFFECT OF GOVERNMENT PLANNING

San Francisco is one major city that has imposed a cap on office building construction, allowing only 900,000 sq ft per year. The establishment of this quota has generated competition among rival proposals that amounts to a beauty contest judged by local officials. To some extent, the imposed cap has had the intended effects of discouraging new construction and limiting the office population of the city, but it also caused

▼ *Home Insurance Building, Chicago, 1883, by William Le Baron Jenney. The first office building to have steel framing set the pattern for many speculative office buildings of the late nineteenth century. Photo © Bettman/Corbis.*

an extreme escalation of rents that affected the entire Bay Area market for new and existing buildings.

Sometimes governments can have an unexpected negative effect on office building development through zoning and tax laws—for instance, by prompting developers to attempt to beat the deadline for a proposed change to the zoning or tax laws. In New York in the late 1980s the city down-zoned the west side of Mid-town from 18 FAR to 15 FAR (floor area ratio, meaning total building floor area as a multiple of site area). This step caused a panic among developers, who saw a loss of potential project value, and they immediately had large buildings (max-imizing the 18 FAR) designed for their sites and started construction to beat the deadline. Most of these developers would have been better off losing the 3 FAR, because in many cases they lost entire buildings and sites to their financial partners when the market became overbuilt, rents dropped below pro formas, and tenants became rare.

SPECULATIVE VERSUS CORPORATE BUILDINGS

The planning and design of investment office buildings from the mid-1950s to the mid-1970s was typically based on statistics, with little apparent concern for the users or the public. In this investment —or speculative—office market, the goal was to design the most efficient and economical building, however mundane. Most architects did not regard these buildings as architecture.

When Kohn Pedersen Fox Associates was founded in 1976, its partners shared a conviction that serious architectural consideration of the investment building could benefit owners, users, and the public. From the beginning, the firm served both corporate and investment clients, treating the two kinds of projects with equal care. "Spec" buildings received the same attention as other efforts in terms of their sensitive relationship to context, memorable exterior form, efficient and appealing office floors, entrance and lobby sequences, public amenities, and meticulous detailing. Of crucial importance, of course, is presenting a persuasive case to the investment client that the additional effort will have long-term benefits in terms of recognition and revenues.

Investment office buildings numbered among the proudest landmarks of American architecture from the 1880s (Chicago's Monadnock and Reliance Buildings, for example) through the 1930s (New York's Empire State and Chrysler Buildings). The apparent success and widespread recognition of early KPF spec buildings, such as 333 Wacker Drive in Chicago, proved that investment buildings could again be counted among landmark business locations.

Even today, however, many in the real estate business see buildings as assets from which to profit, not necessarily as workplaces for people. Of particular concern are the large real estate investment trusts (REITS) and capital funds investing in real estate and development, because they look at buildings primarily as products to generate a financial return. A building conceived strictly as a financial instrument takes on a different character from one that is viewed as a place of work—a source of productivity and a home during working hours—as well as an important component of the urban or suburban environment.

It is most critical to realize that the tenants and their willingness to pay for quality also influence the product. There obviously must be a balance between the two goals—one is short-term economics, and the other is the quality of the building and the work environment. The best developers and REITS strike this balance. They are confident that companies will pay higher rents for quality buildings, thus yielding a proper return for the investor, the risk taker.

▼ 333 Wacker Drive, Chicago, 1983, by Kohn Pedersen Fox Associates. A structure that reasserted the potential of the speculative office building as an urban landmark. Photo © Barbara Karant.

In the design of a corporate headquarters the architects are exposed to a company's history, culture, growth potential, and leadership styles. Usually, the project is overseen by the CEO, president, chairman, and/or head of corporate real estate, who are talented and very successful people. Finding out what such leaders aspire to in terms of inspiring employees, enhancing productivity, and establishing a public image is not only fascinating for the architects, but also valuable for their future performance.

OFFICE BUILDINGS OF THE FUTURE

Everything we build today must make allowances for continued technological advancement, particularly in communications systems, air-conditioning, and lighting. For office buildings of the future, we can expect improvements in materials, curtain walls, and construction methods, and—through more advanced computer applications—a reduction in the time required for design and construction.

▼ *Rodin Pavilion at Samsung Headquarters, Seoul, Korea, 1997, by Kohn Pedersen Fox Associates. A museum pavilion housing two famous Rodin sculptures is a key part of the architects' renovation of the public areas joining three existing office towers. Photo © KPF/Kim Yong Kwan.*

In regard to program and planning, we can expect office buildings to include more hotel-type features, with lobbies containing a concierge service, a variety of food services, and meeting areas with computer capability. The lobby will no longer be a dead space during non-rush hours but will include interactive functions, perhaps 24 hours a day and seven days a week. Larger floor plates will remain the rule—where permitted—laid out and equipped for adaptability to various work space concepts.

There are several unpredictable developments that may affect the office building of the future. (The intensified threat of terrorism will surely affect safety requirements; see pages 23–24, "After 9/11," and Chapter 9 of this book, on safety and security.) One development with a potentially major impact would be a serious, prolonged shortage of energy. That would cause American developers to adopt some of the energy-conserving concepts now prevalent in Europe, such as double walls, operable windows where

▼ *Rodin Pavilion. Glass with various degrees of translucency forms the walls and roof of the structure designed for sculpture display. Photo © KPF/Kim Yong Kwan.*

▶ *Ford Foundation, New York City, 1967, by Kevin Roche John Dinkeloo. A benchmark for amenities in office buildings was established with the public winter garden incorporated into this structure. Photo © Esto/Ezra Stoller.*

climate permits, higher temperature thresholds before air-conditioning kicks in, and night cooling of the concrete structure to reduce the next day's energy demand. In the United States it is still a difficult economic decision to make exceptional first-cost investments for the sake of energy conservation.

Widespread environmental concerns and rising interest in the "green building" could also be the big change in the United States. Maximizing the use of materials from renewable sources and materials that return to nature when disposed of could have a significant effect on office building design. The use of recycled and recyclable products in office furnishings, already a feature of some product lines, could become more common without causing major changes in design possibilities or cost.

(continued on page 20)

◀ *Ford Foundation. Offices overlook the greenery of the building's winter garden. Photo © Esto/Ezra Stoller.*

IBM Headquarters

While working on the IBM headquarters in Armonk, New York, with Louis Gerstner, CEO, and Swanke Hayden Connell as interior designers, we saw how a company could be reorganized to meet the challenges of the twenty-first century. IBM under Gerstner wanted to shed its old culture, to reduce the luxurious amount of space per person provided in its previous headquarters, and to create a more democratic environment with a predominantly open office plan. Senior people were assigned small offices adjoining conference rooms. With an average of 75 sq ft per person and workstation partitions of glass above a low wood partition, all staff members are able to see their neighbors, to feel like a team, and to enjoy the view of the surrounding natural wooded environment. Gerstner located his own office in the center of the building, well related to all.

▲ *IBM World Headquarters, Armonk, New York, 1997, by Kohn Pedersen Fox Associat Folded forms of the office building fit into a wooded sit along the edge of a ravine. Photo © KPF/Vergara.*

◀ *IBM World Headquarters. Angular building forms clad in stainless steel appear to rest lightly on a stone base. Photo © Esto/Peter Aaron.*

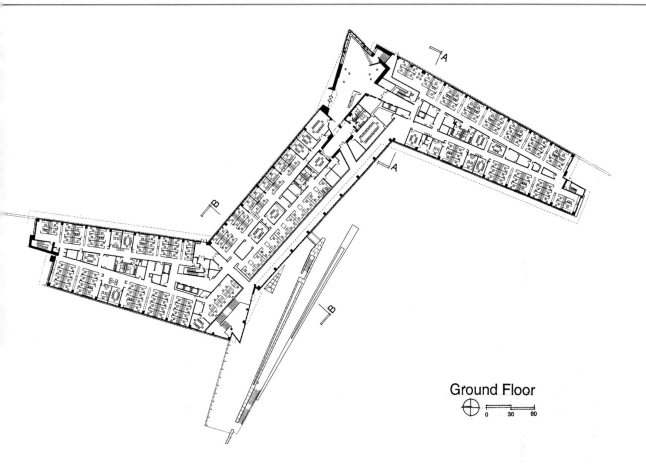

Ground Floor

0   30   60

The IBM staff has numerous opportunities to gather and talk—in breakout areas, at the café, in dining areas, at the fitness center, and in the galleries installed in circulation areas. Museum-like displays of the history of IBM's products support team identity.

The boomerang-shaped form of the building fits snugly into its wooded site, atop a rock formation with a steep ravine below. In contrast yet in harmony with nature, it is clad in stainless steel and glass, befitting an advanced technology corporation. Despite its high-tech look, however, the building does not necessarily embrace today's advanced technology; specifically, it does not have raised floors for communications links, because Gerstner believes wireless

equipment will soon render these obsolete.

A distinctive aspect of this project was Gerstner's decision to reduce the number of headquarters staff to make it manageable in size, then to make no allowance for expansion or any concessions to an exit strategy such as selling or leasing the building to others.

Designing its headquarters has been part of IBM's strategy for success. This is more than a building: It is a home for its employees, a friendly place to conduct business, efficient and team-oriented, intended as a center for ideas and leadership. It establishes an image for a highly successful and profitable twenty-first-century IBM. –A.E.K.

▲ *IBM World Headquarters. The building's narrow linear floor plate, bent to fit its site, locates all workstations close to window walls, with cores of shared facilities adjusted in width to meet needs. Courtesy KPF.*

▲ Washington Mutual Tower, Seattle, Washington, 1988, by Kohn Pedersen Fox Associates. Among the amenities possible in an urban office building is a dining terrace at an upper-floor setback. Photo © KPF.

Just as buildings must have built-in flexibility to accept upgraded mechanical, electrical, lighting, and communications systems, they must also be flexible to accommodate continually changing concepts of the way work is to be accomplished. The current trend toward warehouse-like space that is highly flexible, where workers can spend any hours they like, bring the dog or cat, and so on, may or may not become the standard. In any case, such a building is not revolutionary in terms of its architectural envelope. The increased density of people per square foot, which seems to satisfy users as well as management, is likely to be a long-term trend.

BELOVED OFFICE BUILDINGS

It is fascinating to contemplate that New York's Chrysler Building, which is almost 70 years old, has greater value today than ever before. The nearby Seagram Building, at some 43 years of age, continues to demand the highest rents despite being behind technologically. Maybe the real reason that the design of the office building, like that of the home, changes slowly is that human beings and their habits change very slowly—certainly not at the speed of technology.

Then too, Chrysler and Seagram are prime examples of architectural icons that make unique contributions to the urban scene. An individual or a company can aspire to be located in these buildings. The experience of entering the Chrysler lobby or walking across the Seagram plaza can be a source of pride and joy. Ultimately, the greatest thing any building can do is make you feel good.

(continued from page 16)

Two forces will act to moderate any quantum leaps for most owners of office buildings, however, whether they are investment or corporate properties:

1. Strong concerns about cost and a reluctance to tie up large sums of capital in real estate

2. Designing for an exit strategy so that many companies can use the same building if the initial owners or tenants decide to leave

◀ *Chrysler Building, New York City, 1930, by William Van Alen. The world's tallest building for only a few months, at 1048 ft, it is a perennially popular icon, embodying the exuberance of pre-Depression years. Photo © Museum of the City of New York/Corbis.*

▼ *Seagram Building, New York City, 1958, by Ludwig Mies van der Rohe and Philip Johnson. It remains one of the most admired office buildings of the past half century because of its elegant proportions and meticulous details. Photo © Esto/Ezra Stoller.*

▶ World Bank Headquarters, Washington, D.C., 1989–1997, by Kohn Pedersen Fox Associates. An amenity of this full-city-block building is a 150-foot-square skylighted atrium. Photo © Michael Dersin.

▶ World Bank Headquarters. Atrium as setting for after-hours banquet. Photo © KPF.

AFTER 9/11

As this book was in progress, an unprecedented act of terrorism took place on September 11, 2001, in New York City. Terrorists hijacked two commercial airliners and intentionally crashed them into both World Trade Center towers, two of the world's tallest office buildings.

After resisting the initial impact of a B-767 fully loaded with fuel, the North Tower withstood the jet fuel fire, with temperatures of up to 2000°F, for well over an hour, while the south tower remained standing for a little less than an hour. During that time the majority of the people in the towers were able to escape. (The normal occupancy was about 50,000, but many had not yet arrived at the time of the impact.) The collapse of the towers then killed approximately 3,500 people remaining in them, including hundreds of firefighters and emergency workers who had entered the buildings or were gathered at their bases. (See Chapter 4, on structural systems, for a fuller explanation of the collapse.)

The destruction of the World Trade Center towers started debates on the future of tall buildings, particularly structures of 100 or more stories. Are such buildings safe? Can they be made safer?

Among the issues being discussed is whether exceptionally tall buildings, as attractive targets for terrorism, would any longer appeal to occupants. (Height is not a requirement for a terrorist target, as is apparent from the September 11 attack on the five-story Pentagon building in Arlington, Virginia.) More pragmatic issues include the maximum height of a building that can be evacuated before structural systems fail, and what steps can be taken to make the structure and escape routes more effective in case of natural or human-made disaster.

I have participated in these debates with many architects and engineers. One of the first steps was to consider the advantages of tall buildings in our dense urban areas and to review fire safety codes and structural solutions in tall buildings around the world. In Europe and East Asia the codes are more conservative than in the United States. They include such requirements as dedicated firemen's lifts —fireproof and pressurized—and fire stairs with pressurized vestibules. In Japan there must be fireproof corridors leading to fire stairs.

In Hong Kong there must be a fireproof refuge floor (its only use) every 25 stories, and in China refuge floors must occur every 13 stories. These floors, with their own air systems and communications serve as places of assembly in emergencies, where people can gather to be evacuated in an orderly way following instructions. They are safe havens, like the compartments in a naval vessel that can be isolated from parts of the ship that are taking on water.

Also in China, Hong Kong, and Japan, two-hour fire-rated partitions drop from the ceiling to separate areas of 10,000–20,000 sq ft to confine fires. In Germany such fire-rated partitions between subdivisions of floors are permanent, with fire doors for circulation under normal conditions.

As a result of these discussions following September 11, I am sure that codes for fire safety, exiting, and structural systems in the United States and other countries will be reviewed and eventually modified.

It is critical that we not abandon the construction of tall buildings, which are essential to dense urban areas.

High-density urban development encourages economic and cultural activity and the conservation of land and resources. Tall buildings related to transportation nodes make efficient public transportation possible and provide efficient work environments for large organizations that may occupy 400,000–1,000,000 sq ft.

Tall buildings also offer exceptional resistance to earthquakes, high winds, and even car or truck bombs. (Witness the 1993 attempt to bring down a World Trade Center tower with explosives in a basement.) Because these buildings have great structural mass at their bases, they resist such attacks far better than smaller structures.

Views of and from tall buildings have a positive role in identifying organizations and cities such as New York, Chicago, Hong Kong, and Shanghai. Many become widely recognized icons.

We cannot design any of our buildings —tall or otherwise—as fortresses to stop airplanes or missiles from penetrating, because to do so would create a working environment like an underground bunker. We can, however, consider how to design exterior walls and central cores to limit damage from such impacts and prevent subsequent total collapse.

We are seeing a major change in the corporate location strategies of investment banks, stock and bond traders, and other users of large spaces who until recently concentrated their offices in Lower Manhattan. Some have had to relocate their workforces to other parts of Manhattan and the New York metropolitan area, and a more dispersed pattern is likely to prevail. The New York City region, not just the Wall Street district, will become the world's leading financial district.

It is possible that the concept of mixed use in tall buildings—with retail, offices, hotel, and residences sharing towers— will become less popular than it has recently been in the United States and Asia. Living above a high-profile office occupant may give residents concern for their safety, and office tenants may be concerned about who might occupy or gain access to apartments or hotel rooms above.

In the weeks after September 11 the threat of biological warfare has raised other concerns. The fear is that diseases can be introduced into an air-conditioning system to affect occupants throughout the building. Another advantage of tall buildings is that each floor can be supplied directly with outside air, drawn far above the ground.

Terrorist action is probably going to be a real threat for years to come. The built environment all over the world will obviously reflect what has taken place and will be influenced by our success at thwarting terrorists. We must not allow their actions to influence us to give up the rich interaction of high-density cities or to isolate ourselves in fortresses. We must show the world that we will continue to live a full life in an environment of free interaction, which will continue to include prominent office towers, some of them recognized as icons.

THE OFFICE BUILDING TYPE: A PRAGMATIC APPROACH

PAUL KATZ *Kohn Pedersen Fox*

The office building may well be the defining building type of our lifetime. After the home, it has become the most important setting for modern adult experience. Throughout the twentieth century the proportion of the workforce employed in offices has steadily increased, and mid-century prophesies of shorter work weeks have not proven accurate. One of the few artworks dedicated to the modern workplace, Edward Hopper's *Office at Night,* although painted in 1936, is an indicator of the psychological and social importance of the modern work environment. Hopper's image deftly captures the tension between the economic and social dimensions of our lives.

The relationship between economic growth and the design of the workplace—in which the architect's role is decisive—has gotten little scholarly attention. In fact, relatively recently, the great historian Nikolaus Pevsner in *A History of Building Types,* published in 1976, did not consider the office building a separate type but a subset emerging from a number of older types: government buildings, banks and exchanges, warehouses, and factories. Admittedly, Pevsner's book focuses particularly on the development of building types during the nineteenth century, following the rapid urbanization caused by the Industrial Revolution. Especially germane to this subject is the discussion on the emergence of utilitarian types influenced more by function and material (or technology) than by style. These earlier types were, in various respects, precursors to today's office building.

- Government buildings appeared when the bureaucracy outgrew the more symbolic city halls and other seats of government. Government offices as such were being built in architecturally distinct form in the late 1500s, when the Uffizi (originally government offices, now a museum) was constructed in Florence. It was characterized by extensive, repetitive work spaces, expressed in a regular pattern of windows.

- Banks and exchanges developed when banking and trade demanded organizations with employees, which happened as long ago as the Middle

▲ Office at Night, by Edward Hopper, 1936. A noted American artist's commentary on the relationship of work to life. Collection Walker Art Center, Minneapolis; Gift of the T.B. Walker Foundation, Gilbert M. Walker Fund, 1946.

Ages in Europe (and at least as early in other parts of the world). In the fifteenth century these establishments took architectural form in the palazzo of Florence's banking families. Evolving from family palaces, they afterward retained characteristics of the palazzo, including imposing façades, prominent central entrances, and differentiation in the scale of various floors.

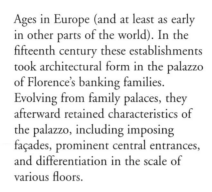

▼ *Palazzo Vecchio, Florence, Italy, 1314. Government offices representing a Renaissance city-state. Photo © Paolo Sacchi/Corbis.*

- Warehouses occurred in the most ancient civilizations, and they contributed to the development of the modern office building when, at some undetermined time, they spawned the concept of leasing floor areas to a variety of tenants.

- Factories emerged with the development of printing. Pevsner cites the earliest in Nuremberg in 1497, illustrating the connection of information technology to the advance of architectural invention. Factory buildings were innovative in terms of construction (steel frames, large scale, long spans, fireproofing) and social reform and urban planning (utopian factory towns). Of particular importance to the office building type is the early use of glass and metal curtain walls in two early modernist examples: the AEG factory by Behrens (1908) and the Fagus factory by Gropius and Meyer (1911).

The office building, as a structure reserved for commercial offices, emerged in Chicago and New York around 1880 with the development of the fireproofed steel frame and the elevator. It was contemporaneous with the emergence of the modern urbanized, capitalistic state. Since then, each economic growth cycle has seen an evolutionary transformation of the office building.

By about 1900 the principal characteristics of the office building type were emerging. Three American buildings of that time exemplify the three fundamental but often conflicting concerns that are relevant to this day: the needs of the individual employee, the functioning of the organization, and the identity of the company with the building.

- The Guaranty Building, Buffalo, New York, 1896, is architect Louis Sullivan's quintessential expression of the office building as a cellular structure of individual offices. This building with homogeneous space on repetitive floors anticipates post–World War II North American speculative office buildings. Tenants could take as much space as needed.

- The Larkin Building, Buffalo, New York, 1904, by Frank Lloyd Wright, accommodated substantially the entire company staff in one vast "organic" space—the ultimate expression of corporate unity. (Of these three archetypal buildings, the Larkin is the only one to have been demolished, perhaps because its unusual one-big-room concept had little appeal to other corporate managers. The Johnson's Wax Headquarters in Racine, Wisconsin, of 1936, also by Wright, is similar in concept and does survive.)

- The Woolworth Building, New York City, 1911–1913, by Cass Gilbert, perfected the concept of a corporate skyscraper as a "Cathedral of Commerce," proclaiming the power of its owners (in this case a retail chain) as an icon in the city skyline.

Until the Great Depression of the 1930s put an end to new construction for almost 25 years, there was an unprecedented building boom in this type, particularly in New York and Chicago. For an in-depth understanding of this period, see *Form Follows Finance,* by Carol Willis (1995). This work traces the development of the American office building, focusing on the regulatory and entrepreneurial forces that to this day guide commercial development in the United States.

By the 1950s the European utopian vision of modernism was blended with commercial architecture, notably in New York. The United Nations Secretariat (1952, by Wallace K. Harrison and an international board including Le Corbusier) displayed the first all-glass curtain wall in a high-rise office tower. It was closely followed by Lever House

▼ *Woolworth Building, New York City, 1913, by Cass Gilbert. Tower proclaiming the company's importance on the skyline. Photo © Corbis.*

▲ *Palazzo Piccolomini, Pienza, Italy, 1462. Renaissance aristocrats' residences, often housing banks, set precedents for later office structures. Photo © Ruggero Vanni/Corbis.*

◥ *Guaranty Building, Buffalo, New York, 1896, by Adler & Sullivan. Uniform expression of cellular offices, with different treatment for first and top floors. Photo © G.E. Kidder Smith/Corbis.*

(1952, Skidmore, Owing & Merrill) and, a few years later, the masterpiece of this period, the Seagram Building (1958, Mies van der Rohe and Philip Johnson), structures that introduced the tower-in-the-plaza concept for office buildings. None of these three buildings followed the forms typical of New York buildings governed by the zoning regulations. These buildings used considerably less than the available zoning area. In 1961 the zoning regulations were changed to allow for the tower block on a plaza, which could fully utilize the zoning area. The prototype of the modern office block thus established was quickly adopted throughout the United States and in much of the world.

Unlike the design of houses and cities, which have emerged from centuries of history and are as different as the various languages spoken, the design of modern office buildings has developed from a few models within the last century, and the various office buildings around the world may be viewed as many dialects of essentially the same language.

Within a relatively short period, innovations in the three "stories" defined by Pevsner—function, material, and style—transformed the prototype. The possibilities were suddenly enlarged, and for architects the challenges were greater. The office building has indeed taken its place as a key building type and is central to any debate on modern architecture. The purpose of this book is, rather than to pursue theoretical discussions on the office building, to outline the practical considerations common to this building type, which will be of use to anyone involved in creating an office building.

Although there are no universal prototypes or formulas for responding to a client's specific needs or to local influences such as climate, culture, codes, or construction methods, the fundamental elements that need to be considered in every office building are identical.

The first decision to be made is the total floor area of the building. As the preceding brief historical review begins to show, the development of the type is closely linked to the utilization of area. This is clearly the fundamental factor in the cost, the potential value to the owner, and the approval by building authorities. There is, in fact, no one way to measure floor area, but a variety of ways, from the point of view of the zoning officials, the engineers and cost estimators, and the

tenants or corporate users of the building. And these ways of measuring area vary from place to place as well.

The basic unit of measure—in effect, the currency—of all commercial property is floor area. The Builder Owners and Managers Association (BOMA) has established a means of measurement, "Standard Method for Measuring Plan Area in Office Buildings," initially developed in 1952. It may seem that the idea of area is universal and absolute. But a closer examination reveals that even this fundamental concept can be confusing, because each interest group in the development process has a different interpretation of it.

The architect and client must establish at the outset a common definition of area. The four most common methods of calculating area, and some of their variations, are discussed in the following section.

◣ Uffizi, Florence, Italy, 1560–1580s, Giorgio Vasari. Extensive offices assembled of repeating modular sections, later adapted as an art museum. Photo © Bettman/Corbis.

▼ Larkin Building, Buffalo, New York, 1904, by Frank Lloyd Wright. Solidarity of the office staff expressed in a single vast room. Courtesy Buffalo and Erie County Historical Society.

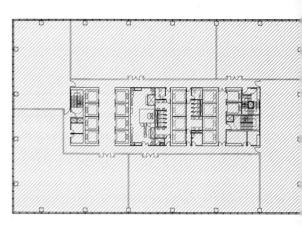

GROSS FLOOR AREA

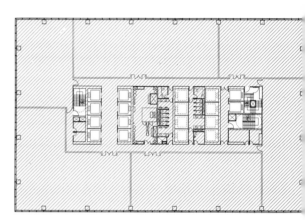

RENTABLE FLOOR AREA

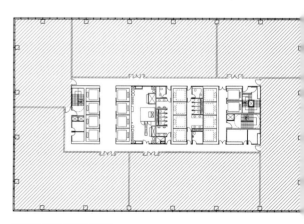

USABLE FLOOR AREA

CALCULATIONS OF AREA

Governmental authorities typically define the maximum size of a building in zoning gross floor area (zoning GFA or ZFA). Zoning area is usually measured to the exterior of the building wall. In many jurisdictions, the ZFA is fixed for every site. In New York, for instance, the ZFA is established by multiplying the site area by the maximum FAR (floor area ratio; that is, the ratio of ZFA to site area) for that location. Floor area allowances can be transferred from nearby sites that meet certain qualifications or can be increased by bonus percentages in return for amenities such as public passages or open space, but all this is mathematically calculated in terms of the established FAR for the site.

In many other locations, however, there is a degree of negotiation in establishing the allowable GFA for a particular site. In London and in Washington, D.C., for instance, the prime concern has been to protect key views to landmarks such as the domes of St. Paul's Cathedral and the U.S. Capitol, and floor area is negotiable.

In some cities the mechanical rooms, shafts, and mechanical floors can be excluded from the zoning area. In others, all area must be included, even below-grade spaces. Regulations covering the measurement of building area obviously play a part in the design of the significant elements, such as the exterior wall and mechanical systems, because building owners need to maximize the area developed on their property, especially when land prices are high in proportion to the project cost.

To establish costs, contractors and estimators measure the construction area, often called the construction gross floor area (CFA). This includes all the areas of the building, including the basements, mechanical floors, loading areas, and penthouses. In New York, a rule of thumb is that the construction gross floor area of a typical office floor is about 5 percent greater than the zoning floor area at any given floor. Typically, this construction gross floor area is the largest measured area and is the basis for the engineering calculations as well as fees.

Landlords and agents are typically most concerned with the rentable (leasable) area of the building. The rentable area is calculated differently in every market. The landlord measures the efficiency of the office building by dividing the total rentable office area on the office floors by the zoning area of those floors.

In New York, however, rentable area of a floor is measured to the center line of the exterior wall. Depending on the design of the curtain wall, this can make a difference of 2 percent, as compared with the measurement to the inside of the glass as practiced in London, for instance. In New York the rentable area can also end up being greater than the construction gross because of an unusual concept, the "loss factor." This factor is a percentage by which the actual rentable area is increased when the lease is negotiated between owner and tenant. It was developed during the 1970s, when companies were leaving New York because of high rents. Landlords wanted to keep the published rents down while retaining the ability to raise rents in the future. Application of the loss factor in leases caused the total rentable office space in New York to grow during the 1990s without any new buildings being built, as in an improving market landlords could increase the loss factor percentage when negotiating leases.

◀ Generic plan illustrating three methods of floor area calculation, used by zoning authorities, owners, and office tenants. Courtesy KPF.

◀◀ United Nations Headquarters, New York City, 1952, by Wallace K. Harrison with an international board of design. The secretariat tower included an influential use of the glass curtain wall. Photo © Esto/Ezra Stoller.

◀◀ Fagus Factory, Alfeld, Germany, 1911, Gropius and Meyer. Early demonstration of the unadorned glass curtain wall, illustrating the key elements in industrial buildings. Photo © Ruggero Vanni/Corbis.

In Hong Kong, as another example, rentable space is measured to the inside of the glass, but the ZFA is measured to the edge of the floor slab—and the exterior wall is allowed to project up to 300 mm (1 ft) beyond the slab without being included in the ZFA, which can increase the rentable area by almost 4 percent.

The facility managers for the tenants are most interested in the usable area. This is the area that the tenant can utilize for day-to-day functions. Often, it is referred to as the "carpeted" area, inasmuch as it excludes the toilets, vestibules, multi-tenant corridors, elevator lobbies, and the like. In evaluating the space, the facility manager typically hires an independent interior designer to determine the number of employees who can be housed on a floor. The architect often prepares test layouts for hypothetical tenants to assure the developer that the proposed typical floor will adequately serve the targeted tenant type.

TEN KEY CONSIDERATIONS

The design process for office buildings is a team effort, possibly more so than for other building types, because of the relative speed required by commercial imperatives and because the issues involved demand calculations and decisions that are beyond the expertise of the architect alone. Consultants must be brought into the process at the outset.

To complete the schematic design, the team must resolve a number of inter-related elements quickly, anticipating solutions to problems that will arise in the later phases. These elements are common to all office buildings, and some are unique to the building type.

1. Core Configuration

The core of the building comprises all of the elements of the office floor that serve the "usable area." In early office buildings these elements tended to be dispersed on the floor rather than concentrated, as is now typical. The elements now included are the fire stairs, elevator shafts and lobbies, toilets, machine rooms for the air-handling units, electrical and telephone closets, and a number of risers for air, water, electricity, and communications. Many of the key structural elements, such as the shear walls that provide lateral bracing, are integrated into the core; elevator shaft walls and stairwells are ideal for this purpose. Depending on the client's or tenant's requirements, the area of the core elements can vary greatly for buildings of equivalent total area, affecting efficiency.

The starting point in designing the core is usually to lay out a prototypical floor that is the most efficient and largest possible on that site, given the owner's leasing depth (exterior wall to core) requirements and special program needs. This floor plate must then be tested with hypothetical interior layouts, and the likely worker population per floor must be determined, to establish a typical floor that meets the owner's needs. This determines the approximate number of floors and their areas. With this information, the architect, with the assistance of the elevator consultant or, often, the manu-facturer, can provide options for the elevator system and the number of shafts. Until the number of elevators and the floors each group serves is established, the core development cannot progress.

The core design and coordination is an iterative process that continues through to the working drawing phase, but the essentials of the core have to be established and approved as early as possible. Buildings planned for single users have different priorities, typically requiring a greater level of service in elevators than those for multiple tenants, and that is often reflected in the arrangement of the core elements. In recent years, however, North American corporations have increasingly been requiring an "exit strategy" that allows the building to be easily converted to a rental property.

The location of the core or cores in a building is affected by several factors, and buildings can be categorized by where the cores are placed:

Center-core building

A center-core building is the most typical office building type, particularly for high-rises. The advantages of this type include the following:

- Central structural core to resist wind loads, opening up the perimeter for light and views
- Mechanical services located in the center of the floor
- Ease of construction
- Flexible arrangement for multitenant situations

The center-core configuration may not be the most appropriate for buildings with smaller typical floor plates, buildings with certain site conditions, or buildings with special functions such as trading floors that are not suited to central-core configuration.

Side core building

A side-core is typical for smaller office floors or those built up to a party wall. The advantages of this configuration are as follows:

- The core can open to the exterior environment, allowing for natural ventilation of the common spaces.
- The core can shade the office space from the harshest sun.
- The mechanical system can easily introduce fresh air at each floor.
- The usable area is homogeneous and can usually be organized into one space.

This building type is often very attractive to users without cellular offices and has until recently been the standard in Japan and Korea. However, on large floor plates its use is limited, usually because travel distances to the fire stairs and elevators do not meet time or code requirements.

Multicore building

Multiple cores are common in low-rise buildings, those with very large floor plates, and those with narrow floor plates. These configurations are quite usual in Northern Europe, where cellular offices are the norm, building depths are often limited to 15 m (50 ft) glass to glass, and sites are irregular.

The advantages of multicore configurations are as follows:

- Travel distances to the core are short.
- The floor plate can be adjusted to difficult site conditions and contexts.
- Building elements can be smaller in scale.

The disadvantages include the likelihood of more total elevators and a more complicated lobby and circulation design, requiring a greater area.

2. Floor Plate

The size and shape of a building's floor plate have the greatest impact on its

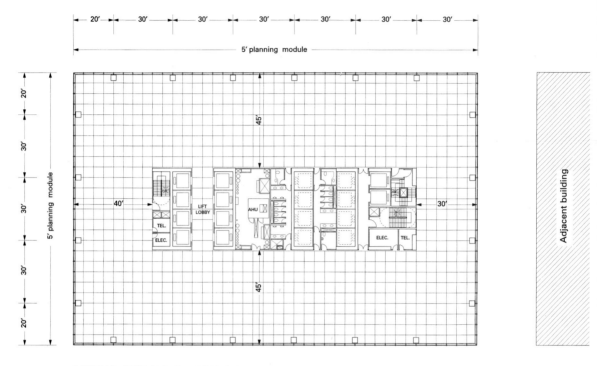

DEPTH–TO–CORE AND PLANNING MODULE

▲ *Depth-to-core measurements, structural bays, and planning modules, as illustrated on a typical office floor plan, with a linear core and an asymmetrical layout that takes the adjacent building into account by maximizing leasing depth on the other three sides. Note that the low-rise elevators are located to open up desirable space on the higher floors. The linear floor plan illustrated here is the most efficient for multitenant buildings in most markets. Courtesy KPF.*

internal effectiveness and its external character. Two major determinants of the floor plate are the client's desired leasing depth and the internal planning module.

Leasing depth is the dimension of the usable area between the outside wall and the core or the multitenant corridor. In some cases the leasing depth will be measured to another exterior wall, if it is a windowless party wall, or to another window wall, in which case the leasing depth is half the wall-to-wall dimension.

Determining the leasing depth can be one of the most frustrating aspects of office building development. It is always difficult for the developer to anticipate the market's ideal leasing depth two years or more prior to leasing. In build-to-suit structures, this is much easier, because the user determines the preferred leasing depth at the outset of design. The

difficulty with build-to-suit owners is that there is usually little leeway for the variations in this depth typical in high-rise towers (as elevator shafts drop off). The space that varies is less efficient because it is unlikely to conform to the owner's work space modules. The leasing depth varies considerably in different markets, for reasons to be discussed later. In Northern Europe the leasing depth is typically no more than 8 m (about 25 ft), and in Tokyo it is now typically 18 m (almost 60 ft).

Planning modules are the basis for the design of the vast majority of office interiors. Because furniture systems and tenant space standards usually correspond to the module, it is essential to lay out as many of the building elements as possible on the planning grid — in particular, columns and exterior wall mullions — as this will greatly facilitate the efficient and flexible use of space. The leasing depth must also accommodate the desired planning module.

The modules of lighting and air supply/return systems often do not match the exterior wall module. These are usually coordinated with the 2-ft grid of typical ceiling systems, whereas the typical planning grid in the United States is 5 ft (1.5 m).

Typical planning modules

United States	5 ft (1.5 m) module now the standard, although older buildings typically have smaller modules.
Japan	1.6 m and 1.8 m (5' 3" and 5' 11")
Europe and Asia	1.2 m (3' 11"), and 1.5 m (5' 0")

Considered together, leasing depth and planning module will determine a rectangular and repetitive floor plate, which almost all developers and users prefer. But floor plates are also affected by other considerations, such as site con-figuration and zoning regulations. In high-rises, upper floors necessarily vary, as elevator shafts are reduced, and they may also be affected by setbacks required by zoning.

3. Floor-To-Floor Height

The floor-to-floor height of an office building is typically the same on all the occupied floors except for the lobby and those with specially designated functions, such as trading floors. In low-rise buildings extra floor-to-floor height usually comes at little additional cost, whereas in higher buildings additional

floor-to-floor height entails significantly greater costs of structural systems, cladding, mechanical risers, vertical transportation, and so forth. The major factors governing the floor-to-floor height are discussed in the following paragraphs.

The intended finished ceiling height, which is typically 2.6 m or 2.75 m (8' 6" or 9' 0"), although the trend during the 1990s was to increase this height to allow for:

- Reflective artificial lighting, particularly in offices with intense use of computer screens

- Reflective ceiling lights, which require an additional 10 in. (25 cm) of depth, as compared with standard fluorescent lights

- Greater office depths, where higher ceilings allow sunlight to penetrate farther and provide psychological relief

The depth of a raised floor, if used. The standard raised floor is 150 mm (6 in.), but variations are frequent. Although raised floors are accepted in most parts of the world, provisions for raised floors in U.S. speculative office buildings are very much the exception, the actual floor not being provided by the owner.

The structural depth, which is dependent on the depth to core and the structural material. Obviously, the deeper that dimension, the deeper the structure and the greater the floor-to-floor dimension. Deep floor structure can actually reduce floor-to-floor height if the mechanical ducts run through the structure (as in One Raffles Link, pages 251–262) rather than below it.

The air delivery system, which can be either in the ceiling zone below (or partly passing through) the structure or — increasingly in Europe and for single-user

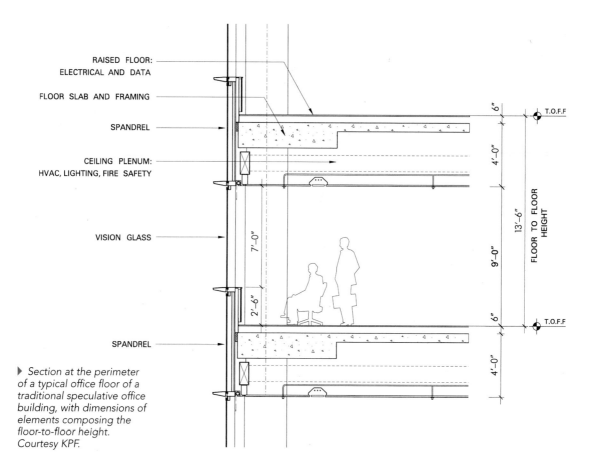

RAISED FLOOR:
ELECTRICAL AND DATA

FLOOR SLAB AND FRAMING

SPANDREL

CEILING PLENUM:
HVAC, LIGHTING, FIRE SAFETY

VISION GLASS

SPANDREL

6" — T.O.F.F

4'-0"

13'-6" FLOOR TO FLOOR HEIGHT

7'-0"

9'-0"

2'-6"

6" — T.O.F.F

4'-0"

▶ Section at the perimeter
of a typical office floor of a
traditional speculative office
building, with dimensions of
elements composing the
floor-to-floor height.
Courtesy KPF.

buildings—in the raised floor. The larger the exterior-to-core depth, the deeper the air supply ducts.

The ceiling system, usually integrated with the lighting system, which requires at least .15 m (5 in.).

The sprinkler system—now a standard feature (.07 m or 3 in.). Typically it can be threaded between the ceiling lights.

Tolerance for deflection. Deflections result from building movement and vibrations. The tolerance required is dependent on the structural system, the height of the building, and the local codes, but should be no more than 1 in.

In the United States and Asia, the floor-to-floor height of typical high-rise office buildings is between 13'0" and 13'6" (4.0 to 4.2 m). For buildings with shorter structural spans and concrete construction, as in Germany and France, the typical dimension is 3.75 m (12'4").

4. Exterior Wall Systems

The exterior wall has been an area of continuous innovation and experimentation for architects, as it requires consideration of the aesthetic, technical, and functional performance of the building. The technology of the curtain wall and the materials used in its fabrication have improved rapidly over the last decade, particularly as the limitations in the design and longevity of earlier systems began to be addressed. The exterior envelope of the building

- Controls the interface of the interior with the surrounding environment
- Affects the utilization of the interior space by the tenants
- Usually defines the aesthetic character of the office building

Particular attention must be given to the interior environment immediately adjacent to the exterior wall. Difficulties often arise with regard to solar glare, radiant heat and cold, condensation, acoustic pollution, and air supply. There are no universally acceptable levels of human comfort. In the United States, for example, there is an unquestioned expectation of all-year air-conditioning, whereas in Europe there is greater acceptance of warmer interiors in summer months. In Japan the standard of lighting is direct fluorescent tubes. Proposals for indirect lighting are rejected on the assumption that office workers there strongly prefer bright, direct lighting, a condition unacceptable in the United States and Europe.

The wall is usually designed to meet interior partitions precisely at mullions. This is one of several reasons why the wall is typically dimensioned to match the interior planning module. Despite the long-predicted demise of the private office, almost all office buildings still have to be planned for at least some perimeter offices. Single-use buildings are exceptions, as they are typically planned either for all perimeter offices or for none.

The primary material of the curtain wall is glass, usually supported by an aluminum frame. Sometimes masonry elements such as precast concrete, brick, stone, or ceramic tile are used. Recently, the overwhelming aesthetic preference has been to utilize much greater expanses of glass than ever before. The increased emphasis on transparency, while allowing natural light to penetrate into the space and affording views from the interior, increases the solar heat gain and glare considerably.

Various adhesives, fasteners, gaskets, tubes, sealants, and fireproofing materials are required to complete the system. The great increase in the number of available glass types expands options and complicates the final selection and procurement of glass. The appearance of the glass is difficult to predict under various light conditions, so a visual mock-up, if possible, is often helpful. Glasses used today often have soft coatings that reduce the nonvisible spectrum entering the building and heating the interior. These coatings are nearly invisible and thus very appealing to architects, who previously used tinted or reflective glass to achieve these properties. In the future these coatings will be hard, applied by a pyrolitic method, and therefore will not need to be used only on the inner surfaces of insulated glass lites.

The last decade has seen unprecedented developments in glass technology, and these can be expected to continue, with innovation led as before by needs of the automobile industry. Future innovations in the structural properties of glass and coating technology promise new opportunities that will further transform the design of curtain walls.

An area of great interest is the active wall—that is, a curtain wall with multiple layers allowing air to pass between the surfaces, often with operable windows and shading devices built in between the layers. These walls are designed to minimize or eliminate the need for air-conditioning in office buildings. The increased cost of the walls is offset by the decrease in the expenditure on mechanical equipment and the lower energy costs. This is indeed possible in Northern European countries with benign climates, shallow leasing depths, low occupancies, and high energy costs.

Currently, a number of large commercial developments in Japan are using these systems for the first time, but because of certain drawbacks, including greater maintenance demands and the loss of the rental space to the thickness of the double wall, these systems have not been widely adopted outside Europe. In the United States and some other countries the relatively low cost of energy has discouraged such systems. As public officials become more aware of the need for energy savings in commercial buildings, these systems will become more common in other markets. (See also Chapter 7.)

5. Elevators and Mechanical Systems

The critical system in design, as well as in the procurement process, is the elevator system, because it requires a longer lead time than any other equipment. In establishing the number and types of elevators, it is important not to rely on rules of thumb or elevator company representatives—except for relatively small buildings—but to include an independent elevator consultant early in the process. It is almost impossible to improve the elevator service of a building later.

The mechanical specifications of a building are studied very carefully by prospective tenants and their advisers. The owner must make adequate provisions but also consider the running costs of these systems. Each air-conditioning system has ramifications in the planning of the entire building.

It is essential to chart all the systems that require vertical distribution—usually through the core—everything from rainwater drainage to telecommunications. During the schematic design phase, the core of the office building is developed to contain these vertical systems, without necessarily fully coordinating all of them with the structural and architectural layout of the core. Sufficient coordination must be done early on, primarily to establish the dimensions of the core and to confirm the viability of the scheme.

In addition to the mechanical areas on the office floors, there are mechanical equipment needs distributed throughout the building and necessary links to the utility infrastructure. The building's mechanical equipment must be separated from usable office space to avoid acoustical and electromagnetic interference with operations. There must also be convenient access to this equipment for maintenance.

The location and design of mechanical facilities can affect the exterior wall, where there may be a substantial requirement for intake and exhaust louvers. The locations of the centralized mechanical areas are governed in some cases by local zoning regulations, so as to be exempt from the building's zoning gross area.

In recent years the area taken up by the mechanical equipment has increased, partly as a result of the greater demands of the new technology. In fact, in some recently constructed financial services buildings in New York, up to 20 percent of the construction floor area is dedicated to mechanical equipment, although the typical proportion is closer to 12 percent.

Except for the elevators, final design of most of the numerous necessary systems takes place only after most of the architecture and the structure design has been done. Because the mechanical systems are typically enclosed between the architectural and structural elements, care must be taken to make allowance for all these systems in the early phases of the design.

6. Structural System

To complete the schematic design, certain structural elements should be determined to allow the design to proceed without later adjustments in key dimensions:

- The type of construction must be confirmed. In some areas and for certain building configurations, either steel or concrete is virtually inevitable. In other situations, a comparative evaluation of steel and concrete structure is of value.

- Column sizes, location, and spacing affect the quality of the rental spaces and exterior wall design. Interior columns are typically viewed negatively but often cannot be

▼ Representative framing plan for a typical floor, assuming a post-tensioned concrete floor slab, with dashed boxes representing predesigned slab opening for possible stairwells between floors. Note that the elevator and stair shafts are ideal for shear walls, allowing for small perimeter columns. Note also the absence of corner colums to maximize the views from internal offices. Courtesy KPF.

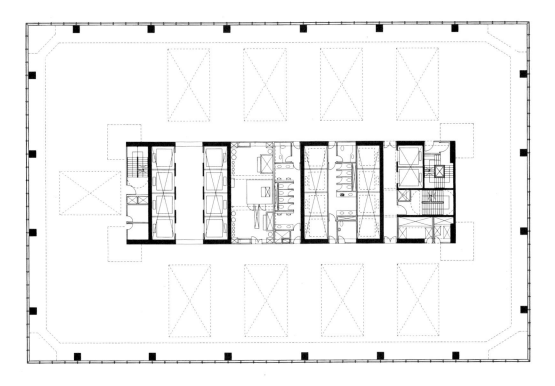

FRAMING PLAN

avoided, so their locations have to be considered.

- The core typically provides resistance to wind by means of shear walls. These affect the design and location of the primary elements in the core such as elevators.

- The determination of a structural grid assumes that the needs of garages and loading areas at the base of the building have been determined, so that the relationships of lower-floor and typical-floor structural systems can be considered.

- The preceding decisions should be summarized in a framing plan for the typical floors. Unfortunately, this is often neglected, but even minor adjustments in the framing plan during the later phases can have wide repercussions.

For many tall buildings, a wind tunnel analysis should be performed in the initial phases. Its findings can affect not only the structural system, but the floor plate shape and size, the exterior wall details, the location of mechanical intakes and exhausts, and the design of plazas and entrances.

It is the architect's responsibility to coordinate the various consultants' work and the architectural design. In most building projects today the structural design is completed prior to the rest of the engineering and architecture. In fact, the below-grade structure is often bid (tendered) separately before the above-grade design is final.

In the case of steel structures, the lead time is much longer than with concrete, and there is far less flexibility to make subsequent changes during design and construction. However, steel-framed office buildings have a number of advantages, the most important of which is the relative ease of modification after completion.

Besides tolerating changes later in the design and construction process, concrete has the advantage of greater weight, which can be useful for damping building movement, particularly in taller structures. Concrete also has excellent thermal storage characteristics, and there are systems that use this property to cool the building when chilled water is run through pipes embedded in the floor slabs. Although concrete construction is available, usually at lower cost, in most markets, it also has a number of disadvantages, particularly for larger projects. Concrete structural members are larger than comparable steel members, and the erection process is slower and more labor intensive.

Some buildings use combinations of concrete and steel, utilizing the advantages of both. In high-rises a core is often constructed in slip-formed concrete and the floor beams and perimeter columns are steel. In mixed-use projects it is not uncommon for the podium housing retail and parking to be built of concrete, with steel-framed office floors rising from there, and even concrete residential or hotel floors above the offices.

It is important to note that the most elegant or efficient structural system is very often not the most desirable one to meet the client's needs. The most obvious example is that owners typically prefer to minimize structural elements on the perimeter of the building, even though that can be the most efficient location for lateral bracing. From the owner's viewpoint, the leasing value and flexibility of the interior space is usually the governing consideration, overriding possible structural savings.

7. Code Conformance

The codes that most affect the initial stages of the design are those governing the bulk of the building—its height and setback from streets and property lines. Cities have different codes governing these issues. In some cities they are carefully prescribed (as in New York and Hong Kong), and elsewhere they are negotiable (as in San Francisco and London). These codes originated to preserve sunlight and fresh air for the streets and adjoining buildings. In some cities there are height restrictions to preserve important view corridors, particularly in historic and capital cities where certain views are of particular importance, such as Washington, Paris, and London, where the development of tall office buildings is strictly controlled.

The other codes that define the design of an office building are the fire codes established to save lives in case of fire. These codes also vary considerably from city to city. Certain fire codes require elevators adjacent to the escape stairs for access to every floor by firefighters (United Kingdom, Hong Kong, and Singapore). Many codes require the stairwells and vestibules to be pressurized. Both of these requirements increase the size of the core. Some cities do not allow elevator lobbies to serve as a means of escape, and some even require a fire-protected corridor between the two escape stairs (Paris and Tokyo), thus significantly reducing the efficiency of the floor. In China and Hong Kong there is a requirement for ventilated refuge floors within a specific number of stories, where people can congregate in the case a floor

has to be evacuated. Interestingly, none of these precautions are in place in New York, the world's largest office market.

Perhaps the most significant code requirement that affects the shape and size of the floor plate are the rules relating to the maximum travel distance to the escape stairs—rules found universally, but with different specific distances. These essentially limit the leasing depth and floor size. Even with a small floor plate, however, these requirements can create the need for unanticipated corridors in multitenanted layouts, reducing the efficiency of the floor.

8. Parking and Loading

In a typical suburban office building in the United States, the area dedicated to parking is equal to or often even greater than that of office space. The developer standard is normally three to four cars per 1000 sq ft of office floor area. Each car typically requires 300 sq ft for surface parking, which includes parking space and driveway; and 350 to 400 sq ft for structural parking, which includes allowances for ramps. Whether on the surface or structured, parking greatly increases the complexity of the planning and demand for land. In urban locations where parking is allowed, it usually has a significant effect on the structural design. Ground-floor loading areas, particularly on small sites, can affect not only structural design, but even the location of the cores. Where codes or clients require off-street loading, it can greatly complicate the design of the building.

Some of the densest cities have begun to limit parking spaces as a way to discourage an increase in cars. In Manhattan, for instance, new office buildings cannot add parking spaces beyond the existing number. One of the greatest challenges facing the workplaces of the future is for them to become less dependent on the automobile. There is little advantage in designing environmentally sensitive buildings that require large parking structures for employee vehicles that consume unconscionable amounts of fuel.

9. Area Schedule

The apportioning, measuring, and analysis of the areas of a building should be constantly updated. An area schedule must be developed to confirm that all of the zoning area has been used, but not exceeded. An ongoing record must also be kept of total rentable area, the efficiency of the building, and the total construction area of the building.

As mentioned earlier, the apportioning of the areas is particularly important in order to determine the elevator design, as the location of the usable spaces determines the location of the population.

The area schedule is essential to determine the cost estimate. The owner must approve the sizes of all the floor plates. Nearly every building will have floors of different sizes in terms of rentable area.

All owners are concerned with the building efficiency. Efficiency is a relative notion depending on a number of factors besides skillful design and coordination, such as the building services standards required by the owner, the method of calculation, and whether the building is for a single user or multiple tenants. Therefore, all charts comparing efficiency of office buildings are of limited value.

10. Cost and Schedule

The prime motivation for commissioning almost all speculative (not for a corporate owner user) office buildings is profit. Therefore, clients will expect cost and schedule to outweigh other issues. The owner's first priority is to maintain the budget, which is probably part of a financial model behind the decision to proceed with the project. The architect, however, must make it clear that a design is a first essential to confirm the validity of the client's proposed budget and schedule.

Monitoring the cost of the design is typically the final responsibility of the client, who usually calls on a combination of in-house experts, consultants such as project managers, quantity surveyors (in the British Commonwealth), cost estimators, and general contractors. As the design develops, it is imperative that the cost of the project be monitored continuously, a procedure that may seem obvious but is often neglected. At the end of each design phase, the architect should request confirmation that the design meets the client's budget before proceeding to the next phase.

One pitfall in regard to cost is that the budget is often determined on the basis of the cost of a comparable existing building, but often during the design process the program expands and standards are upgraded without an increase in budget. Another danger is the expectation that the client's negotiating skills can lower subcontractor prices. Moreover, because office buildings are usually planned during periods of economic growth, construction prices are likely to be rising.

All building projects involve a balance between short-term capital expenditures

OFFICE CONSTRUCTION COSTS

Effect of Building Height and Floor Plate on Cost

Source: DLS Quantity Surveyors

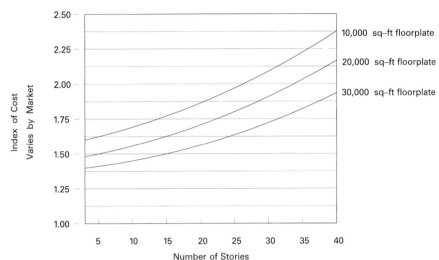

10,000 sq–ft floorplate

20,000 sq–ft floorplate

30,000 sq–ft floorplate

◀ *Graph showing how building costs might vary with floor and story height. © DLS Quantity Surveyors.*

and long-terms costs of operation and maintenance. The approach to first cost is likely to vary among clients, depending on whether the building will be owned over the long term or sold once it has been leased. Many design innovations—particularly in the area of energy consumption—involve anticipated operating savings. Costs and payback period must be calculated and made clear to the client.

The schedule is critical too, because the financial model always assumes a delivery date and a commencement of income. If the building is preleased, as is increasingly typical, there will be financial penalties, as well as damaged reputations, if completion is delayed. In some cases the schedule may in fact be the foremost consideration—particularly in markets where the land cost is high relative to construction cost. Schedule concerns may affect design, particularly in the choice of systems that

shorten construction time. Even the sequence of producing design documents can significantly influence the time required for bidding and construction.

LOCATION AND MARKETS

During the twentieth century a fundamental pattern of the preceding five millennia of human history was changed, as the proportion of urban to rural populations was reversed. This process first took place in the developed world and is now apparent across the developing world. In fact, today more than one million people a day are migrating to cities around the world. The image of the future in these places inevitably includes the high-rise building to support many aspects of life, in particular the workplace.

Despite the convergent pressures of globalization, each country—often each city—tends to develop unique characteristics in the design of office buildings that are resistant to foreign fashions or technological developments. These result from a combination of priorities specific to that place, including climate, geography, local culture and religion, economic history, local codes, and construction practices. A consideration of these distinctions is instructive for office building designers, even if they are not working on overseas commissions.

The world today can be divided into four major markets for office buildings, each with distinct regional characteristics: the United States, Europe, Japan, and Asia.

For the present, all other markets can be considered derivatives of those. Significantly, the Asian market is rapidly increasing in size and eventually will probably be the biggest, especially in tall and large projects.

At the risk of oversimplification, we can see these four markets as having certain characteristic power relationships and design priorities.

In the United States, the performance of mechanical systems, which can account for more than 25 percent of an office building budget, is considered vital to competitive survival. Competitive advantage—at both corporate and personal levels—is the primary concern in office building design. This is manifested in the almost obsessive need for efficiency in the design of the typical floor plate and in the redundancy of power and telecommunications systems. Air-conditioning is often required first for computers, then for employees. In the United States, employee mobility is an accepted fact, and there is hardly any expectation of organizational stability. The typical lease in the United States is 10 to 15 years, allowing tenants to move easily.

In continental Europe it is established by law that every office worker is entitled to work in natural light. This effectively limits the depth-to-core dimension to 8 m (about 25 ft). There is also an almost exclusive use of cellular offices, as well as an overwhelming cultural preference for natural ventilation and an acceptance of summer temperatures that American workers would find uncomfortable. The temperate climate of Northern Europe accommodates these priorities. As a source of natural light and ventilation, and as a key energy-conserving feature,

GLOBAL VARIATION, RELATIONSHIPS AND PRIORITIES*				
Power Relationships	United States	Europe	Japan	Other Asia
Owner	1	2	3	1
Designer	3	1	2	2
Contractor	2	3	1	3
Design Priorities				
Exterior wall	3	1	2	1
Structure	2	3	1	2
Mechanical systems	1	2	3	3
* With 1 designating the most important party or priority and 3 the least.				

the exterior wall is a crucial component, justifying greater design consideration and greater investment in this region than in other parts of the world.

London is a laboratory of the modern office building. As London's office stock undergoes rapid rebuilding within a rich historic context, almost the entire range of possible office building types can be found there, from the conventional North American center-core high-rise through the shallow, naturally ventilated continental European type. This range in quality and type cannot be found anywhere else. Tenants in London have long leases of 25 years, making it potentially difficult to move but allowing owners to invest in higher-quality buildings.

In Japan, pervasive concern about earthquakes gives highest priority to structural stability. In fact, the bulky proportions of so many buildings probably have a comforting effect on many Japanese people, which those who have not grown up with the fear of earthquake devastation cannot understand. The more the buildings have the proportions of sumo wrestlers, the better. In terms of power relationships, contracting companies—some of them more than 200 years old—are granted enormous authority. Owners and architects generally accept their determinations of cost, design feasibility, and details. One of the reasons the contractors are so powerful in Japan is that building owners are not invoiced for construction as it proceeds, but pay only when a building is completed.

The maintenance of buildings is a national priority in Japan. Coupled with what to Westerners must seem as an obsession with hygiene, this tradition of caring for buildings results in spotless but dated structures still in use, where the linoleum floors are paper thin from endless polishing. One need only enter a fire stair, open a service closet, or walk on the roof of even a modest building to recognize that this is not just good management, but a cultural phenomenon. The landlord of commercial property in Japan washes every window in a building at least once a month.

The developments in Asia tend to be larger and more ambitious in scale, taller and bigger than seen elsewhere. Until the economic crisis in 1998, the majority of high-rise office buildings were being built in the cities of Asia. Although the quality of their commercial development is mixed, Hong Kong and Singapore in particular exhibit the best examples of integrated infrastructure and urban planning, and some of the most advanced construction, surpassing the achievements of Europe, the United States, and Japan.

TENANTS, OCCUPANTS, AND INTERIOR ENVIRONMENT

Before finalizing the typical floor plate, it is good practice to develop test layouts of the interior design for hypothetical tenants to be sure the design is sufficiently flexible to meet a variety of needs. The tenant's facility manager will be concerned with the head count, or the number of employees or desks that can be positioned on the floor.

The owner will also be concerned that the design can accommodate multiple tenants in a practical, attractive, and efficient way. If excessive corridor space is required to link possible tenant subdivisions of the floor to the elevator lobby, fire stairs, and rest rooms, the efficiency of the floor will be too sharply reduced.

What is the strategy of the tenants filling these office buildings? Today corporate policies influencing the design of the office building are primarily related to the interior environment and less to the exterior image of power that was a prevalent objective in the 1980s.

The corporate strategy of most companies relative to their real estate is to preserve valuable capital resources—to reduce expenses while increasing productivity and revenue. The typical objectives of a United States company are as follows:

▼ *Office interiors, Union Carbide Building, New York City, 1960, by Skidmore, Owings and Merrill. One of the first office interior systems shows modularity and uniformity.*

- Limit costs, to avoid tying up capital in real estate.

- Maintain the same standards wherever the company operates globally.

- Attract the best people to work for the company and keep them.

- Get these people to communicate and interact with each other, both in person and electronically.

Partly as a result of these pressures, an entirely new model of office tenancy is emerging. In a concept pioneered by companies such as Regus, we are beginning to see office space marketed similarly to hotel space.

Could the success of U.S. corporations over the past ten years be partially attributable to the American workplace? Or is there no correlation between the productivity of the corporation and the design of its workplace? Japanese and European corporate workplaces have not changed as rapidly as those of American enterprises. In Japan the persistence of traditional organizational patterns and life-long employment has, at least until now, discouraged workplace change. Ironically, the heightened European concern for workplace quality has tended to perpetuate the established pattern of cellular offices along exterior walls, and innovation takes the form of increased employee amenities.

The great engine of change today is, of course, the creation of the electronic workplace, which has revolutionized the way we work, communicate, entertain, inform, and so on. Although the electronic revolution has radically affected the design process, vastly expanding analytical capacities, our repertoire of design solutions, and our building team communications, its greatest effects on building design are less tangible. The real challenge for workplace design is to see the implications beyond the obvious ones.

ADAPTABILITY AND LONG-TERM VALUE

Architects and developers tend to conceive buildings for hypothetical scenarios of the first year or two to speed the initial leasing, whereas not enough time is spent considering the entire life of the building, or how to sustain the building in the distant future, assuming that the future is at all predictable.

It is hardly easy, of course, to design buildings that satisfy today's requirements, much less to try to anticipate the requirements of the years to come. This is particularly true of the office building, which is subject to cyclical changes in the commercial world. When we consider the period of business cycles and the uncertainties of currency and interest rate fluctuations, which affect the demand for space and cost of construction, respectively, we can understand the risk involved over even the few years required to design and construct office buildings. One method of promoting the building's value in the more distant future is to consider the adaptability of the design to the broadest range of subsequent occupancy.

Long-term adaptability of buildings is sometimes fortuitously integrated with urban growth and regeneration. Today the most desirable housing in New York is in renovated office buildings in the Wall Street area, where wonderful structures dating from 1890 to 1940—with floor plates too small for today's office market—are being transformed into apartments and so creating true mixed-use neighborhoods. In Chicago, the 1894 Reliance Building, a pioneering curtain-walled office building, has just been renovated as a chic hotel (named The Burnham, for its architect), as has another modern landmark, the 1932

▲ Office interior, Thames Court, London, 1998, by Kohn Pedersen Fox Associates. Contemporary trading floor, with flat computer screens that allow greater density of staff. Photo © H.G. Esch.

PSFS Building (now the Loew's) in Philadelphia, and in London obsolete office buildings from the1960s are being transformed into trendy hotels such as The Sanderson and St. Martin's Lane. In Midtown Manhattan, Lever House, the 1952 icon of the post–World War II modern office building, though obsolete technologically, is being renovated as office space that is leasing for rents equal to the highest in the city, demonstrating the value of location and architectural uniqueness.

TRENDS

Three major issues seem to be driving the design of office buildings today and in the near future, as discussed in the following sections.

Provisions for New Technology, Especially Communications

Electronic technology has, on the one hand, made it more important for cities, especially those with established infrastructure, to quickly absorb the

▲ *PSFS Building, Philadelphia, 1932, Howe and Lescaze. Built as the headquarters for a bank and now a Loew's hotel, the building illustrates the adaptability of modular office spaces, as well as original lobby, banking, and retail spaces. Photo © Esto/Jeff Goldberg.*

and time. We see the possibility of decentralized work not only in the developed economies but also in the developing world. The Internet has the potential to slow, if not reverse, the migration to large cities by bringing opportunities to secondary cities and rural areas around the world.

Companies can organize in such a way that not all work need be done in the inner city but can be done in or near the workers' homes, reducing their commutes and the cost to the organization as well. In the developing world we can already see the benefits of work being outsourced, with the help of electronic communications, to lower-cost but literate labor pools, increasing the need for knowledge workers and for new office buildings there. State-of-the-art buildings are now being proposed in places we would not have imagined only a few years ago.

New technology and e-commerce will have a profound effect on how we build, use, and maintain buildings. The air-conditioning demands of electronic equipment are far more critical than those of employees, because such equipment often needs cool air 24-hours, and mechanical inadequacy can be devastating. With the introduction of wireless technology into mechanical equipment, buildings will operate based on higher levels of information. Companies will be able to monitor buildings owned, space rented, and equipment installed.

"Green" Aspects and Sustainability

As we see in Europe, "green" environmental and ecological concerns can lead to exciting opportunities in the design of exterior walls and to a high ratio of envelope-to-floor area, but such features

demand of emerging companies. In her 1991 book *Global City*, Saskia Sassen brilliantly anticipated the increased importance and dominance of the inner city, especially of the cities that could establish themselves as global. On the other hand, globalization and the Internet, in particular, have eroded the traditional relationship between place

drive up the initial costs of buildings. Apparently, these costs are justified in Europe in terms of lifecycle costs. The following factors have contributed to the development of green office building design there:

- Social priorities favoring the ecologically sensitive

- The relatively high cost of energy

- A preference for cellular offices

- Workers' legal right to work within 25 ft (8 m) of natural daylight

- A strong preference for natural ventilation over uniform air-conditioning

- A relatively temperate climate

It is unlikely that buildings with these characteristics will be commercially viable in other parts of the world unless some of the listed conditions are in place. But there is no doubt that we can learn from the investigations performed for European office buildings and integrate some if not all of these concepts. Ironically, many of these ideas were developed by U.S. firms during the oil crisis of the 1970s.

Human comfort issues are manifested in a variety of features that often work together, such as the exterior wall that not only allows for higher energy savings but also provides natural ventilation, affording greater individual control.

Assuming fuel prices increase in the future, we may see governments in America and Asia adopting stronger energy conservation policies and more educated workforces pressing for green buildings. The solutions in these markets, however, will have to fit the building standards prevalent there, notably large and deep floor plates.

The health effects of working in office buildings, especially the impact of

mechanical ventilation, is a subject of growing concern in the United States. There are also concerns about the environmental impacts of much of the technology and new materials being introduced into the workplace.

Changing Role of the Office Building

The office building is playing a vital role in defining the changes occuring in cities around the world. In nearly every city new office buildings are adding to the density of the urban core. Even European cities, which until recently opposed high-rise office buildings as foreign and insensitive, are now embracing them. Some urban areas in the United States and Europe will soon approach the hyperdensity that we associate with Asian cities such as Tokyo and Hong Kong, which continue to increase their own density—made possible by new technology and increased investment in infrastructure.

Meanwhile, the overlap of work, leisure, and home has created what is sometimes referred to as the "experience economy." The compression of discretionary time results in a great proliferation of places for mixing business, entertainment, and dining. A typical example—combining business, art, recreation, and culture—is the new museum, catering to the business world with high-end restaurants rather than mere cafeterias. Breakfast, lunch, and dinner business meetings and functions happen in museums and themed restaurants. Increasingly, eating, socializing, and active recreation and fitness facilities are being given ample, prominent spaces within the corporate office itself.

A number of social factors are at play here, including the following:

▲ *Nihonbashi 1 Project, Tokyo, Japan, 2002, by Kohn Pedersen Fox Associates. Facing busy Ginza Street, the retail spaces in the base of this office tower are plainly expressed and distinct from the office provision directly above, which houses a major financial services company. Courtesy Kohn Pedersen Fox/Nihon Sekkei.*

- The breakdown of conventional hours for work
- The weakening of traditional family structures
- The change in food and dining culture
- The increased emphasis on health

The ideas about public space that were developed in the 1980s could not take hold until the late 1990s, as retailing and lifestyles had not yet sufficiently evolved. Barnes & Noble, Starbucks, and the Gap have in some ways made these planning concepts possible. During the 1990s retail developers and architects renewed an emphasis on an architecture of placemaking. Although the resulting projects were typically heavily themed, the success of these developments did renew interest in traditional urban experiences.

Consider how mixed-use development has changed since the 1980s, when projects such as Copley Place in Boston or 900 North Michigan in Chicago were built. They turned inward, away from the street, in the manner of suburban shopping malls, and their various functions were distinctly separated. In new developments, the retail opens to the street, the office space is secondary to ground-level

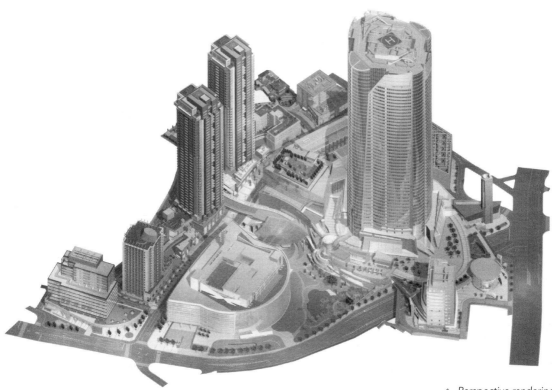

activity, and all of the uses share the place-making function. Increasingly, office tenants feel they need to be connected with these vibrant urban places. In New York, this trend can be seen in the drift of corporate uses to areas that are vital with retailing and cultural activities, such as Times Square.

Buckminster Fuller stated that the largest waste in our society was the office building, which used up so much of our resources and was used only eight hours a day. Today, however, the place of work operates all hours of the day all week, and the building it occupies may accommodate numerous other commercial, cultural, and entertainment facilities, thus greatly extending the usefulness

of its common spaces and service infrastructure, as well as expanding its role in the larger community.

It seems that the global economy and its pervasive technology are indeed driving toward a convergence of building standards in different markets, and superficially office buildings worldwide do share common elements and are occupied, bought, and sold by powerful institutions. However, possibly stronger forces of context, culture, and climate operate to maintain significant distinctions and variations. Moreover, each building results from the personal motivation, imagination, and decisions of willful individuals, thus ensuring ongoing diversification and evolution of the type.

▲ *Perspective rendering of Roppongi Hills, a 27-acre redevelopment in a commercial and entertainment district of Tokyo, with the Roppongi Tower, by Kohn Pedersen Fox Associates, on the right. The mixed-use building incorporates over 3 million sq ft of office space and a variety of retail and cultural uses. The retail component and the 550-room Tokyo Grand Hotel surround the base, and a large museum of contemporary art is at the crown of the tower. With its own independent entry sequence, the rooftop museum can handle a high volume of visitors. A television broadcast center, gardens, and housing complete the project, which provides a new model for development in dense urban environments. Courtesy Kohn Pedersen Fox/The Mori Building Company.*

Office Building Checklist

Listed below are the principal matters addressed by architect and client in the earliest stages of the planning and design of an office building.

Overview of Issues

1. Description of project
2. Project scope
3. Development objectives
4. Planning criteria
5. Specifications
6. Building structure
7. Building envelope
8. Building services
9. Vertical transportation

1. Description of Project

- Site location
- Dimensions of site
- Planning requirements governing design (FAR, height and setback, bulk, street wall requirements, open space, etc.)
- Legal constraints such as property easements and covenants
- Unique conditions such as existing structures or foundations, environmental pollution, required subway connections, etc.
- Approval process
- Construction budget and schedule
- Bidding process (guaranteed maximum price [GMP], design build, fast track, etc.)
- Client organization chart and responsibilities (architects' role relative to client, owner's representative, developer, construction manager [CM] and general contractor [GC])
- Description of consultant team
  - architect(s)
  - structural engineer

- mechanical engineer
- cost consultant (or quantity surveyor)
- vertical transportation engineer
- geotechnical engineer
- civil engineer
- parking consultant
- acoustic engineer
- curtain wall consultant
- exterior wall maintenance consultant
- lighting designer
- landscape architect
- specification writer
- code consultant
- graphic and signage design
- fountain consultant
- wind tunnel laboratory
- curtain wall testing facility

2. Project Scope

- Description of building use(s)
- Anticipated area of each use and number of floors (stacking diagram and program)
- Target tenant types and sizes (For example, large multifloor financial institutions with trading requirements require a very different building than smaller service business.)
- Key design issues for the tenants, possibly including:
  - regularity of floor plate shape
  - efficiency of floor space
  - flexibility of layout—raised floor, easy divisibility, cable management
  - building services:
    - 24-hour operation
    - maximum capacity and redundancy
    - backup cabling
    - quality and reliability of power systems
    - vertical duct availability for power and communication cabling

- building maintenance system (BMS) and security
- telecommunication systems, including satellite
- concierge services
- vertical transportation
- car parking
- Other uses in project
  - retail and entertainment space criteria
  - cultural program such as galleries, exhibition or museum space
  - hotel program

3. Development Objectives

- Ownership objectives (lease buyback, own, exit strategies, build to suit)
- Level of finish (shell and core, full build-out, partition and finish)
- Target tenant mix
- Level or grade of the building relative to competition and/or other buildings in that market or elsewhere
- Design priorities
  - flexibility and quality of interior workplace
  - maximizing views
  - creating column-free space
  - distinctive and memorable form
  - integrating (or contrasting) with immediate context
  - utilizing most advanced technology available
  - respecting environmental considerations
  - level of finish in lobbies and elevators
  - minimizing approval period
  - minimizing construction period
- Target efficiency or total net renewable (usable) space in the building
  - 76–80% mid-rise
  - 80–84% high-rise

85–90% low-rise
- Relationship of other uses and parking to office space

4. Planning Criteria
- Plot ratio (New York City very defined, but often negotiated)
- Building height (governs in London and Washington)
- Car parking (not permitted in New York City, but critical in many cities)
- Loading (varies from city to city)
- Design occupancy (varies from market to market and building to building, but is a critical aspect of decision making. It is unwise to compare efficiencies of buildings without taking this into consideration. On a trading floor, one can anticipate a density of 70 sq ft (7 sq m) net rentable per person. In Asia the design densities are often less than 100 sq ft (10 sq m), whereas in the United States they are usually greater, closer to 140 sq ft (14 sq m).
- Environmental standards (notably in Europe, Hong Kong, and Singapore)
- Typical floor criteria
  floor plate size
  floor plate configuration—shape requirement for corner offices, number of tenants per floor
  core position
  dimension, glass to core wall
  planning grid
  column layout
  natural light
  finished ceiling height
  raised floor
  ceiling type (lighting, acoustic tiles, and plenum requirements)

5. Specifications
- Office space
  floor loading
  raised floors
  ceilings
  walls
  lighting
  sprinklers
  air-conditioning
  toilets
  cleaner closets
  pantries
  electrical closets
  telecommunication and TV distribution closets
  service elevator and lobbies
- Public space facilities
  public space finishes
  building management
  main lobby
  reception and security desks
  elevator lobbies
  carport, elevators, and lobbies

6. Building Structure
- Substructure (define special conditions, top-down construction, effect on schedule)
- Superstructure (concrete or steel)
- Floor loads
- Environmental considerations such as flooding, hurricanes/typhoons, earthquakes, snow and ice

7. Building Envelope
- Base, shaft, top zones
- Exterior wall systems (unitized, stick, etc.)
- Glass criteria and character
  color
  reflectivity
  insulated or monolithic
  coatings

- Spandrel material (stone, metal panel, precast)
- Available suppliers
- Critical dimensions
  sill height
  column location
  mullion spacing
- Storefront
- Louvers for mechanical equipment
- Shading methods (exterior louvers, blinds)
- Window washing

8. Building Services
- Air-conditioning
- Ventilation
- Fire services
- Plumbing and drainage
- Electrical services—high voltage and low voltage distribution
- Lighting
- Standby power
- UPS
- BMS
- Security systems—closed-circuit TV (CCTV) and access alarm and control
- Communication
- Telecommunication system and distribution

9. Vertical Transportation
- Elevator service criteria:
  maximum interval (typically 30 sec)
  5-min handling capacity (typically 12.5%)
  loading assumption (typically 80%)
  population density
- Service elevator requirement
- Car parking access
- Escalators
- Double-deck elevators
- Security controls
- Emergency power

CONSULTANTS' ISSUES

▼ Modern information technology makes it possible to work almost anywhere.

◀ Interior of S. C. Johnson and Son Administration Building, Racine, Wisconsin, by Frank Lloyd Wright, a highly innovative office dating from 1936.

◣ Weyerhaeuser Headquarters, Tacoma, Washington, by Skidmore, Owings & Merrill, 1971.

▲ Worker at a desk designed by Frank Lloyd Wright for S.C. Johnson and Son Administration Building, 1936.

◢ Open office planning for all employees, including top executive at Weyerhaeuser Headquarters, Tacoma, Washington. Building and interiors by Skidmore, Owings & Merrill, 1971.

▼ Pioneering modular partitions in interior of Connecticut General Life Insurance Building, Bloomfield Connecticut, by Skidmore, Owings & Merrill, with interiors by Knoll Planning Unit.

INTERIOR ARCHITECTURE

DEBRA LEHMAN-SMITH *Lehman-Smith+McLeish*

THE EVOLUTION OF TODAY'S OFFICE

To understand the components and factors involved in the interior architecture of the office, we should first briefly review a the history of the office.

As recently as the 1960s, a state-of-the-art office meant central air-conditioning, a telephone at every desk, an IBM electric typewriter for each secretary, and a new Xerox photocopier on each floor. By the late 1980s, however, two relentless forces—the rise of high technology and the competitive global economy—had changed the workplace forever. As the office hierarchy flattened, more executives occupied open office workstations, computers appeared on every desk, conference rooms expanded as private offices shrank, e-mail globalized and intensified business communications, laptops and cell phones extended work hours into travel and leisure time.

In the 1990s employers extrapolated these trends with workplace strategies like telecommuting, satellite offices, and "office hoteling," which shifts workers from desk to desk based on scheduling and work requirements. Industry experts predicted the death of the traditional office. But something unexpected happened: Many workers did not like telecommuting, preferring face-to-face interactions and collaboration, and they wanted their own spaces in which to work.

These cutting-edge approaches began to lose their appeal, but interior architects found themselves designing for an exceptionally wide variety of workplace programs. The office interior had never been less standardized.

CLIENT OBJECTIVES AND INDUSTRY TRENDS

Office configurations, trends, and buzzwords come and go. Although no one can predict what changes the future will bring to office buildings, two basic strategies can help guide the office planning and design process.

▲ *Connecticut General Life Insurance Building, 1957.*

▼ *Open office at Chiat Day Building, Venice, California, by Frank O. Gehry & Associates, 1991.*

First, office planning and design should be impelled by the client's unique corporate identity, culture, and business goals. These factors cannot be stressed enough as a driving force behind the office design. Before even approaching an interior architect, the client organization should first determine its own goals and objectives for the new or renovated office space. Typical goals include the following:

- Increased worker efficiency and productivity
- Increased worker satisfaction
- Increased customer or client satisfaction
- Greater profitability margins
- Benefiting from tax incentives
- Improved corporate image
- Allowing for future growth
- Accommodating office politics
- Integrating new technology
- Creating sustainable office design

The client should also estimate a project budget and determine whether the space is to be leased or owned. Once the client has made decisions on these issues and knows how it plans to run the project—whether in-house or through an outside project manager—it can then begin to select an interior architect.

Second, the planning and design should address trends in the client's business sector. With tomorrow's directions in mind, the design team can better design an office that will accommodate the client for many years to come. This effort is best accomplished jointly by the interior architect and the client, as each can contribute to a different aspect of the research:

- The client has a good understanding of trends in its specific industry and new industries that it may plan to expand into.
- The interior architect has experience in designing spaces for various industries and adapting them to current trends.

As Heraclitus said, "Nothing endures but change." Corporate goals change. Customers and clients change. A company should continually restudy and adapt its workplace to the ever-evolving technology, work patterns, and challenges of its particular business. Thus, the interior project team must understand this business evolution and create designs that will improve the client's business practices and meet its business goals.

THE DESIGN PROCESS

The planning and design of an office interior that serves a company's business goals, while remaining within the budget, is often best accomplished through an inside-out process—planning the interior before designing the exterior. Through this "form follows function" method, the building design will be based on the requirements of the client. Alternatively, many companies choose to design an office located in an existing building or in a new structure whose interior volumes have already been established. In any case, the first task is often finding the right interior project team for the job.

Selecting the Project Team

To find the best interior project team, the company must state and prioritize its goals for the project (such as those listed in the previous section) in its Request for Qualifications (RFQ), which is sent to the interior architecture firms selected for consideration. To determine which firms are to receive an RFQ, the company most often draws on past experience and gets references from business associates and friends. Depending on the size, scale, and prestige value of the project, an RFQ may be sent to two firms, or as many as thirty.

Firms that respond to the RFQ submit a written document stating how they meet the qualifications required for the project. Generally, the information submitted in an RFQ includes the following:

- Firm background

- Descriptions and graphic representations of similar projects

- Proposed team members, including consultants

- Proposed core team members' résumés

- Current and future firm workload

- Firm's financial status

- Number of firm's employees

After analyzing the submissions of all responding firms, the company creates a short list of suitable applicants, which may range from two to about eight firms. Then the company interviews these firms, evaluating them and selecting those most appropriate within the established parameters. The company should also ensure that the personalities of the proposed project team can work well with the personnel running the project for the company.

A Request for Proposal (RFP) can also be issued as part of the selection process.

The information requested from potential candidates in the RFP further details the information provided in the RFQ, including proposed team members' relevant project experience, letters of recommendation, proposed fee structure, and the like. Companies may choose to issue the RFP either before the interviews, to all potential interview candidates, or after the interviews to the final two to three firms.

Each project team selection process is different. The decision to issue an RFP and its timing are largely determined by the corporate culture of the company and the personality and organizational practices of the company's contracting officer. On many projects, the RFQ and RFP are combined into one document request.

It is advisable for principals of a firm answering an RFP and appearing for an interview to stress their value as problem solvers and professionals who can analyze problems in light of corporate objectives and come up with solutions. "Design" skill as such—although essentially encompassing the same attributes—may be perceived by the client as much less essential. It is also important, when a firm wins the commission, for the design team to determine where the project has the strongest support—or resistance—within the corporate hierarchy. It is the role of the design team to get the client's senior management to understand the project process and design and to get them excited about the project so that they champion it within their organization. This approach will make the entire project process much more successful for all parties involved.

Freddie Mac's Selection Process

Freddie Mac had been developing its corporate campus in northern Virginia for 13 years. Each of the three buildings so far completed had been treated separately, and different architectural teams had participated. When it was decided to add a fourth building, a high priority was to create one that would look to the future. Responding to the changing business environment, and especially the recent real estate trends in the northern Virginia area, Freddie Mac wanted the new building to represent its position as a progressive leader in the home financing market as well as a corporation that gives back to its community.

The design team selection process was based on the corporate goals and objectives of Freddie Mac. After reviewing RFQ submissions from a number of interior architectural design teams, Freddie Mac sent out an RFP to five teams. This RFP clearly stated the client's evaluation criteria and requirements for the new project as follows:

- Design excellence
- Technical capability
- Commitment to quality
- Use of minority- and women-owned businesses
- Fee

Further, Freddie Mac defined its objectives for the new building as including flexibility, as well as technical, functional, and aesthetic integration with the existing campus and an environmentally state-of-the-art workplace.

After reviewing the RFP submissions, Freddie Mac held interviews involving key members of the proposed project team. This allowed the client to determine firsthand

▶ *Main entrance, Freddie Mac corporate office building, McLean, Virginia; architecture by AI, interior design by Lehman-Smith + McLeish.*

whether the project team met its selection criteria. To enhance its selection capability, Freddie Mac included nationally recognized architects with base building and interior architecture experience on the selection committee. With a solid set of project goals and the aid of these architects, it was able to select a firm that it believed would help to realize the organization's goals and lead it into the future.

Once the team was selected, Freddie Mac took time to express the benefits of teaming and scheduled team-building meetings. All team members took the Myers Briggs test for personality assessment. The personality profiles were compiled and evaluated to create a group profile, which served to assist both the team and the client to avoid any potential pitfalls during the design process. "Design charrettes" and nontraditional collaborative meetings, attended by all members of the project team, replaced traditional project meetings, with agendas divided by subject matter. In this way the design team was given responsibility to ensure that all areas of design, from the lighting design to the mechanical systems to the furniture specifications, were coordinated and successfully met or exceeded the project goals set forth by Freddie Mac. Every member of the team was empowered to initiate design concepts.

▲ *Main lobby, Freddie Mac corporate office building.*

Team Members

An interior project team is composed of the interior architectural team members and their consultants. The interior architectural team is headed by the project designer and the project manager. The project designer and manager may be the same person, depending on the size and scale of the project. The project designer is responsible for all design services throughout the project, providing the vision and direction for the entire team, creating the overall organization and design of the interior spaces, and ensuring that the client's objectives are met.

The project manager—supported by the project architect, the strategic planner, the staff architects, and the interior designers—manages the design team and all consultants, is in charge of construction administration, coordinates all project activities, and directs development of all technical criteria.

It is beneficial for the client to have the design team involved throughout the entire project from the programming stage through the construction administration stage, so that the initial design concept is sure to be incorporated in the completed offices. Some clients, however, choose to turn the project over to a team involved solely in construction administration during construction to gain a more objective view on field construction issues.

Every interior architectural project team must collaborate with a number of consultants to complete all facets of the design. These consultants may be members of the architect's office, or they may be outside firms. Consultants in the following fields typically make up an interior project team:

- MEP (mechanical, electrical, plumbing) engineering
- Structural engineering
- Telecommunications/data
- Technology
- Life safety and codes (local and federal)
- Lighting
- Acoustics
- Audio/visual
- Signage and graphics

Additional consultants, such as those in the following fields, are often added to project teams, depending on the complexity and special requirements of the project:

- Budget and schedule control
- Sustainability and environmental issues
- Food service
- Construction management
- Public relations
- Specifications
- Procurement
- Relocation
- Feng shui
- Allied arts
- Workplace psychology

Any consultant selected for an interior office project should have the following qualifications:

- Experience with a similar project type
- Ability to meet the budget and schedule
- Understanding of the client's culture and business goals
- Understanding of the project's goals and design aesthetic

- Understanding of global challenges
- Cutting-edge expertise in the field
- Potential for innovative solutions that enhance the project
- Strong communication skills
- Collaborative work ethic
- Previous successful collaboration with the architectural team

Analyzing the Client Organization

Once an interior architect is selected, that firm must begin the project by analyzing the client organization and its goals. This analysis is the most important step in the design process and will become the driving force behind all subsequent decisions. Depending on the expertise of the interior architect, a different firm may be hired as a consultant to work with the interior architect on this strategic planning process.

Strategic plan

The design of a corporate office offers a unique opportunity to improve upon the existing efficiency and productivity levels of the business while reflecting the distinct corporate culture in the space. The first meetings with the design team should review the client's strategic plan for the project. Most often this plan is generated directly from the corporate strategic plan, which will give the design team invaluable knowledge of how to approach a project.

Responding to the strategic plan, a forward-thinking project team can introduce innovative ideas and suggest paradigm shifts that will have a lasting impact. For example, General Dynamics was interested in renovating its existing headquarters in Falls Church, Virginia.

After several initial meetings, it became apparent that, in addition to updating and modernizing the look of the offices, the facility should promote the collaboration of the different operating units at the executive level and introduce the rich General Dynamics history into the design. The company had begun as Electric Boat in the late 1800s, and upon acquisition of the aircraft company Canadair, Ltd., had changed its corporate name to General Dynamics, with Electric Boat remaining as a subsidiary. The project team resurrected and brought to the forefront the strong corporate image of a global corporation. Models of General Dynamics ships and submarines were mounted on corridor and conference room walls, a history wall outlining more than 100 years of business was incorporated as a design element, and posters from the General Dynamics-commissioned "Atoms for Peace" campaign of the 1950s were rediscovered and framed for display in the training room.

The best interior plan and design are developed from an in-depth analysis and understanding of what makes a specific company's workforce perform to its maximum potential, within the framework of the company's culture and goals and the workforce members' lifestyles. The final strategic plan that evolves from this process is often different from the initial direction.

Understanding how an organization works involves more than constructing an overall picture. Groups within the company work, behave, and interact differently, depending on their responsibilities and individual needs. Thus, the initial meeting with the client should be accompanied by a tour of its existing facilities to see how various parts of the organization operate. A group of computer programmers, for example, has a different culture from a group of advertising executives. The computer programmers work, for the most part, independently and require a significant amount of solitude and privacy in a structured setting. The advertising executives, however, constantly collaborate and brainstorm to meet fast-paced deadlines, requiring spaces that support speed, flexibility, and collaboration.

The European approach to office interiors is to create a healthful and supportive work environment that includes a maximum amount of fresh, as opposed to recycled, air; individual control of lights, temperature, and airflow by workstation or zone; and invigorating design elements and details. The value of these benefits is becoming more widely appreciated in the United States.

Program

An office interior program is based on an analysis of the client's business goals and objectives. It defines the physical requirements of the workplace and allocates space for every use and employee. The interior project team begins programming by interviewing client executives and staff to determine the following:

- Current staff and future projections
- Current and future departmental responsibilities, work processes, and functional requirements
- Individual personnel functional requirements
- Critical department adjacency requirements

- Department support space requirements (workrooms, computer rooms, meeting spaces, training rooms, etc.)
- Office and workstation space standards
- Technology requirements specific to departments
- Base building requirements (structural, HVAC, plumbing, ceiling height, etc.)

From this information and the design team's understanding of the client's organization, the program can be created to define the physical requirements of the workplace.

Workplace analysis

Once the project program is established, the interior project team must delve deeper into the requirements for the project. The following topics related to the project organization should be covered:

Flexibility

The team must determine how often a company shifts departments and/or changes teams and how simple this process needs to be. This assessment can lead to discussions regarding movable or fixed partitions and the cost impacts of flexibility.

Uniform office/workstation sizes

The amount of open versus closed office space and the sizes of offices and workstations that are required to support various office functions must be determined. A standard office/workstation size or a limited number of sizes to delineate hierarchy in an office is an important factor in any project. These workstations can be composed of various components that can become a "kit of parts" to aid in their flexibility. Such methods will help to keep costs down and provide a module for space layouts.

Technology

One of the most expensive investments for a corporation and one of the largest components of the construction budget is technology. It is essential that the amount of flexibility needed, redundancy requirements, needs for multisite operations, reliability of the system, employee accessibility (home or office), and the type of distribution (wireless or broadband) be taken into consideration in the strategy for integrating technology into the facility.

Security

The visibility of security and how it is best integrated into the building management systems and architecture must be consistent with the corporation's philosophy regarding security. The increased risk of violence in the workplace, caused by employees or coming from outside, has changed the way security is viewed. For example, after the Oklahoma City bombing, the General Services Administration (GSA) enhanced security at its facilities around the country, but the visible enhancements changed the character of those workplaces and created a negative first impression for visitors. The GSA is now better integrating the security systems into the interior architecture, keeping the protective measures but making them less obvious.

Acoustics

There are fundamental conflicts between productivity and the acoustics of open office designs. Studies now define high-intensity and low-intensity noise. This helps in deciding what building systems

and products can make open office space more productive.

Shared conference facilities

The interior architecture team must understand fully how conference rooms are used, what sizes are most functional, and who the users are. Decisions can then be made about whether there are to be centralized or decentralized conference rooms or a combination, what services must be adjacent, and whether they are used by the public or not. The amount of real estate required for departmentalized conferencing is greater than that needed for a central conference facility, but the choice must be appropriate to the corporate culture.

Support spaces

Support spaces are critical to the operation of a facility; they can include mailrooms, records storage, stockrooms, and catering kitchens. Again, the amount of real estate dedicated to their use has a cost impact, but their functionality is equally important. The company must assess where these spaces should be located and consider alternate solutions such as off-site storage or less costly basement or windowless space.

Communication areas

One of the most important programming objectives for today's companies is increasing communication among employees through spontaneous interactions and strategies like teaming. Companies have found that the faster information is shared, the faster it is processed. The faster ideas are communicated, the faster they are improved. Closed-door sessions are now rarely the preferred method of working. The New

Jersey–based M&M/Mars candy company has an open office plan in which department heads sit surrounded by team members in a wagon wheel arrangement, which provides easy access and communication throughout the office.

Amenities

Additional amenities and services within the workplace are becoming increasingly common. The following amenities may be incorporated into the design to raise worker satisfaction and productivity:

- Dry cleaner
- Fitness center
- Child care
- Café
- Outdoor running trail
- Cafeteria with take-home meals
- Employee-interest courses (non-work-related)

The following services can be provided to improve morale by saving workers time outside the office:

- Dog walking
- Vacation planning
- Flower delivery
- Elderly care option analysis
- Medical facilities and personnel

All of these amenities and services are viewed as extremely valuable by employees, as many of them are working extended hours and have little free time to spend with family and friends. The Gap, Inc., headquarters has a fitness center and a lap pool to encourage employees to exercise and relieve stress without leaving work. The John Hancock Mutual Life Company in Chicago has found that its child

care facility has alleviated family pressures for its staff, allowing workers to concentrate better on the business at hand. More and more companies are asking for interior areas that encourage creativity. Nortel Networks, a leading global supplier of data and telephone network solutions and services, has an Internet café and a Zen garden in its Brampton, Ontario, office facility. The 120,000 sq ft Los Angeles headquarters of the TBWA/Chiat Day advertising agency has an indoor basketball court.

Special equipment

Every company has special equipment requirements unique to its culture, business, and work process that directly impact an office building's architecture and systems. Vaults, library shelving, and high-density file storage, for example, require increased structural strength for their floors.

Budget

Every project has a budget that it must correlate with the design. Regardless of the budget, the architect should strive to accommodate all required project goals. Often, it is the projects with the most limited budget that result in the most creative and interesting designs.

Planning

Too many companies occupy outdated office facilities that do not necessarily reflect their culture or corporate identity, do not support the work now being produced, reduce the ability of workers to operate effectively, and negatively impact real estate value. Several key planning strategies, however, can break those ties to the past and create an office that supports a company's culture and business goals. These strategies include determination of location and office configuration, organizational methods, and use of building components.

Location and configuration

The selection of a location for an office is based on issues of immediate and long-term costs, politics, business goals and objectives, corporate image, and the ability to serve and attract clients and customers. These factors contribute to choosing where a company settles, whether it is a city center or suburban site, a speculative building, a new campus, or a virtual office.

Because the interior program and plan are driven by the client's culture and busi-ness goals, the building size and shape are as well. Before programming was done for Gannett's new headquarters in Tyson's Corner, Virginia, the client had anticipated building a 30-story tower. But the programming showed that most of the company's departments need the adjacencies that come with fewer, larger floor areas, thus pointing toward the mid-rise campus concept that was ultimately carried out.

Organizational methods

Strong organizational concepts established in the early stages of planning provide clear guidelines throughout the planning and design process. To produce an efficient, dynamic, and cost-effective facility, the design team must consider the way people circulate within the building, how adaptable the building is to changing needs, and the standards to adopt for offices and workstations.

Circulation

The way people move through a building is a key organizing element of the interior space. Both horizontal and vertical circulation can be designed to create maximum opportunities for chance meetings and interactions. Placing common pantries and support centers adjacent to the main circulation path, for example, is one way to encourage interaction.

Establishing common travel patterns and prioritizing paths—for instance, creating a primary hallway or "main street"—give definition to flexible spaces and create a consistent traffic pattern. A main street also means that less secondary circulation is required, saving space for other uses. Perimeter circulation is beneficial because, unlike traditional internal paths, it does not break up office areas, it improves communication within and between departments, and it permits more efficient space planning and cost-effective reconfigurations as work processes and organizational needs change. At AmSouth Bancorporation's corporate campus there are informal teaming areas just off the perimeter circulation paths on each floor, offering views to the adjacent woods.

A vertical circulation system (stairs, elevators, escalators) can ensure critical vertical adjacencies and communication. Escalators provide the main vertical circulation in Alcoa's Pittsburgh headquarters, creating a visual connection between floors and establishing a traffic pattern that increases staff contact and chance meetings. The elevators are reserved for use by disabled persons. Designing visual links between floors also fosters improved communication.

(continued on page 70)

AmSouth's Location and Design

As a result of rapid expansion in the early 1990s, AmSouth Bancorporation almost doubled its assets, growing from $9.5 billion to $18.6 billion. During this expansion it underwent numerous office reconfigurations throughout its eight buildings. By 1992 it was time to find a better way to deal with the churn in the workplace. Lehman-Smith + McLeish was brought in first to help the company in this effort. Together, they created a new corporate complex that met all of AmSouth's goals. Instead of maintaining the multiple offices located throughout Alabama, the firm decided on a centralized corporate complex to increase departmental communication and corporate unity. The 350-acre wooded site selected for the complex provides desired views and ambiance for the employees, thus enriching their work environment. The new complex was composed of 100 percent open office spaces to provide a flexible space with a serene and intimate appeal.

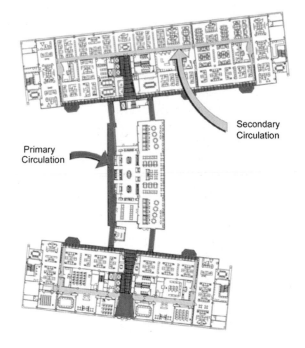

Primary Circulation

Secondary Circulation

▲ Plan showing main circulation along exterior walls at AmSouth Bank corporate complex, Birmingham, Alabama; base building by Lohan & Associates, office interiors by Lehman-Smith + McLeish

◀ Perimeter corridor at AmSouth, by Lehman-Smith + McLeish. Photo © Hedrich Blessing.

▲ Perimeter office partially enclosed
by movable partitions at AmSouth,
by Lehman-Smith + McLeish.
Photo © Hedrich Blessing.

◀ Cafeteria with broad view of site at
AmSouth, by Lehman-Smith + McLeish.
Photo © Hedrich Blessing.

(continued from page 67)

Because stairs and escalators are expensive, companies may want to consider the use of the exit stairs for internal vertical circulation. These can be upgraded or secured as need be to meet the company's requirements.

Components of the overall interior architecture, including circulation paths, flooring patterns, ceiling patterns, ceiling height changes, the expansion and contraction of spaces, and the angling of walls, are the most important wayfinding devices of interior architecture. To enhance architectural wayfinding clues, graphics and signage should be integral to the overall aesthetic and be displayed at appropriate locations throughout the building. The forms of graphics and signage used should respond to the client's image and the architectural design of the space and provide detailed information, such as office and room numbers and names, building egress plans, and the like.

Flexibility

A flexible interior that supports change cost-effectively is a key concern for companies that are growing, shedding groups or subsidiaries, or acquiring new ones. A standardized plan with uniform office and workstation sizes provides an organizational framework that can be reconfigured as required. The design should also support technological change. Provisions for long-term flexibility can ultimately be more economical than short-term solutions. Movable partitions may have a higher cost initially, but if a company is constantly reconfiguring, the money spent relocating drywall partitions can exceed the cost of movable partitions.

Modular workstations—standardized, self-supporting modules, each with its own operating systems—provide the flexibility that supports change. More of them can easily be assigned to an expanding group or department. Renovating an entire floor does not require demolition and starting over. It simply means unplugging in one place and plugging in at another. These modular workstations can also be personalized by each employee from a kit of parts, creating a more varied office environment that addresses individual work styles.

Floor power and data boxes should be strategically located so that workstations have a central spine, with power and communications feeding from a particular floor box. The workstation configurations can vary along that spine, because all of the less flexible power and communications components are carried within it. In this way, the spine walls become organizing elements of the design.

Underfloor systems, once used primarily for data and telecommunication cabling, are now incorporating complex HVAC systems. Underfloor air ducts not only offer greater individual control and higher air quality, but they also increase the flexibility of an interior space. These floor systems are further discussed in the section on mechanical systems.

Regardless of the client's particular needs for conference and training rooms, these facilities and related support functions should be centralized on the floors where they occur. They should be concentrated at the core of the building or at one end of the floor. Through such grouping of these facilities, the client will receive greater economies of scale for the electrical, HVAC, and other systems that are often more specialized, hence more expensive than those for a typical office space. This also allows the rest of the space to be more flexible for future reconfigurations. In addition, the conference and training rooms can be designed to be flexible enough to serve two or more different uses. Movable partitions allow the rooms to accommodate various meeting sizes.

Standardization

Standardizing different components of the interior plan has several benefits. It establishes corporate space standards that can reduce the number of reconfigurations generated by promotions and organizational changes. It creates greater efficiency and ultimate cost savings. And it increases interior flexibility, inasmuch as a particular office can serve a computer programmer or an executive. Common components that can be standardized are furniture, office sizes, lighting systems, mechanical systems, and electrical systems. Standardization can have a dramatic impact on a company's culture, for example, by creating the perception and reality of greater equality.

Too much standardization, however, can have a negative impact on the company culture. If the office layout becomes too monotonous, with little differentiation of materials or components in the workstations or within the general office environment, the employees may feel as though they are working in a factory. Standardized components must be interspersed with architectural design elements, such as changes in ceiling heights, wall angles, materials, colors, and textures, to maintain a dynamic office environment.

Building Components

All of the physical elements of the office interior—visible and concealed—present opportunities to improve efficiency, employee satisfaction, and projection of the company's intended image.

Structural systems

The ideal open office plan is column-free to provide maximum flexibility. Although this objective is seldom accomplished because of the special structural effort it requires, there are ways that columns can be located to facilitate office layout. After the standard office and workstation sizes are determined, an efficient floor layout should be created that incorporates the standard-sized workspaces and allows for sufficient circulation space. When combined with the basic structural loading and related factors, this layout will aid in determining the most effective and efficient column spacing, which will provide flexibility for future reconfigurations.

A cost-effective solution that also improves flexibility is the incorporation of increased structural load capacity adjoining the core area of any floor or floors. Generally, if the floor loading capacity is 100 lb per sq ft, the increased capacity is 150–300 lb per sq ft. This solution allows for a central area to be set aside for the office's heavy equipment and dense storage, leaving the rest of the floor area more adaptable for future reconfigurations.

Mechanical systems

A conventional mechanical system provides air distribution and return at the ceiling. The alternative of underfloor air plenums is being considered increasingly, because they provide better air distribution to the individual workstations, with more personal control and decreased energy consumption. At Freddie Mac's corporate campus, a raised flooring system was already standard, as in many places, for flexibility in relocating cabling and power. In this case, integrating an HVAC system into the established raised flooring system was a logical choice. When the floor layout is changed, the company can easily tap into a duct at a new location without the expense or inconvenience of relocating a duct run, and employees are given control of the HVAC in their work areas.

The initial cost of an underfloor system is higher than that of a conventional system, but the difference can be made up over the long term in energy savings, employee satisfaction and productivity, and cost savings on reconfigurations. The real challenge is installing underfloor systems in existing buildings and in certain cities. Buildings constructed in the early 1900s, for example, may not have the necessary slab-to-slab heights an underfloor system needs. Some cities, such as Washington, D.C., have height restrictions on their buildings. This results in reduced floor-to-floor heights in order to maximize the number of floors.

Telecommunications

The ever-changing and complex world of technology strongly impacts how a company wants to be wired and what it costs. It is critical that systems be flexible enough to change with the times. Flexible infrastructures must be created that can accommodate wireless technology. Technology that supports alternative work styles and offers more advanced and efficient means of communication improves employee quality of life.

The high-tech revolution has directly affected office interiors. An interior program must include a technology program that addresses integrated technology, the amount of flexibility and redundancy the technology or business goals require, the number of multisite technology operators, how employees will access the technology (at home vs. on-site), and the type of distribution (wireless or broadband).

At IBM corporate headquarters in Armonk, NewYork, the building network used category 5 cables (two voice, two data), as well as multimode fiber to support video and future needs. IBM plans to change to a wireless system in the future. To support mixed requirements, wired digital, analog, and ISDN systems were provided to the workstations, including Ethernet, Token Ring, and ATM protocols. The bandwidth for the ATM is planned for 25 mb. RF capability was provided throughout the building on support laptops. Redundant fiber backbones were designed within the building as well as redundant network switches, hubs, and firewalls, all with full backup power management systems. Lucent Technology telephone switches and CTI/telephony technology are utilized to join voice and e-mail. This allows users to call in and retrieve e-mail, whether voice or data—part of the company's effort to support telecommuting. Video and data presentations are available in conference rooms, which are further outfitted with digitalized white boards and video conferencing equipment.

An increasing number of companies are accommodating technology not just at workstations, but throughout their workplaces. Data ports, for example, can be placed in teaming areas, cafés, and lounge seating areas to give individual workers and groups, meeting or collaborating in those spaces, access to their company network, e-mail, and the Internet. At Owens-Corning, laptops have become standard equipment, so employees can move easily through the building, plugging into a data port whenever and wherever necessary or expedient. Alcoa's Pittsburgh head-quarters has "Communication Centers," teaming areas with teleconferencing equipment, computers, data ports, faxes, and audiovisual equipment to support collaborative groups and teaming processes.

Security

The kind, extent, and sensitivity of the security measures used are based on a company's culture and philosophy. Some companies, for example, may simply use standard latch bolts and door key locks on its office floors and install tighter security measures at the public entrances to the building. For companies that want a greater level of security, electronically controlled keyless access is becoming more common. For example, companies with a high churn (employee turnover) rate can simply change the key card, rather than changing locks and issuing new keys.

Corporate culture and business goals also determine how visible a security system should be and how it should be integrated into the building architecture and management systems. Many companies require different levels of security on different floors. To work on government contracts, RAND Corporation, a nonprofit think tank in Arlington, Virginia, must meet rigorous security requirements. All lobbies are controlled by access card, except the main reception floor, which is accessible to employees and guests alike during normal business hours. Exit stairs are controlled by access card so employees can use them as communication stairs. Some offices have keypad locks. The classified workrooms are protected by turn combination locks, similar to those on vaults.

Acoustic control

There are three primary areas to target in an open office program for acoustic and sound control, starting with the mechanical systems. Sound levels can be controlled by the type of fan used, the ductwork layout, a fan discharge design that creates smooth aerodynamics for airflow, an increased length of duct in the mechanical room, and the use of acoustic lining in the duct, particularly in ductwork that is downstream from the fan power boxes. Using low-noise diffusers and properly sized diffusers also helps reduce noise.

Sound-masking systems such as white noise can provide another level of sound control in an open office. White noise is a low-level background noise that is broadcast throughout the office space. The white noise is not easily distinguished and thereby serves to mask the more distinct noises generated by the passage of air through the ductwork, liquids through the plumbing pipes, and so on. This helps to reduce the distraction level of the building systems' noises for the employees working in the office.

The second primary area of acoustic control is in the architectural systems—doors, partitions, and ceilings. Frameless doors, for example, are difficult to seal against outside sound. Solid-core wood doors with overlapping frames are preferable. Sound separation between rooms can be improved by putting acoustic insulation in the partitions, taking drywall to the underside of the slab, and adding layers of drywall. Both private and open offices should have highly absorptive ceiling tile made of fiberglass. Workstation layouts and panel heights also establish walls of acoustic privacy and sound control for personal workspaces. Fabric-wrapped panels provide increased acoustical control; a 60–66 in. panel height is the minimum requirement for speech privacy.

Third, finish materials can also aid or hinder sound control. Hard materials like wood flooring and wall paneling, or stone and metal panels on walls or furniture systems, should be used only in areas where sound control is not important. In sound-sensitive areas such as an open office, soft, sound-absorbent materials are best.

Lighting design

Lighting design should support the interior architecture, enhance the workspace environment, and provide energy efficiency. Different work and break areas need different lighting, both to differentiate the spaces and to serve the needs of various users. Uplighting and fluorescent lighting may be used in an open office environment to accentuate the openness and scale of the space, and downlighting and incandescent lighting solutions are effective in reception areas to create a warm and inviting feeling. Flexible lighting is needed in conference rooms to serve the various uses of the space, including audiovisual presentations.

The following are three of the primary goals for a successful workplace lighting design:

- Maximum use of daylight
- Use of indirect light
- Inclusion of innovative lamps and fixtures like T2/T3/T5 (high-energy, long-lasting, better-color fluorescent lamps), occupancy sensors, and dimming electronic ballasts for greater energy efficiency and lower operating costs

Natural light can be brought into the interior through the traditional use of windows. By designing narrow floor

---

DIRECT AND INDIRECT LIGHTING COMPARISONS

Direct Lighting

Pros	Cons
Most energy efficient (0.8–1.5 watts/sq ft)	Architecturally bland and common solution
Wide range of manufacturers, ensuring low costs	Careful planning required to avoid glare on monitors
Low initial ($34 per sq ft) and maintenance costs	Not cutting-edge technology
Can be integrated into HVAC system	Requires more wiring/mounting points

Indirect Lighting

Pros	Cons
Fixtures can be architectural feature or completely concealed	Least energy efficient
Best for glare control	Higher initial costs ($4 per sq ft concealed; $7 per sq ft pendant)
Innovative fixtures and technologies available today	May require local task lighting to meet requirements

plates and inserting glass clerestory windows at full partition height, along with glass doors and sidelights for enclosed perimeter offices, natural light can be brought into almost any space within an office floor.

Artificial lighting should be used to supplement natural light. Indirect lighting is preferable in an open office because it is less severe, reduces glare on computer screens, and maximizes the flexibility needed to accommodate future reconfigurations. Individually controlled desktop lighting and individual task lights save energy and give employees personal control of their work environment. As a method of combining natural and artificial lighting, automatic dimmers can be used to sense a reduction in natural light and add artificial light.

Sustainability

Sustainablity is an increasingly important business issue, and architectural design issue. Sustainable design reflects a company's decision to be environmentally responsible by setting clear environmental performance goals, minimizing material waste, using green products, and incorporating energy-efficient mechanical and lighting systems. Ultimately, this effort translates into better facility management and can, over the long term, be very cost-effective.

Sustainable actions a company should consider for employee and global benefit can include the following:

- Improving air quality through building systems
- Eliminating unhealthful materials that give off harmful gases
- Increasing natural light and reducing reliance on artificial light

- Using efficient building systems and lighting components
- Using natural, recycled, durable, and low-maintenance materials
- Emphasizing the use of locally manufactured materials and environmentally friendly products, especially those that are biodegradable or created from postconsumer waste
- Installing components and furniture that can be adapted and reused in new office configurations
- Using nontoxic finishes and wood products harvested from ecologically friendly sources

As companies become steadily more aware of the long-term environmental and health impacts of the materials and furniture in their offices, more environmentally-friendly products are appearing. Paint manufacturers, for example, now produce low- to zero-VOC (volatile organic compound—i.e., toxic gas emitting) paints and paints made from natural resins and nontoxic pigments. Natural floor coverings such as natural linoleum and natural carpeting are now being rediscovered for their environmental qualities. Many furniture manufacturers are designing environmentally sensitive products made from recycled and biodegradable materials.

Materials

How materials are perceived and the way they are used is constantly changing. The following paragraphs discuss some of the key considerations in choosing materials.

Image

A company's corporate image can be defined, refined, or magnified through the careful selection and use of materials and finishes. An office can incorporate a wide range of materials such as wood, glass, stone, and metal. How and where these materials are used will determine the effect on the office design and environment. For example, many of the "dot-com" companies tend to use a combination of materials to create an edgy and progressive image. To be successful, the image projected should be focused on the client and its industry.

Sustainability

Materials that are environmentally friendly and energy efficient are sought by many clients who want to project an image as benefactors to their communities. Through the use of sustainable products, the client is also often able to gain long-term cost savings in their materials and building systems such as mechanical and electrical systems. Sustainability was discussed in more detail in a previous section of this chapter.

Operations and maintenance

The most frequently underestimated costs of any project are the operations and maintenance costs over future years. Materials should be selected that are durable and easily cleaned, resist damage, and require a minimum of upkeep procedures such as painting. It is important to fully describe these future costs to your client when working on the design of a space. Many clients are most concerned with the initial project costs and do not want to look to the future costs. In the long run, however, your client will be glad that you took time to explain the potential for these costs so that it can be addressed during the initial project design and construction.

Regionalism

The location of an office will affect material choices. The local weather patterns and the base building or nearby architectural styles are key components that should aid in the determination of some project materials. For example, an office building in Miami will have very different requirements from an office building in Chicago. The interior architecture should also reflect the environment, culture, and history of the facility's geographic location. In Bangkok, for instance, the use of teak, silk wall panel fabrics, and local artisan crafts are prevalent means of reflecting the local region and its culture.

Cost benefit

If all or even a few of the items discussed in the preceding paragraphs are taken into consideration in selecting a material, there will be greater long-term cost benefits. Some of the products that are selected on the basis of these criteria are even less expensive than less effective alternates.

Artwork

Artwork should be selected or created to reflect the client's identity, culture, and business goals, as well as the building's interior and exterior architecture. An ad agency, for example, may use some of its ads as artwork throughout its office, particularly in client spaces like the reception and conference areas. A high-tech firm may use abstract and futuristic artwork to reflect its culture or image.

Integrating the Interior and Exterior Design

The best office plan requires close collaboration between the client, the interior architect, the base building architect, and the landscape architect to ensure that a building's interior, exterior, landscape, graphics, artwork, and other visual elements are integral components of one design solution.

A basic integration strategy is to use on the interior the same or similar materials and details found in the exterior architecture. Lehman-Smith + McLeish's interior architecture for the Gannett headquarters, for example, translated the different uses of glass on the façade into many different interior components, such as translucent glass walls that bring in natural light and opaque mirror glass that gives rooms an expansive feeling.

Even in renovating an existing office facility rather than constructing a new building, more and more clients want the interior office design to reflect the exterior building architecture and landscaping. For the renovation of Jones Day's Washington, D.C, office, for instance, the exterior and interior architectures were integrated by incorporating the existing façade and lobby materials throughout the office. A roof terrace and garden courtyard were added to provide additional gathering places for employees. Because the building is located near the Capitol, this terrace now provides excellent views of the Capitol and other city landmarks.

▼ *Washington, D.C., office building that helped set architectural objectives for offices of Jones Day inside. Photo © Hedrich Blessing.*

▲ Main lobby of Jones Day's Washington, D.C., offices, by Lehman-Smith + McLeish. Photo © Hedrich Blessing.

RENOVATION/RESTORATION/ ADAPTIVE REUSE

Renovating, restoring, or adaptively reusing an existing building requires much the same interior planning and design process, with some further considerations peculiar to redesigning an existing building.

The first step is to determine the company's strategic plan, programming requirements, and workplace needs. Then a survey must be made of the building components—from mechanical systems to technology infrastructure and security —to find out whether they will support the proposed renovation and future client needs. It often happens that upgrades or entirely new systems will be necessary.

Phasing is a key element of an office renovation. When Kirkpatrick & Lockhart, (K&L), an international law firm in Pittsburgh, decided to renovate its existing offices, the main challenge was to perform major interior alterations and infrastructure upgrades without disrupting the firm's work. K&L had looked at several new office buildings but could not find any that met its financial, spatial, and identity goals as well as its

▶ Conference room at Jones Day offices, by Lehman-Smith + McLeish. Photo © Hedrich Blessing.

existing space in a historic Burnham-designed building in a key downtown location. What the building offered in historic value, however, it lacked in all major structural, mechanical, electrical, code, and technological aspects. Remaining in the existing building presented another set of issues regarding how to renovate while living in the space. The solution was a very complex phasing schedule that took construction and coordination of moves into account simultaneously. Although this project is ongoing, the major reception floors are complete and have given K&L an identity that it was unable to envision even during the design process. The company now wants to use the new imagery and office standards throughout its offices nationwide.

INTERNATIONAL CHALLENGES

In this era's global economy many American companies have overseas offices. Although it is important to incorporate regional influences into each office design, standardization of the basic layout, furniture, and office technology is essential to reflect a company's culture and business goals wherever the office is located. Providing a uniform technology platform, for example, enables employees to move from facility to facility without loss of productivity.

Designing offices in foreign countries presents interior planners/architects of the United States with many challenges. In some Asian countries, for example, even commonly used U.S. materials such as gypsum wallboard can be difficult or extremely expensive to obtain.

Every country has its own building codes and construction laws. In Germany, for example, workplace environmental

▲ Remodeled elevator lobby and reception desk at Kirkpatrick & Lockhart, Pittsburgh, by Lehman-Smith + McLeish. Photo © Hedrich Blessing.

▶ Remodeled restroom at offices of Kirkpatrick & Lockhart, Pittsburgh, by Lehman-Smith + McLeish. Photo © Hedrich Blessing.

standards are codified. Some countries have a building development culture that habitually circumvents such codes. In Taipei, building owners may specify balconies on new office construction. When the building is completed and occupied, they then enclose the balcony space, adding to the overall square footage. Countries often have different construction techniques and processes, which can affect cost, materials, and fixtures. In Asia, for example, drywall ceilings are often installed before the light fixtures.

Before planning a single wall, the interior architect must first understand the local culture and the client's organization and culture, as well as the prevailing building technology.

KEY COST FACTORS

Interior architecture costs vary tremendously from company to company and from location to location. Renovating a floor in an existing building can cost as little as $5 a sq ft or as much as $1000 a sq ft. A company moving into an existing building may choose to keep costs to a minimum by simply moving its existing furniture and putting its sign on the door. At the other end of the scale is the company that embarks on a complete renovation, including new mechanical, electrical, and plumbing equipment, new structural provisions, and a new technology infrastructure.

Now, more than ever before, companies are focusing on long-term cost-effectiveness rather than immediate savings or gains from office construction or renovation. If a facility is completed $2 million under budget but is not a pleasing and efficient place to work, it is a failure, despite the cost savings.

Companies increasingly recognize that investing in better facilities with more amenities and advanced technology will have a direct and positive impact on the bottom line by increasing the performance of their greatest asset: their employees. In a recent survey, 86 percent of employers reported they had difficulty attracting employees and 55 percent said they had trouble retaining them.

Speaking about the offices of GSD&M, an Austin-based advertising agency, communications director Eric Webber says, "The numbers speak for themselves.

▼ *Skylighted circulation axis of Federal Realty Investment Trust offices, Rockville, Maryland, remodeled from former bowling alley by Lehman-Smith + McLeish. Photo © Hedrich Blessing.*

There's been a dramatic increase in our business." The "Idea City" concept of the firm's offices provides an environment that is fun and stimulates collaborative creativity. The cost of an interior design is best evaluated by how well it serves the company's goals.

At the same time, budget constraints are a reality that interior architects respond to by providing cost-effective solutions. For example, inexpensive and innovative materials like plywood and metal decking can be used to enhance a project. "High-end" materials such as marble or slate can be reserved for public areas like the main reception space, the elevator lobbies, and a conference center. Less expensive materials can be used in the more private spaces.

Federal Realty Investment Trust (FRIT), a real estate specialist in the ownership, management, and development of retail properties, began its search for a new corporate headquarters with an interesting yet economical design by selecting a windowless bowling alley on the lower level of a strip mall. Executives are located in offices with 7½ ft high walls and 15 ft high ceilings; administrative and support staff are located at flexible workstations; mechanical, electrical, and plumbing elements are exposed throughout; and most of the flooring is a tinted concrete.

Another example of a company that reduced costs is RAND, a nonprofit research company in Arlington, Virginia, with a very restrictive budget, that wanted its office design to project a professional image. RAND decided to have slate floors in the main reception space, at all elevator lobbies, and at borders in the conference center. Maple wall panels were used in the reception area and on furniture throughout the project. An exposed ceiling was

used for the library to add a spatial design element while also saving the cost of installing a ceiling.

Time is often an overlooked factor in determining cost estimates for projects. Lead times for ordering materials such as carpet and light fixtures are often extremely long and can affect the final cost of the product and design time. If the selected product cannot be received on-site in the time allowed, the design team will spend extra hours reviewing and selecting alternative products. The architect should work directly with the

▼ Offices of Federal Realty Investment Trust by Lehman-Smith + McLeish. Photo © Hedrich Blessing.

contractor at an early stage to identify potential long-lead items and ensure that they are ordered far enough ahead of time to meet the schedule.

CONCLUSION

The most important thing to remember about design is that it should always be a collaborative effort. Each member of the design team, from the mechanical engineers to the lighting designers to the interior designer, plays an important part in achieving the final design product.

Without a successful relationship among the project team members, the project itself will not succeed. The project team should strive to be the "problem solvers" of the project, recognizing the important features of each project that are unique.

Recall the beginning of this chapter, with the focus on the client, its culture, and its project goals and objectives. Together, the project team can create workplaces that deliver clear messages about the client's image while producing efficient yet energetic environments.

CHAPTER 4
STRUCTURAL SYSTEMS

LESLIE E. ROBERTSON AND SAW-TEEN SEE *Leslie E. Robertson Associates, R.L.L.P.*

With this chapter we introduce some of the fundamental concepts of structural systems for office buildings. We delve as well into some of the interfaces between the structural system and the other building systems: architectural, electrical, mechanical, and vertical transportation.

The primary function of the structural system is to support safely, efficiently, and economically the gravity and lateral loads imposed on the building and to carry those loads to the foundations.

The structural system must also provide acceptable levels of performance associated with floor vibrations, the swaying motion induced by wind or earthquake, and a host of other factors. Resistance to fire and blast and other untoward events is an important characteristic of any good structural system. All of the these functions must be accomplished while allowing for the efficient distribution of electric power, communications, HVAC, and plumbing.

Omitted from this chapter are a myriad of excellent structural systems that are not commonly found in this building type over a wide geographic area. Wood framing, often used in low-rise office buildings, is not discussed.

RESISTANCE TO GRAVITY LOADS

For high-rise office buildings, it is interesting to note that the wind load pressures, reaching to 200 pounds per sq ft (psf) (10 mpa), are sometimes larger than the floor load pressures, normally 70–100 psf (3.5–5 mpa) or less. For low-rise buildings, the wind loads are smaller, whereas the floor loads remain more or less the same, making floor loads dominant. Even so, all or nearly all components of

the structural system are required to resist gravity loads, so that the gravity load systems are important for all office buildings. The systems described here can be and often are mixed and matched.

Floor Framing

For reasons associated with the rental of office space, the distance from the services core to the exterior wall is seldom less than 30 ft (9 m), with spans up to 60 ft

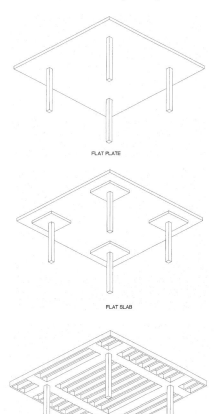

FLAT PLATE

FLAT SLAB

ONE-WAY JOIST

◀ *Concrete floors of uniform thickness. Examples include flat plates, flat slabs with drop panels, and pan joist floors with girders matching depth of joists.*

▶ *Bank of China, Hong Kong, with diagonal structural members carrying loads of 72-story tower to four corner columns, each 5 m (16' 5") square.*

▼ *IBM Seattle, Washington, under construction, showing numerous small columns acting as bearing wall.*

(18 m) not uncommon for larger tenants, particularly in the United States.

For lower-rise buildings, concrete floors of uniform thickness are commonly used. These systems include flat plates and flat slabs with drop panels, pan-joist floors with girders matching the depth of the joists, and the like. It is difficult to alter these concrete floors later to make them capable of carrying an enhanced live load or to create large floor openings. Conversely, the two-way nature of this type of construction allows local areas to carry an enhanced load, with perhaps a modest reduction in permissible load in other areas. Because of the creep characteristics of concrete, these floors tend to continue deflecting with time; flat slabs are particularly prone to substantial long-term deflections, sometimes resulting in undesirable sag in the floors.

Beam-and-slab systems, with spans up to 60 ft (18 m) and longer, are found in structural steel and in both conventionally reinforced and posttensioned concrete. For use with structural steel, a profiled steel deck is commonly employed, with depths usually of 2 in. (50 mm) or 3 in. (75 mm); a modified metal deck (cellular floor) is used in some office buildings for the distribution of electrical power and communications.

Steel trusses for longer spans and open web joists for shorter spans have been used with considerable success. These components are more expensive to fireproof than steel beams, but the need to provide fire-rated construction must not be neglected in establishing the cost and design implications of using trusses and joists. Available systems include the application of contact fireproofing and fire-rated ceilings.

Particularly where floor systems are of structural steel, they can be designed so that later structural enhancement is both viable and economical. These steel-framed floors also allow the later introduction of large floor penetrations as may be required for tenant stairs and the like. It is interesting to note that longer-span floors, requiring deeper beams, may result in a reduced floor-to-floor height while maintaining the same ceiling height, because ducts can penetrate deeper beams.

Columns, Walls, and Hangers

Columns and walls of structural steel, reinforced concrete, and combinations of the two are used to resist gravity loads as well as the lateral loads from wind or earthquakes. Columns are sometimes smaller than assumed possible. For example, 4 in. pipe columns can support a 20-story reinforced concrete building. Conversely, columns are sometimes rather larger than generally expected: Steel sections are used in pairs to support the 20,000 ton (180,000 kN) load of the corners of the services core of the United States Steel Building, now known as the USX Building, in Pittsburgh.

The four corner columns of the 72-story Bank of China Tower, Hong Kong, each carrying 440,000 kN (50,000 tons), are of reinforced concrete; each of these columns is 5 m (16' 5") square, with each "reinforcing bar" consisting of a bundle of four reinforcing bars 50 mm (2 in.) in diameter.

Column Transfers

The need to transfer column loads seems to become more prevalent with the passing years. Column transfers are made in order to create more open spaces at the street level or to obtain large column-free spaces (ballrooms or trading floors, for instance) at the interface between building occupancies (residential over or under office space) and similar conditions. Columns are transferred with girders or trusses or by sloping the columns.

The use of posttensioning, whether in concrete or in structural steel, is particularly effective in reducing both the short- and the long-term deflections of the transfer system. Almost any column transfer involves the use of deep structure, commonly detrimental to increasing

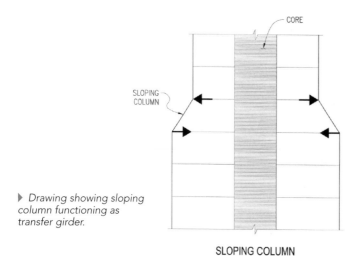

CORE

SLOPING
COLUMN

**SLOPING COLUMN
AS TRANSFER GIRDER**

▶ *Drawing showing sloping column functioning as transfer girder.*

M   2M

7
6
5
4
3
2
1

**HANGING
BUILDING**   **HUNG
LOAD**   **MATERIAL
REQUIRED**

▶ *Diagrammatic drawings showing relative efficiency of hanging vs. conventional structural systems.*

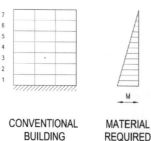

7
6
5
4
3
2
1

**CONVENTIONAL
BUILDING**   **MATERIAL
REQUIRED**

M

building cost and (usually) creating interference with other building systems.

Suspended Structures

A suspended structure is generally used to create a column-free space at the base of a building. Although other means of creating the desired space may be available, the architectural effect of suspended structures can be striking.

Usually, the hangers are supported at the top of the building, being carried on trusswork or the like cantilevered from the service core. The suspended system requires that the weight of the building be first carried upward and then downward to the foundations. The net result is a tripling of the cumulative load times distance traveled, seldom a move toward improving the economy of a structure.

Another approach to the suspended building is the suspended catenary. In the former Federal Reserve Bank in Minneapolis the catenary is composed of W36 beams bolstered with post-tensioned cables, all to minimize overall building deflection. The clear span is 60 ft by 300 ft (18 m by 90 m). The building was designed to carry a 50 percent vertical expansion atop the existing portion, but spanning free from the structure below.

RESISTANCE TO LATERAL LOADS

For very tall office buildings, the lateral force from the wind dominates the concept of the structural design, as seen in the comparison of loads for a hypothetical building 1000 ft (300 m) high. Here you can see that even in the very mild wind climate and the significant seismic conditions of Los Angeles, the wind forces are as large as or larger than the earthquake forces. Annual maximum

◀ *Federal Reserve Bank, Minneapolis, Minnesota, under construction, illustrating suspended structural system.*

wind speed in Los Angeles is about 53 mph, and the 100-year maximum is about 77 mph, whereas New York and Hong Kong can expect winds in excess of 100 mph at 20-year intervals.

Although all structural systems for office buildings must resist the forces imposed by gravity, it is often the lateral forces imposed by wind or earthquake that establish the fundamental nature of the structural system. The following sections describe a variety of the more commonly used structural systems, with emphasis on their resistance to lateral forces.

Rigid Frames

The fundamentals of rigid frames should not require an introduction. The stiffness of rigid frames tends to be proportional to the depths of the columns and girders, but inversely proportional to the column spacing and to the floor-to-floor height. Greater economy and increased stiffness,

then, are generally achieved by decreasing the column spacing and/or by widening the columns.

Where a given column is to be found in two more or less perpendicular frames, that column will undergo bending about both of its axes. For H-shaped columns, the bending strength and stiffness about the weak axis are low, a deficiency that often leads to the use of box columns.

In areas subjected to significant earthquakes, the structure must be designed so that in an earthquake, the girders of the frame yield well before the columns. This requirement effectively limits the depth of the girders in relation to that of the columns. It has led as well to imaginative solutions both in structural steel and in reinforced concrete, all designed to ensure the early yielding of the girders, without the collapse of the frame. An example of such a solution with structural steel is the "dog bone" connection. This strong-column/weak-

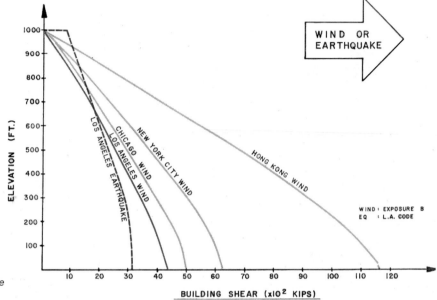

WIND OR
EARTHQUAKE

WIND : EXPOSURE B
EQ   : L.A. CODE

▶ Graph comparing shear forces on tall buildings caused by wind in several major cities and by earthquake in quake-prone Los Angeles.

▶ Dog Bone connection, a device that assures that girders will yield before columns under earthquake and other exceptional loads.

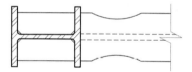

DOG BONE
CONNECTION

girder concept, required to resist the forces from an earthquake, applies to all of the structural systems described in the following sections.

Because of the limitations associated with the strong-column/weak-girder approach, economy is generally achieved with deeper girders and wider columns and with reduced column spacing and story height.

Shear Walls and Braced Cores

Shear walls, sometimes formed into hollow boxes or tubes, are efficient in carrying lateral forces. Such walls can be of concrete or structural steel and may be more or less solid or may be braced.

Steel plate shear walls have found their way into buildings such as the AT&T headquarters building (now SONY) in New York, the Bank of China Tower in Hong Kong, and many other buildings. Such walls can be stiffened against buckling with a concrete overlay, which also acts as a sturdy backup for stone cladding. The thickness of the steel plate in these shear walls is commonly ¼ in. (6mm) to ⅜ in. (10mm), but occasionally thicker.

Braced cores in structural steel have been used in the United States Steel Building and in many other buildings. Reinforced concrete and reinforced unit

masonry can form efficient and economical shear walls and are frequently used. Economy is generally found in longer lengths of individual walls.

Where openings are made through shear walls, a critical interface with the other design disciplines occurs. An unduly optimistic appraisal of the need for openings can later result in extensive and painful redesign on the part of all the disciplines involved.

Braced Cores with Outriggers
In structural steel construction, the outrigger truss system was introduced

with the United States Steel Building; here the outrigger system is located in the mechanical space just below the roof. Likened to an umbrella standing on its handle, with the perimeter tied to the ground, the system has a distinctive pattern of wind-induced deformation. Whether in steel, concrete, or a mixture of the two, the concept remains the same.

Penetrations into the service core are an impediment to the efficiency of the structural system. Although door openings through the walls of the service core are determined early in the design, of particular concern is the late introduction or

▼ AT&T (now Sony) Building, New York City, showing steel plate shear walls being erected.

▲ Construction photo of United States Steel (now USX) Building, Pittsburgh, Pennsylvania, which used braced structural core.

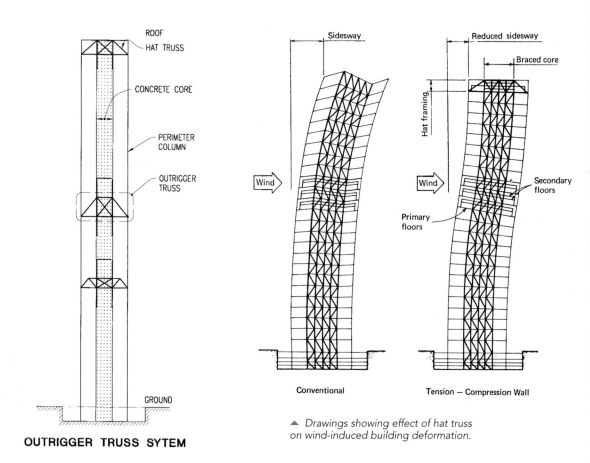

OUTRIGGER TRUSS SYTEM

▲ *Drawings showing effect of hat truss on wind-induced building deformation.*

▲ *Drawing showing hat truss and outrigger truss used to brace structural systems.*

enlarging of penetrations for the HVAC systems. Clearly, the fewer the openings, the more efficient and more economical the structure. Architects are often amazed at the level of complexity (and hence the cost) of the reinforcing steel required as a result of such wall openings.

More commonly found in East Asia, reinforced concrete services cores with outrigger walls or trusses now form perhaps the most cost-effective structural system for high-rise office buildings. The outrigger trusses are usually located in the mechanical floor, but are sometimes used architecturally at elevator transfer floors, sky lobbies, or other special floors.

This system is generally more economical with larger plan dimensions in the critical (usually the narrower) direction of the service core and with deeper outrigger trusses. Belt trusses, described later, may be important adjuncts to this structural system.

Framed Tubes
Used for the first time (probably) in 1962 for the twin towers of the World Trade Center in New York City, the framed tube has found extensive use in both structural steel and reinforced concrete.

Shear lag, a condition understood first in aircraft structures, can be a serious

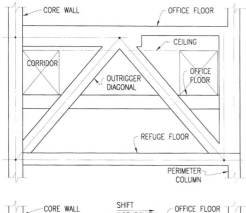

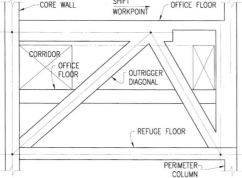

OUTRIGGER TRUSS ELEVATION

▼ *Drawings showing ways to fit outrigger trusses into buildings.*

▲ *World Trade Center under construction, showing load-bearing exterior wall and central core.*

limitation of framed tubes. This condition results in decreasing the stiffness of the system, often significantly.

Economy is generally increased with reduced floor-to-floor height, a reduced spacing of the columns forming the framed tube, and the widening of those columns.

Framed Tubes with Belt Trusses

The problems with shear lag are a serious limitation on the efficiency of, and the height that can be reached by, the framed tube. Accordingly, the system is often bolstered with the use of belt trusses. For the World Trade Center, a similar effect was achieved with the use of a space-frame "hat," also acting as a kind of outrigger truss, just below the roof level. Belt trusses are commonly placed in the mechanical floors, well hidden behind the louvers. On occasion, the trusses are used architecturally, perhaps being placed at an elevator transfer floor, a commercial area, or a sky lobby.

For taller buildings, it is common to find two or more levels of belt trusses. To increase stiffness and to reduce cost, the belt trusses should be as deep and placed at as frequent intervals as is practical.

Braced Tubes

Braced tubes are not unlike framed tubes, but the column/spandrel frames are

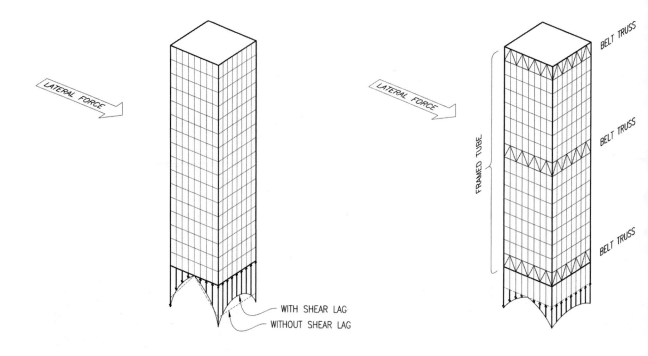

SHEAR LAG

BELT TRUSS

▲ Drawing of framed tube, showing shear lag.

◥ Drawing of framed tube with belt trusses, showing effect on shear lag.

replaced with trussed frames. The system is expressed in structural steel in the John Hancock Building, Chicago. An unusual example is the Bank of China Tower, where the braced tube is geometrically complex and composed of mixed and composite members and connections of steel and concrete.

Where acceptable to both the builder and the architect, for most building geometries and occupancies these braced tubes are as efficient a structural system as is known today.

Bundled Tubes

Without question, the best-known example of the structural system using bundled tubes is the 110-story Sears Tower in Chicago, executed in structural steel. Here we see a bundle of nine tubes

at the foundations, cantilevered up to the roof, with two tubes for the uppermost stories. This is a development of the framed tube, with many of the same limitations and advantages. Its principal disadvantage is that the columns of the various tubes must pass through the interior spaces of the building. At the top of each tube in the bundle, significant vertical distortions and stresses may be introduced, arising from the structural discontinuity.

With a bundled tube, as with a framed tube, improved economy is achieved in closing up the column spacing and widening the columns in the plane of the tube.

Tube-in-Tube

With the service core more or less centered in a building, it is possible to

▲ *Framed tube structure, illustrated by John Hancock Building, Chicago.*

◀ *Bundled tube structure, illustrated by Sears Tower, Chicago.*

construct a tube around the service core and a second tube around the building perimeter. The system is particularly effective in seismically prone areas of the world, where it may be judicious (or may be mandated by code) to provide two systems to resist the lateral forces from earthquakes. One aspect of the system, then, is the provision of a level of structural redundancy, affording extra safety in the event of a major earthquake. The most common form of this system is found with a service core of reinforced concrete walls and a perimeter tube of concrete or structural steel.

An unusual example of a tube-in-tube is the proposed 7 South Dearborn Project, Chicago. Here, both tubes are of reinforced concrete shear walls and both have limited openings through them. This is possible only because the outer tube extends upward through parking floors, which do not require extensive openings at the perimeter.

P-Delta

For taller office buildings (and some lower buildings as well), as the structure is displaced from the true and plumb position, the weight of the structure, now displaced from the vertical, creates an additional overturning moment, but not a shear. Termed *P-Delta,* the magnitude of this additional moment is

▶ Tube-in-tube structure, illustrated in proposed 7 South Dearborn project, Chicago.

commonly found to be about 10 percent of the moment creating the original displacement, but has reached a level as high as 50 percent in some overlimber structures.

The phenomenon is particularly important for buildings not subjected to significant lateral loads. Examples of such buildings include those outside earthquake-prone areas and those that are more or less completely shielded from the wind. Because of the low wind load against the narrow face, resulting in low structural stiffness, very long but thin buildings can be P-Delta-sensitive in the long direction.

PERFORMANCE CRITERIA

It is thought by many that structural systems for office buildings are designed solely to some level of strength, required to resist forces including gravity, wind, earthquake, fire, and blast. Although it is true that the ability to carry loads is essential in the design of any structural system, the more important and more difficult to realize are a series of performance-based criteria.

Lateral Sway Induced by Wind or Earthquake

Induced by the wind or by earthquake, some degree of swaying motion is observed in all office buildings. The motion induced by earthquake has only a dynamic or oscillatory (no steady-state) component of motion. Under wind-induced excitation, both a steady-state and a dynamic component can be seen. For very tall office buildings, the dynamic component is likely to prove to be the driving force in development of the structural system; the structure must counter the undesirable effects of excessive lateral oscillation in order to limit human perception of the swaying motion. Partitions and the exterior walls are affected by the sum of the steady-state and swaying components of building motion.

Floor Vibrations

All floors vibrate, but some floors vibrate more severely than others. Generally, steel-framed floors of structural steel are lighter, hence their level of vibration can be higher. These vibrations occur because of footfalls and the effects of oscillating equipment.

Steel-framed floors for office spaces tend to have a frequency of vibration in the range of 5Hz (cycles per second). Particularly where the floor framing is repetitive, it is important to tune the floor system away from the frequency of any known source of oscillatory energy.

The deflection of floor beams is related more or less linearly to the frequency of vibration, with the stiffening (usually by deepening) of floor framing leading to a higher frequency of vibration.

Floor Deflections and Column Shortening

The acceptable level of deflection of floor beams is associated with the wall and partition systems that may be supported by the beam framing, with excessive deflection leading to structural distress or lack of top support of the wall or partition. The acceptable level of deflection of floor beams is associated as well with ponding on roofs.

Because of the (often brittle) nature of exterior walls, the deflection of spandrels is almost always an important consideration. An acceptable level of the deflection of spandrels depends largely on the characteristics of the supported wall. For example, a wall of granite or limestone, with joints as small as ⅜ in. (10 mm) or even ¼ in. (6 mm), will almost surely require very stiff spandrels. For spandrels of reinforced concrete, it is essential to consider both the short-term (instantaneous) and the long-term (creep-related) deflection characteristics of the spandrel.

The shortening of columns and bearing walls, particularly the long-term shortening of concrete columns and concrete walls, may have a profound effect on the design of beams, girders, and spandrels. Partition systems have failed or cracked as walls or columns shortened, because of the lack of adequate clearance to the framing above.

With long-span beams, excessive live load deflection and inadequate "bite" of the supported partition system to the floor above has been the cause of the partitions simply falling over.

Noise Transmission Through Floors

The limitation of noise transmission through floors, with only occasional exceptions, is not a significant problem in office buildings. Generally, the floors and the ceilings of mechanical floors are constructed to a 100 psf density (5kPa), with about 8 in. (200 mm) of stone concrete generally being satisfactory.

TERRORIST ATTACK

A special consideration for more important office buildings is the possibility of terrorist attack. The most noteworthy of these attacks took place in Oklahoma City in 1995 and at the World Trade Center, New York City, in 1993 and 2001. Detailed design recommendations concerning these extraordinary events are beyond the scope of this chapter. For the structural system, commonsense approaches will often result in good designs. The introduction of gases or biotechnical weapons is not considered here.

Bombs and Other Explosive Devices

The most effective approach to limit loss of life and property damage due to a bomb or other explosive device is to increase the standoff distance, that is, by keeping any such device as far from the office building as is possible. Two methods are obvious: Limit or prohibit vehicular access under the building and move the mail room to a nonsensitive area, because explosive devices can arrive by mail.

Structural solutions are to be found in the toughness and the redundancy of the structural system. It follows that structures designed to resist earthquake loads are commonly known to be effective in resisting the shock waves from a bomb. Detailed designs can be accomplished where the nature of the threat can be defined—the energy of the bomb, standoff distance, and the like. As demonstrated by the very minor damage suffered by the twin towers of the World Trade Center in 1993, properly designed high-rise buildings can have considerable resistance to damage from conventional bombs.

Aircraft impact

Most office buildings struck by aircraft are low-rise structures. Because of the large amount of energy in the speeding aircraft and the limited structural resources economically available in low-rise buildings, there is little that can be done in design to protect either life or property.

Depending on the mass and the speed of the aircraft, medium- and high-rise office buildings have the ability to resist such impacts, but not without the potential for loss of life and structural damage. The Empire State Building was struck by a small military aircraft, a B-25, during the Second World War. Loss of life was limited, the fire was contained in a few hours, and structural repairs were straightforward. Today's aircraft, however, are much larger, carry significant amounts of fuel, and are able to travel at high speed.

The airplanes that struck the twin towers of the World Trade Center in 2001 were speeding Boeing 767s. The design condition we used for the World Trade Center was for a Boeing 707, flying at low speed, perhaps lost in the fog and seeking to land. It is important to recognize that the energy of impact is proportional to the product of the mass of the aircraft and the *square* of the speed. That is, a doubling of the speed of the aircraft results in a fourfold increase in the energy that must be absorbed by the structural system.

The twin towers were first weakened by the impact from the planes and then ulti-

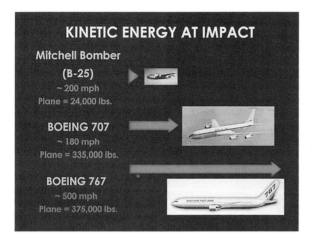

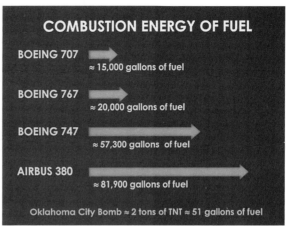

mately destroyed by the raging fires. The towers were fully sprinklered and fire protected in conformance with the requirements of the building code, but were not designed to resist the fires created by the burning jet fuel.

Comparisons of the relative energy of the impact for various aircraft and the relative energy contained in the jet fuel provide convincing evidence that it is futile to attempt to design buildings to resist these larger aircraft. That is, although the structural systems of the World Trade Center were sufficiently ductile and tough to resist the impact of a Boeing 767, a circumstance well beyond the design criteria, it is unlikely that they would be able to resist the impact of the fully loaded larger aircraft found commonly in our skies. When the energy of the jet fuel is added, it becomes totally impractical to design an office build-ing for such an event. It is said that even atomic power plants do not have this capability.

WIND ENGINEERING

As designated by building codes around the world, wind loads are commonly (and

properly) conservative in considering the *strength* of the structural system. It does not follow that building codes provide adequately for the *serviceability* characteristics of the structural system. Serviceability characteristics include the dynamic performance of taller buildings and the floor-to-floor shearing that can damage interior and exterior walls.

Office buildings prior to the World Trade Center were designed more or less intuitively to resist wind loads, relying on prior experience and on building codes. These older buildings were designed for steady-state forces taken from the building code, with an occasional foray into aeronautical wind tunnel studies. Indeed, the technical literature of the past contained lively discussions as to whether the steel frame of a high-rise building had to be designed for *any* wind load. This detached attitude toward the forces of the wind is supported by the fact that many of these older buildings have performed well for most of the last century.

In the fire-rated partition system, however, there is a significant difference between the buildings of the past and those of today. The older buildings

▼ *Relative combustion energy of fuel for selected aircraft.*

▲ *Relative kinetic energy at impact of selected aircraft, including bomber that struck Empire State Building in the 1940s and Boeing 707 at moderate low-altitude speed, which was condition specified in design of World Trade Center towers.*

▶ *Wind flow around a high-rise building, as demonstrated by model in wind tunnel.*

performed well in the wind because the masonry partitions stiffened the steel frame to perhaps five times the stiffness envisioned by the analysis of the steel frame alone. The Shaftwall partition system we conceived for the World Trade Center, and similar systems, have replaced unit masonry as the dominant partition to be found in the service core. With the introduction of Shaftwall, the partition no longer stiffened or strengthened the frame, making the methodologies of the past no longer acceptable.

The Boundary Layer Wind Tunnel

It was two Danish engineers, Jensen and Frank, who demonstrated that the wind pressure on farm buildings could be properly modeled in a boundary layer wind tunnel. This new wind tunnel replicated the surface roughness of the ground, thus generating in the tunnel a turbulence akin to that of the real atmosphere. With the World Trade Center, this new technology was catapulted from the study of barns into the everyday technology of the structural engineer.

Contemporary wind engineering studies are designed to capture both the steady-state and the dynamic wind pressures for the design of the cladding, the structural loading and response of the overall building, the wind loads at street level, and other considerations.

In the past, we and other authors have proposed designing holes through a building and other techniques for leaking air through a building. The goal here is to reduce the dynamic response of the building by altering the airflow around it. By and large, except where governed at least in part by architectural considerations, such systems are likely to be less than cost-effective.

It is important to note that the wind flow around a high-rise building is generally thought to be around the building, but it is both upward and downward. Something of the turbulent nature of the flow can be seen in photos of wind tunnel tests.

EARTHQUAKE ENGINEERING

The total amount of energy released by an earthquake is measured on the familiar Richter scale. Of greater pertinence to structural engineering, the severity of ground motion is measured on the Modified-Mercalli (MM) scale, with modest earthquakes being of magnitude MM-3 or smaller and the very largest earthquakes being MM-8.5 or larger. The ground motion is complex in nature, consisting of movement in both the horizontal and the vertical directions. There is a risk of earthquake activity in nearly all areas of the United States, as well as in other countries. Although earthquakes of the greatest intensity in the United States have been found most commonly along the West Coast, severe earthquakes have occurred in the Midwest and in the Northeast.

The protection of architectural finishes, although not practical in anticipation of great earthquakes, can be enhanced by designing such systems for a floor-to-floor shearing motion equal to the story height divided by about 500 or less, say not less than ½ in. The lateral bracing of ceilings, partitions, and the like is essential. Seismic mounts for mechanical and electrical equipment are in the normal vocabulary of design. Seismic actuators to shut off potentially dangerous utilities (gas, oil, etc.) are commonplace.

ENERGY DISSIPATION AND ENERGY ISOLATION SYSTEMS

Oscillations of structural systems include the tremor of floors, the swaying motion induced by wind or earthquake, vibrations generated by mechanical and electrical equipment, and the like. Taller structures subjected to wind loading and all structures subjected to earthquakes are stimulated to some level of oscillation.

The level of oscillation achieved by structural components and by the overall building is associated with a host of interlocking factors. Yet in dissipating the energy of oscillation, structural damping is of high importance, as it is the mechanism that does, in fact, dissipate most of this energy. Structural damping is the primary role of the shock absorbers of automobiles, door closers, and such devices, all designed to absorb the energy of oscillation.

Critical damping can be imagined as that level of damping that permits a

displaced object to return to its point of zero displacement without displaying any of the characteristics of oscillation. For example, the pistons of door closures exhibit generally slightly less than critical damping; the worn-out shock absorbers on an automobile can exhibit significantly less than critical damping. Intrinsic structural damping in real buildings seldom exceeds 1 percent of critical damping.

Viscoelastic Dampers

The twin towers of the World Trade Center, New York, were the first buildings to incorporate damping devices as an essential part of the structural system. Effective both in wind and in earthquake, and in reducing the vibration or tremor of the floors, about 10,000 viscoelastic dampers were used in each tower. Incorporating a material developed by the 3M Company and a concept and detail design that we developed, these devices are not unlike the closer of a screen door, except that viscoelastic material in shear is substituted for the air plunger and the outlet venturi. The system more than doubled the damping of these towers, bringing the total to about 2.5 percent of critical damping.

Tuned-Mass Dampers

Much later, the Citicorp Building in New York was the first building to make use of a tuned-mass damper. Designed to reduce the swaying motion under wind-induced oscillation, an 820 kip (3700 kN) block is mounted on oil bearings and tuned laterally with nitrogen springs. Similar dampers were retrofitted in the John Hancock Building in Boston.

▶ *Details of viscoelastic dampers used to damp swaying energy caused by turbulent wind or earthquake forces.*

Viscoelastic layers

DETAIL OF DAMPER

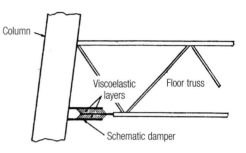

Column

Viscoelastic layers

Floor truss

Schematic damper

▶ *Drawing of tuned-mass damper as used in Citicorp Building, New York City.*

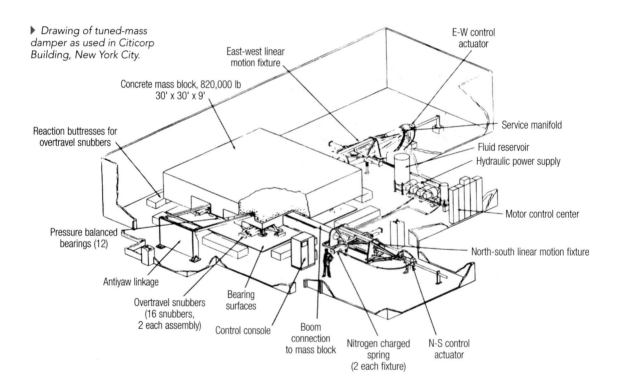

E-W control actuator

East-west linear motion fixture

Concrete mass block, 820,000 lb
30' x 30' x 9'

Reaction buttresses for overtravel snubbers

Service manifold

Fluid reservoir

Hydraulic power supply

Motor control center

Pressure balanced bearings (12)

North-south linear motion fixture

Antiyaw linkage

Overtravel snubbers
(16 snubbers,
2 each assembly)

Bearing surfaces

Control console

Boom connection to mass block

Nitrogen charged spring
(2 each fixture)

N-S control actuator

Active Dampers

Developed largely in Japan, active dampers are finding limited application. Instead of being driven by an earthquake-induced motion, these devices are driven mechanically to produce a force on the building counter to the direction of an earthquake- or wind-induced motion. In essence, for dynamic loading only, these devices provide a partial lateral support at the level of the active damper that (ideally) moves that point in harmony with the earthquake-induced motion at the base of the building. Very significant amounts of energy must be mobilized more or less instantly in order to resist the inertia forces of the earthquake.

Base Isolation

For earthquake-resisting structural systems, base isolation systems have proven effective. The building is mounted on isolation devices limiting its motion in the horizontal directions while providing full vertical support. These systems greatly reduce energy input into the building as the ground shakes beneath it. Of course, the system is not effective against vertical ground motion (as proved to be important in the last great earthquake in Kobe, Japan).

Application

Both the design of and a sensible description of these various damping devices are particularly complex and thus not suitable for this text. It should be understood, however, that these devices can be effective in improving the performance of office buildings of all heights and in the retrofitting of existing office buildings. Where they are to be used, however, the concept should be introduced as early in the design process as practical.

SUMMARY

This overview is intended to assist the designer in arriving at a basic understanding of the loads affecting office structures, the appropriate performance criteria, the various structural concepts at the engineer's command, and their characteristic responses to the loads of office buildings.

Some performance concerns emerge or increase as a building becomes taller. Structural systems are also affected by the attributes of the materials used to execute them. On the other hand, the structural system and its anticipated behavior may have a significant impact on the materials and design of such nonstructural elements as curtain walls, interior partitions, and HVAC and electrical systems.

Because most of the systems in a building are interdependent, the design of office buildings is a highly collaborative effort.

CHAPTER 5
MECHANICAL/ELECTRICAL/ PLUMBING SYSTEMS

NORMAN D. KURTZ, PE *Flack + Kurtz Consulting Engineers, LLP*

DESIGN OBJECTIVES

The success of the mechanical/ electrical/plumbing (MEP) system, consisting of heating, ventilating, and air-conditioning (HVAC), electrical, plumbing, fire protection, and telecommunications, in a high-rise office building can be evaluated according to its ability to meet the following design objectives:

- *Flexibility*—The ability to accommodate the needs of a variety of tenants/occupants and changes in these needs through the life of the building, while maintaining high performance standards of comfort, reliability, and infrastructure support.

- *Maximizing rentable/usable space*— MEP systems require space in a building, strategically located to meet the performance objectives. There is great pressure to minimize this space and to put it in secondary locations. Hence, good communication is required among the design team members to optimize system performance and space utilization.

- *Serving both interior and exterior spaces* —For HVAC systems, there are dramatic differences in performance requirements: *Exterior* systems are very sensitive to the environment— heating, cooling, solar impact. *Interior* systems primarily require cooling year-round, varying greatly with occupant density and telecommunications equipment heat rejection.

- *Infrastructure performance*—The modern office building is increasingly

dependent on information technology and high intellectual output of workers. The reliability and performance of the MEP systems' infrastructure are key contributors to worker performance and job satisfaction.

- *Cost*—Meeting the preceding objectives must be balanced with the initial and lifecycle cost criteria. For developer office buildings, these criteria must be fine-tuned with the other objectives to fulfill the economic objectives of the project.

DESIGN GUIDELINES FOR MEP SYSTEMS

At the inception of the design effort a design brief, or set of design guidelines, should be prepared that establishes the performance criteria and objectives of the MEP systems. These should quantify the criteria with enough specificity to allow one to ascertain the quality standards of the building and the ability of the MEP systems to satisfy the building objectives.

In addition to describing the basic MEP systems criteria, the design guidelines should indicate the extent to which tenant amenity systems are to be provided. Typical tenant amenities include the following:

- *Supplementary cooling*—Beyond the "base building" HVAC systems, tenants may need additional cooling for (1) special loads of greater density (i.e., data centers, conference rooms, trading floors), (2) areas that may be occupied after normal business hours when base building systems may be off, and (3) areas that are critical and must have the cooling system supported by standby electric power when the base building systems are off.

- *Security systems*—Controlling entry to specific tenant areas.
- *Standby electric power*—Tenants may want generators for backup power to critical areas (i.e., data centers, telephone equipment, technology rooms) when base building power may be off, as in the case of brown outs or fire.
- *Food service*—Kitchens and dining areas require extensive additional plumbing service, electric power, (possibly) gas service, and ventilation. The ability to provide these systems to the desired location(s) in the building is critical.
- *Special communication systems*—Financial service firms, Internet companies, and many other service businesses can be extremely dependent on their information technology systems, which require careful planning for additional cable/conduit pathways and technology rooms, vertically aligned with access to equipment rooms in the basement or to roof-mounted satellites.

Design criteria for a typical Class A building are listed on pages 106–108.

THE BASIC HVAC SYSTEM

The HVAC system is the greatest space consumer of the mechanical/electrical/plumbing group. Its equipment is the noisiest and heaviest, with the greatest architectural impact: It involves floor-to-floor and building height, and openings to the exterior for ventilation air and exhaust of pollutants.

Refrigeration Cycle

The heart of an HVAC system is the refrigeration cycle in which a refrigerant (freon) is (1) compressed into a hot gas (125°F+/-), (2) condensed from a hot gas into a hot liquid (125°F), and (3) relieved or expanded into a cold liquid that (4) evaporates into a cold gas (40°–45°F). This gas then goes back to the compressor to repeat the cycle continuously. These changes of state—gas to liquid—involve significant amounts of heat absorption and rejection that are at very convenient temperatures to cool an office building and reject the heat to outdoors: 42°F for cooling air or chilled water for comfort cooling, 125°F for rejecting heat to a summer ambient environment at 95°F in an air-cooled condenser or via a cooling tower.

Chillers

For large office buildings, the refrigeration cycle occurs in a "chiller," which produces chilled water as a cooling medium, to be circulated via pumps throughout the building at temperatures of 42°F+/- and returning 10–15°F warmer, that is, 52–57°F. The water is used throughout the building in various air-handling systems to cool air, which is supplied to occupied spaces for comfort cooling—"air-conditioning." Chillers require spaces with good acoustic isolation and headrooms in excess of 16 ft clear. Hence, they are often located in basement mechanical rooms or in major mechanical rooms in the office tower—penthouses or midlevel setbacks.

COMPRESSOR
With each stroke of the piston, the pressure of the refrigerant gas is increased as it passes to the condenser. This causes the temperature of the refrigerant to be simultaneously raised and set significantly above the outdoor temperature where it can reject heat.

◀ *Diagram of refrigeration cycle, basis of all air-conditioning systems.*

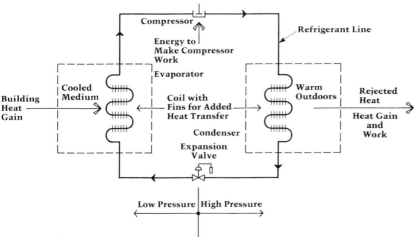

EVAPORATOR
In the evaporator the refrigerant, which has a low boiling point, changes from a liquid to a gas (evaporates, boils) because it absorbs heat from the medium to be cooled. The gas then carries the absorbed heat away from the medium and to the compressor.

CONDENSER
The condenser receives the hot gases from the compressor and cools them with the cooler outdoor air. This causes the gases to liquify or condense and some heat absorbed from the medium and the compressor to be rejected to the outdoors.

EXPANSION VALVE
The hot liquid refrigerant from the condenser, which is at a high pressure level, flows through the orifice of the expansion valve. The orifice causes some of the hot liquid refrigerant to turn to gas at the lower pressure of the evaporator side. This "misting", or boiling, of some of the refrigerant lowers the temperature and pressure of the remaining liquid.

The Compression Refrigeration Cycle

Cooling Towers

The heat that is generated in a chiller is generally rejected to another water circuit, the condenser water. The condenser water typically leaves the chiller at temperatures of 95–105°F and is pumped to a cooling tower, usually on the roof or a high-level setback of the building. This system relies on great quantities of outdoor air to enter the tower and evaporate a portion of the condenser water. The tower is designed to promote good mixing of the air and "sprayed" condenser water, aided by the cooling tower fans. The remaining water is cooled by this evaporation, the way a person is chilled when exiting a swimming pool in dry air. The evaporated water is carried in an air stream away from the building. This is why cooling towers require a free area above them to carry the water/air effluent mixture away easily for an efficient *(continued on page 109)*

Design Criteria, MEP Systems

For a 420,000 gross square foot (GSF) Class A office building, year 2000 vintage.

Heating, Ventilating, and Air Conditioning

1. Design criteria

The building HVAC systems will be capable of maintaining the following environmental standards.

A. Air-conditioned areas

Outside design (ASHRAE, 2.5%):

Summer	Winter
91°F DB†	5°F DB
74°F WB	15 mph winds

Inside conditions:

Summer	Winter
75°F DB	72°F DB
50% RH	25% RH*

B. Other areas

The following spaces will have less stringent inside temperature requirements.

Elevator motor rooms, 85°F
Toilet areas: exhaust only
(air transferred from tenant space)
Plant rooms: ventilation only
for major equipment spaces; control rooms to be provided with air conditioning

C. Ventilation rates

Introduce outside air quantities as follows.

Office areas and public spaces:
20 cu ft/min (cfm) per person*
Provide space ventilation as follows.
Toilet areas: 15 air changes/hr
(transfer air)
Life safety smoke exhaust:
8 air changes/hr/floor
Smoking room exhaust (1/floor):
20 air changes/hr
Nighttime purge:
0.5 air changes/hr/floor

---

†DB = dry bulb; WB = wet bulb; RH = relative humidity; *Requires the addition of humidification

Enclosed parking:
6 air changes/hr

D. Load densities (Heat Rejection Rate) for cooling

Include capacity in the air-handling and chilled/condenser water systems for the following load densities.

Typical office floors:

Lighting	2.0 watts/sq ft
Equipment	3.0 watts/sq ft
Retail:	10.0 watts/sq ft

E. Occupancy criteria

Office areas:	1 person per 100 sq ft
Retail:	1 person per 50 sq ft

F. Acoustic criteria

Typical offices: NC-35 (NC-40 measured within 10 ft of fan rooms)
Toilets, public areas, and circulation spaces: NC-40

G. Supplemental cooling

Provide typical office floors with chilled water or condenser water for tenants' 24-hr supplemental cooling loads at the rate of 30 tons per floor (approximately 1250 sq ft/ton).

2. Office lobby

Provide the office lobby with separate variable-air-volume air-handling system.

3. Retail spaces

Provide each retail space with capped chilled water or condenser water valved outlets for cooling. Outside air, general exhaust, and toilet exhaust requirements will be available for each retail space through an intake louver located in the storefront. Provide shaft space to the roof for retail kitchen exhaust.

4. Miscellaneous systems

A. Electric closets to be exhausted.

---

*If a central outside air system is provided, size it for 25 cfm per person to accommodate extraordinary tenant outside air requirements. If a central air-handling system is provided, provide spare shaft space for future tenant extraordinary outside air requirements.

B. Telephone service entry room to be cooled.

C. Elevator machine rooms to be cooled.

D. Provide a variable-air-volume general exhaust system to accom-modate tenant smoking rooms, excess outside air relief, and night purge.

5. Miscellaneous spaces

Empty shaft space will be provided for future tenant exhaust requirements.

6. Smoke control

For the floor-by-floor system, smoke control for typical office floors will be accomplished by using a dedicated smoke exhaust air fan and a smoke exhaust duct riser to the main roof.

Provide stair and elevator shaft pressurization systems with supply air fans located at the penthouse mechanical equipment room. Provide atriums with dedicated smoke control systems comprising supply and exhaust fans.

7. Parking garage ventilation

The parking structure to be naturally ventilated.

8. Building management and control systems

Provide a microprocessor-based, direct digital control building management system to monitor, control, and optimize the operation of the HVAC systems and the life safety functions of the HVAC systems.

Plumbing and Fire Protection

1. Plumbing systems

A. Domestic water supply system
Water Use
Office: 20 gal per person per day
Retail: 1.5 gal per customer per day
Operating pressure
Minimum: 30 lb/sq in. (psi)
Maximum: 80 psi

Velocity
  Risers: maximum 6 ft/sec (fps)
  Branches: maximum 6 fps

B. Domestic hot water system
Provide domestic hot water at the
following temperature.
  Office tower core: 110°F
  Future tenant: provided by tenant

C. Sanitary waste system
Sanitary and waste minimum slope:
  1/8 in./ft

D. Drains
Drains will be provided at a minimum, in
accordance with the following schedule.
  Mechanical equipment rooms:
  per equipment arrangement.
  Office tower toilet rooms (not
  needed in retail portions)

E. Storm system
The main storm system will be designed
for a 6 in./hr rainfall intensity.
The overflow storm drainage system
will be designed for a 6 in./hr rainfall
intensity.

2. Fire protection

A. Water supply duration: 60 min

B. Flow rate
  Sprinkler, based on standpipe for
  combined system w/1250 gal/min
  (gpm) maximum

C. Pressure requirements
  Sprinkler/standpipe w/100 psi at top

D. Wet pipe systems
  Sized per hydraulic calculations in
  accordance with the following
  schedule.

Hazard (NFPA-13)*	Density (gpm/sq ft)	Remote (sq ft)	Maximum area per head (sq ft)
Tenant offices: light	0.10	1500	220
Storage: ord. GP.	0.15	1500	130
Parking: ord. I	0.15	1,500	130
Mechanical rooms: ord. I	0.15	1500	130
Retail: ord. II	0.19	1500	130

NFPA = National Fire Protection Association

Electrical

1. Design criteria

A. Electrical loads in watts/sq ft (wpsf)
Office areas	6.0
power	4.0
lighting	2.0
Atrium and lobbies	15.0
Service areas	3.0
Parking garage	2.0

B. HVAC and other mechanical loads
will be over and above the load
densities described earlier.

2. Electrical service

A. 480/277 V, 3-phase, 4-wire, 60 Hz
  electrical service will be provided.
  A main utility vault will be provided
  at street level.

B. Mechanical equipment (motors)
  will be supplied at 480V, 3 phase,
  via motor control centers.

C. Vertical distribution to the typical
  office floors will be via rising plug-in
  bus ducts for tenant and landlord
  lighting and power loads. These
  rising bus ducts will be sized for 8
  watts/sq ft to allow for higher density
  of power usage by certain tenants at
  a nominal increase to the initial cost.
  A life-safety power riser, mechanical
  equipment risers, and elevator power
  risers will also be provided.

D. The rising bus ducts, vertical risers,
  and landlord distribution panels will
  be accommodated within two
  electric closets in the core.

E. For tenant fit out, horizontal
  distribution on typical floors will be
  above the hung ceilings and via poke-
  through fittings for power, lighting,
  and telecommunications loads.

3. Metering
Each 3-phase, 4-wire switchboard will be
provided with a current transformer
cabinet for utility master metering.
Utilities of office tenants will not be
directly metered. Check metering will be
provided to allow the landlord to pass
the electrical usage costs to the tenants.

4. Emergency power system

A. The office building will be provided
  with one 800 kW diesel-powered
  emergency generator rated for
  standby power for supplying life-
  safety emergency loads. A complete
  diesel oil supply and storage system
  will be provided for the generator.

B. The system will generate at
  480/277 V, 3-phase, 4-wire, 60 Hz.

C. The emergency power distribution
  system will support the life-safety
  functions of the building, including
  owner-provided emergency egress
  lighting, fire alarm and detection
  system, smoke control systems, stair
  pressurization, elevators, security
  systems, sump and ejector pumps,
  and building automatic systems, as
  well as critical building loads such as
  house pumps, heating system, additional elevators, ventilation fans, etc.

D. Space will be allocated for generators for future tenants.

5. Fire alarm and life-safety system

A. The fire alarm system will be the
  "addressable" type, with each initiating device enunciated as an individual zone. The fire command station
  (FCS) will provide centralized control
  and enunciation of fire alarm zones.

(continued)

Design Criteria, MEP Systems (continued)

B. A voice communication system (VCS) will provide automatic evacuation signaling and selective paging to all areas of the building.

C. A firefighter telephone system (FTS) will provide two-way communication between a fire control center (FCC) and dedicated phone jacks in elevators and at elevator lobbies.

6. Telecommunications raceway system

A. The incoming telecommunications lead-in facilities will enter the building at two locations and will provide a minimum of eight 4-in. conduits in each route.

B. From the service entrance, the cabling will be routed to the main distribution frame and telephone switch (MDF) room via conduits. Service will be routed from the MDF room up the building in two telecommunication closets vertically stacked. Provide a telecommunication grounding system, including grounding risers, in each closet.

C. Provide a satellite antenna room of approximately 100 sq ft in the roof penthouse.

D. Horizontal distribution of tenant telecommunications cables will be above the hung ceilings.

7. Lighting

Provide typical office lighting consisting of direct/indirect recessed light fixtures with energy-efficient lamps and electronic ballast. Lighting levels will be as follows:

Area	Lighting level (footcandles)
General office	35–50
Corridor/lobbies	20
Toilets	30
Storage	20
Emergency egress	2
Mechanical room	20
Stairwells	20
Parking garage	10

▼ *Diagram of chiller and cooling towers. One distribution system circulates chilled water between chiller and fan coil units that cool interior air. Another water circuit carries heat from the condenser to open cooling tower, where some evaporates or spills and make-up water is added for return to condenser.*

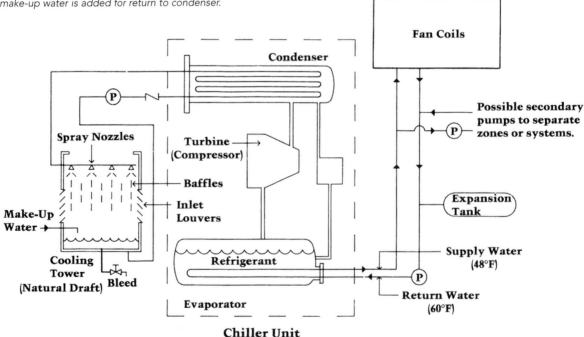

(continued from page 105)
cooling effect. Another reason is that the effluent may contain dissolved chemicals that can stain building materials in or adjacent to its upward path.

Typical HVAC Distribution Systems

Variable air volume system— chilled water

The most common distribution system in the U.S. model of the high-rise office building is the variable air volume (VAV) system. Typically, an air-handling unit (a supply fan with filters and cooling coils) distributes conditioned (cooled, filtered) air at a predetermined temperature in sufficient quantity to offset the heat gains in an occupied space. Because it is primarily a cooling problem, the amount of cooling effect provided can be varied by varying the amount of cool air. As the cooling load varies because of occupancy variations or solar gain through the exterior, a space thermostat will sense the amount of cooling required. It then sends a signal to the VAV terminal to admit the appropriate amount of cool air into the duct system and air outlets that supply the space.

The air-handling unit supplying a certain floor will sense the amount of air that the different VAV terminals call for and adjust its output accordingly. The cooling coil in the on-floor air-handling unit receives chilled water (produced by the central chillers) via a chilled water piping system to produce the cooling effect on the air.

Heating, in climates where required, is primarily a perimeter issue and a function of the envelope design. This function can be met by perimeter baseboard radiation or by a heating coil in the perimeter VAV terminal unit.

Variable air volume system— packaged cooling units

An alternate to the VAV, chilled-water, on-the-floor air-handling unit is an air handler, which includes a self-contained refrigeration package to provide cooling

▼ *Water riser diagram for typical variable air volume HVAC system.*

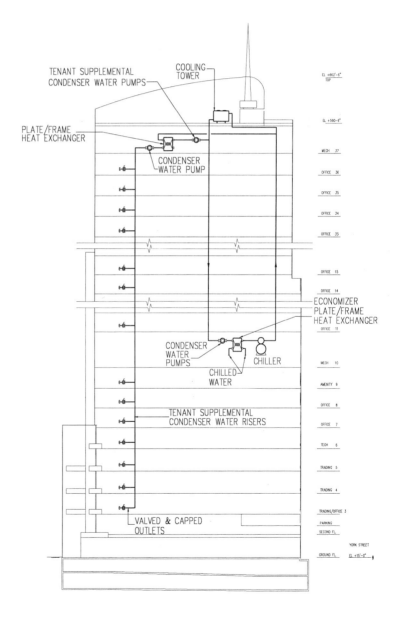

▼ *Diagram of variable air volume HVAC system with chilled water.*

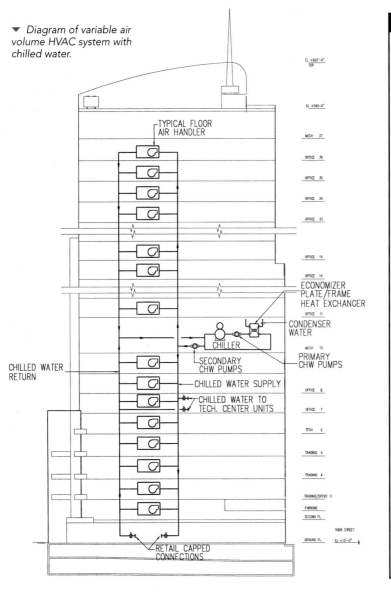

directly to the cooling coil. This system does not have a chiller plant. Like the chilled water system, it requires a cooling tower, but the condenser water from the cooling tower is circulated to the individual refrigeration package in each floor air handler.

Ventilation air

The on-floor VAV system is a recirculating system in which the air from the space is returned above the hung ceiling, acting as a plenum. This air is then returned to the fan room in the core, which is also a plenum. Ventilation air is

Floor	Equipment and Associated Space Requirements				
Roof Garden	Air-cooled chillers, 3200 sq ft	Cooling towers, 7000 sq ft	Tenant standby generators, 1000 sq ft	House domestic water tanks, 600 sq ft	
51		Plumbing room, 400 sq ft		Mechanical equipment room, 1500 sq ft	
50					
49	Electric closets (2) @ 100 sq ft				
48	Electric closets (2) @ 100 sq ft	Telecom closets (2) @ 100 sq ft		Mechanical fan room 400 sq ft	
31	Electric closets (2) @ 100 sq ft	Telecom closets (2) @ 100 sq ft		Mechanical fan room 400 sq ft	
30	Electric closets (2) @ 100 sq ft	Telecom closets (2) @ 100 sq ft		Mechanical fan room 400 sq ft	
29	Electric closets (2) @ 100 sq ft	Telecom closets (2) @ 100 sq ft		Mechanical fan room 400 sq ft	
28	Electric closets (2) @ 100 sq ft	Telecom closets (2) @ 100 sq ft		Mechanical fan room 400 sq ft	
27	Electric closets (2) @ 100 sq ft	Telecom closets (2) @ 100 sq ft		Mechanical fan room 400 sq ft	
26	Electric closets (2) @ 100 sq ft	Telecom closets (2) @ 100 sq ft		Mechanical fan room 400 sq ft	
25	Electric closets (2) @ 100 sq ft	Telecom closets (2) @ 100 sq ft		Mechanical fan room 400 sq ft	
24	Electric closets (2) @ 100 sq ft	Telecom closets (2) @ 100 sq ft		Mechanical fan room 400 sq ft	
23	Electric closets (2) @ 100 sq ft	Telecom closets (2) @ 100 sq ft		Mechanical fan room 400 sq ft	
22	Electric closets (2) @ 100 sq ft	Telecom closets (2) @ 100 sq ft		Mechanical fan room 400 sq ft	
4	Electric closets (2) @ 100 sq ft	Telecom closets (2) @ 100 sq ft		Mechanical fan room 400 sq ft	
3	Electric closets (2) @ 100 sq ft	Telecom closets (2) @ 100 sq ft		Mechanical fan room 400 sq ft	
2	Electric closets (2) @ 100 sq ft	Telecom closets (2) @ 100 sq ft		Mechanical fan room 400 sq ft	
Mezzanine	Electric closets (2) @ 100 sq ft	Telecom closets (2) @ 100 sq ft		Mechanical fan room 400 sq ft	
Ground-level lobby	Fire command station 120 sq ft	Telecom closets (2) @ 100 sq ft		Mechanical fan room 300 sq ft	
Basement 1	Electric service transformers and switchgear, 4800 sq ft	Life safety and tenant generators, 800 sq ft	Fuel-oil storage, 1000 sq ft; UPS system, 1000 sq ft	Boiler & chiller plant, 15000 sq ft; Plumbing and fire protection, 1100 sq ft	Telecom service rooms, 2500 sq ft

TYPICAL MEP SPACE REQUIREMENTS, HIGH-RISE OF 1,500,000 SQ FT

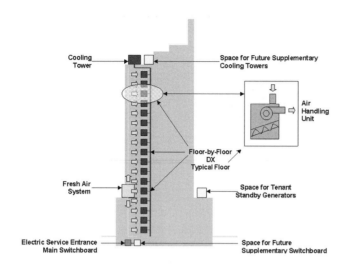

Diagram of typical variable air volume HVAC system with packaged air-conditioning refrigeration units on individual floors.

typically brought in from a separate system in the main mechanical room, requiring substantial exterior louvers. It is supplied to each on-floor fan room directly to mix with the return air. A portion of the return air is exhausted to maintain a proper air balance and good indoor air quality.

Fan coil systems

An alternative to the VAV system, using chilled water, is the fan coil system, which is more popular in Europe than in the United States. In this system, individual units containing fans, coils, and filters are located throughout the occupied space. Each unit can provide individual zone control via fan speed or varying the supply of chilled water. They may be mounted exposed within the space or above hung ceilings. This system usually requires less hung-ceiling space. It also requires more access for maintenance, i.e., changing filters, cleaning, etc., as well as condensate drain pans. Ventilation air in a separate system is also required, since fan coil units are recirculating systems.

IMPACT ON ARCHITECTURAL STRUCTURES
Space Requirements

Mechanical and electrical equipment have unique requirements for space, which are critical to the efficiency of space utilization and system performance. They are equal in importance to the programmatic requirements for a building. Hence, they should be disseminated to the architects and engineers in a similar manner. Early in the project, the MEP engineer should give the architect preliminary information, including some of the important related characteristics: louver requirements, adjacencies, alignment, and so on. For large or tall buildings, there is particularly intense competition for space at the base of the structure, where the demands of lobbies, parking, loading docks, and ancillary retail areas contend with the need to get utilities and communications into the project.

An example of a typical space requirements report is shown on pages 114–115. Space requirements can also be communicated graphically, which is helpful in visualizing the design implications for various parts of the building and in initiating a dialogue on modification.

Very Tall Buildings

In very tall buildings, space utilization becomes even more critical, as the vertical and horizontal tradeoffs have greater consequences. The better the location of mechanical spaces and the vertical distribution, the easier it is to develop an efficient floor-to-floor height. In tall buildings there are great economic pressures and/or zoning requirements for minimum floor-to-floor heights. In the Petronas Towers at Kuala Lumpur City Center, Malaysia, the chillers and cooling

The labels in the diagram read:

Cooling Tower
Space for Future Supplementary Cooling Towers
Air Handling Unit
Floor-by-Floor DX Typical Floor
Fresh Air System
Space for Tenant Standby Generators
Electric Service Entrance Main Switchboard
Space for Future Supplementary Switchboard

towers were located at grade, part of a district cooling plant scheme. Hence, the articulated building top was free of cooling tower constraints. Tall buildings exert high hydrostatic pressures on the water systems. Accordingly, such a building is often organized in isolated pressure zones using efficient plate/frame heat exchangers, which transmit the cooling effect between two water circuits without passing on the pressure; that is, the circuits are independent. This is called a "pressure break" and requires mechanical space within the tower.

The air distribution scheme is VAV, with one on-floor chilled water air-handling unit per typical tower floor. The unit is located in a fan room within the core, with overhead distribution of supply ductwork in the hung ceiling. This is accomplished within a floor-to-floor dimension of 4.0 m (13 ft), typical for tall buildings. In the Petronas Towers, a

ceiling height of 2650 mm was provided above a 125 mm raised floor for cable and wire distribution.

RAISED FLOOR DISTRIBUTION SYSTEMS
Raised floor—cabling only

Responding to the demand for flexibility and change in the modern office, raised floors for horizontal distribution of power and information technology cabling have become increasingly popular. Typically, these are 100–150 mm (4 to 6 in.) in height above the concrete slab and utilize lift-out floor modules covered with corresponding carpet tiles. Cabling and outlet modifications are easily accomplished by lifting floor tiles and making the necessary changes. Owner-occupied buildings use this system more often than speculative office buildings, because the occupant derives most of the benefit throughout the building life.

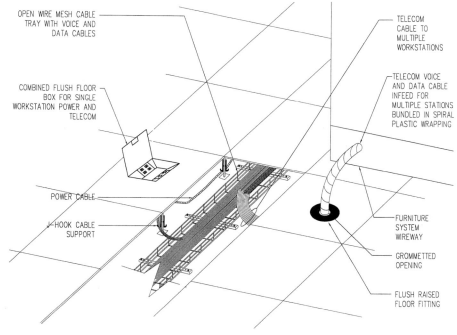

OPEN WIRE MESH CABLE TRAY WITH VOICE AND DATA CABLES

COMBINED FLUSH FLOOR BOX FOR SINGLE WORKSTATION POWER AND TELECOM

POWER CABLE

J-HOOK CABLE SUPPORT

TELECOM CABLE TO MULTIPLE WORKSTATIONS

TELECOM VOICE AND DATA CABLE INFEED FOR MULTIPLE STATIONS BUNDLED IN SPIRAL PLASTIC WRAPPING

FURNITURE SYSTEM WIREWAY

GROMMETTED OPENING

FLUSH RAISED FLOOR FITTING

◀ *Typical raised office floor, for cabling only.*

TYPICAL PRELIMINARY SPACE REQUIREMENTS REPORT*

Area	Space Required (sq ft)	Comments
BASEMENT		
HVAC		
Exhaust	200	Also for smoke exhaust
Supply	200	
Fuel oil tank room	200	10' × 20' vault
Chiller plant room	3000	2500 tons for 3 buildings
Health club, retail HVAC room	2000	
Subtotal HVAC	5600	
Electrical		
Service switch gear	216	12' × 18', 15' headroom, exterior pad
Subtotal Electrical	216	
Plumbing/Fire Protection		
Domestic water RPZ	64	2 rooms @ 8' × 4'
Fire service room	80	2 rooms @ 10' × 4'
Fire pump room	100	10' × 10'
Domestic water pump, central domestic water	105	
Gas room	50	
Subtotal Plumbing and Fire Protection	399	
Telecommunications		
Service entrance rooms 1 @ 225 sq ft	225	
Subtotal Telecommunications	225	
GRAND TOTAL	6440	
GROUND FLOOR		
HVAC		
Typical floor AHU	400	
Pipe shaft	12	
Subtotal HVAC	412	
Electrical		
Telecom closet 1	80	8' × 10' closet to vertically align
Telecom closet 2	18	3' × 6' niche closet to vertically align
Electric closet main	80	Closet to vertically align
Emergency generator and F.O. tank	400	Locate outside building
Subtotal Electric	178	
Plumbing/Fire Protection		
Pipe shaft	10	
Subtotal Plumbing and Fire Protection	10	
GRAND TOTAL	600	
TYPICAL FLOORS		
HVAC		
Fan room	400	2.0
Fresh air shaft	30	40,000 cfm, included in fan room
Smoke exhaust shaft	25	Dedicated rated shaft
Toilet exhaust shaft	10	Per toilet room 10,000 cfm
Stair pressurization	15	Per stair, two shafts
Boiler flue	20	If boilers are used in project
General exhaust	10	
Subtotal HVAC	510	Per floor

*For a 400,000 sq ft office building in Virginia, including parking below grade

Area	Space Required (sq ft)	Comments
TYPICAL FLOORS (cont.)		
Electrical		
Main electric closet	80	8'×10' closet to vertically align
Satellite electric closet	0	Not required
Subtotal Electrical	80	Per floor
Telecommunications		
Telecom closet 1	80	8'×10' closet to vertically align
Telecom closet 2	18	3'×6' niche, closet to vertically align
Subtotal Telecommunications	98	
GRAND TOTAL	688	
PENTHOUSE MECHANICAL EQUIPMENT ROOM		18'0" clear height
HVAC		
Exhaust fans	800	Smoke exhaust, toilet exhaust, electrical closet exhaust, tenant exhaust, 100 sf louver required
Fresh air supply	1800	120 sq ft louver required
Stair pressurization fans	400	120 sq ft louver required
Base building cooling towers	1300	If located on roof
Boiler room	1200	If required, 18' headroom
Subtotal HVAC	5500	
Electrical		
Electrical room	600	15' headroom
Subtotal Electrical	600	
Telecommunications		
Space for antenna room	100	
Subtotal Telecommunications	100	
GRAND TOTAL	6200	
TYPICAL PARKING FLOOR		
HVAC		
Exhaust fan rooms 4 @ 300 sq ft	1200	Outside through wall openings
Subtotal HVAC	1200	
Electrical		
Telecom closets	50	25 sq ft per room, 2 per floor
Electric closets	200	50 sq ft per room, 4 per floor
Subtotal Electrical	250	
Plumbing/Fire Protection		
Pipe shaft/dry pipe valves	10	
Subtotal Plumbing and Fire Protection	10	
GRAND TOTAL	1460	

Some developers are hesitant to invest the higher capital cost in a raised floor, if only the tenant receives life-cycle economic benefit. Of course, market demand can dictate a raised floor for cabling as a requirement. The use of this system varies dramatically among different cities of the world; that is, it is popular in Tokyo and London but not in most major U.S. cities today.

Raised Floor—
Air and Wire Distribution

In a further move toward flexibility, a raised floor can incorporate air distribution as well as wire/cable distribution. For air distribution, the raised floor is treated as a large-supply air plenum. On-floor air handlers can blow air down into the space created by the raised floor via a supply header duct, slightly pressurizing the floor. Air is supplied to the space from floor outlets instead of overhead. Air is returned at the ceiling, which acts as a return-air plenum, back to the air-handling unit room, as in a conventional overhead system. This air circulation is often called a *displacement type* system, in which cooled air is supplied at floor level, gently (low velocities). As it picks up the heat of people and office equipment, it rises through its own buoyancy to the ceiling, where it and the gained heat are carried away to the air-handling unit.

Because air outlets are integrated with the raised floor tiles, they can be relocated as easily as electric outlets. Air supply can be increased or decreased accordingly. In Cheung Kong Center, Hong Kong, the floor distribution used fan-assisted VAV terminals in the floor tiles to gain increased zone temperature control as well as flexibility.

INTELLIGENT BUILDINGS

The term "smart buildings" refers to those that integrate the low-voltage, signal, data, and communications systems into one network. They offer the ability to rapidly control and automate the following systems:

- Life safety
- Building management
- Security
- Elevator controls
- Office telecommunications (information technology)

▼ *Diagrammatic section of typical office floor with overhead air distribution.*

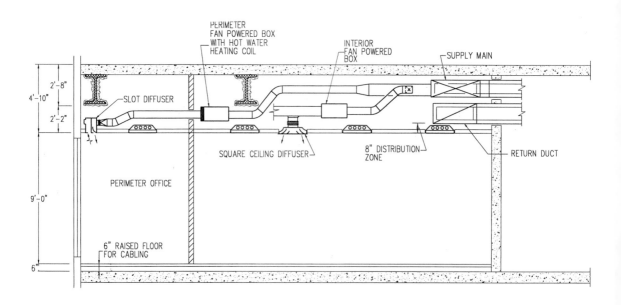

Many buildings incorporate a fiber-optic backbone to carry all the "traffic" at high speeds. Pathways must be properly incorporated into the basic building design (see "Space Requirements" earlier in this chapter) to provide the proper flexibility and infrastructure support.

GREEN ENGINEERING

What is a "green" HVAC system? A green HVAC system has the following attributes:

- It supplies an improved level of comfort throughout the occupied area of the building.

- It provides improved indoor air quality throughout the building.

- It is sufficiently adaptable that it will be able to handle a range of use variations for the building, thus delaying building obsolescence.

- It provides an optimal level of energy efficiency based on first cost and operating cost savings.

A green HVAC system must not only deliver adequate amounts of outside air to the spaces of a building, it must also ensure that the outside air is delivered to the spaces according to occupant density. It should respond dynamically, furthermore, to changes in occupancy. It must remove particulates from the air much more efficiently than is currently common. A green HVAC system must also not only control moisture to avoid microbial growth, it should have positive means of inhibiting such growth.

The use of natural ventilation can sometimes be an important part of a green HVAC system. Some places in the United States, particularly on the West Coast and in the western mountains, with dry, moderate climates, may rely totally on natural cooling. Other locations, particularly on the East Coast and in the South, may have a very limited opportunity for natural ventilation. For most of the Eastern portion of the United States, the prevailing summer dew point

▼ *Diagrammatic section of typical office floor with underfloor air supply.*

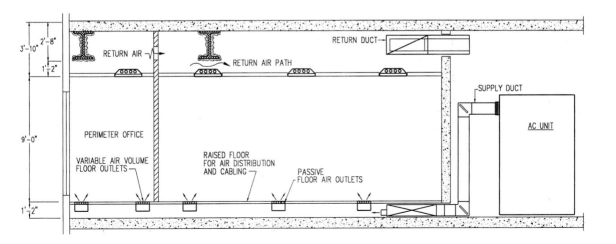

temperatures are far too high for comfort. In fact, studies at the Florida Solar Energy Center have shown that the absence of air-conditioning in very humid climates can lead to unhealthy levels of mold spores in the indoor atmosphere. In other areas, furthermore, particulate levels, either human-made, such as brake dust and soot, or natural, such as pollen, make natural ventilation both a housekeeping and a health problem. The effectiveness of operable windows depends very much on whether occupants will open and close them under the right circumstances. Natural ventilation, therefore, is sometimes green and sometimes not.

Engineers have given intense scrutiny to HVAC energy efficiency since the oil crisis of the mid-1970s. Today most equipment is available at efficiencies far beyond those available only a few years ago. Many energy-efficiency solutions, however, are based only on peak load operating conditions. For most of a building's operating time, the equipment will be operating far below peak demand.

Some Hints for Providing "Greener" HVAC Systems

1. Investigate systems that inherently provide a larger number of control zones than do conventional systems.

2. Consider systems that separate the tasks of dehumidification and sensible cooling. These systems are especially effective for densely occupied spaces and other areas with relatively high dehumidification requirements.

3. Look carefully at other factors that influence comfort. Consider operating the space at a lower relative humidity during the cooling season

to widen the dry bulb temperature comfort band.

4. Look at mean radiant temperatures during peak heating/cooling periods. Greater comfort can result from improved wall insulation or higher-performance glass, reducing unfavorable radiation to/from its surfaces, even though the energy cost saving payback may not be large. The building envelope can help make an HVAC system greener.

5. Provide a separate outside air conditioning system that, in addition to preheating the air, precools it, dehumidifies it, prevents mold growth on filters and coils, filters particulates from the air, and, in some locations, removes ozone and oxides, especially sulfur dioxide, from the air.

6. Equip the outside air-handling unit with ultraviolet sterilizing lamps or with a nonmetal-based brocade treatment to prevent mold growth on filters and coils.

7. Provide a heat exchanger within the toilet exhaust air to reduce ventilation air preheating requirements.

8. Use a humidifier in the outside air stream to keep the coil on the outside air-handling unit wet during swing seasons. The condensate on the wet coils tends to absorb certain pollutants in the ventilation air.

9. Reduce the required flexibility of an HVAC system by intelligent design of the building envelope. The variation of solar heat gain is often the single largest cause of cooling load variability in a building. Using high-performance glass or solar screening to mitigate the variability of solar

loads can ease the required flexibility of the HVAC system.

10. Use daylight-responsive lighting controls to reduce the heat gain from electric lights when solar heat gains are highest.

11. In appropriate areas, consider the use of mixed HVAC systems that can operate in concert with natural ventilation. These systems typically have a dedicated outside air system for ventilation and dehumidification and a separate system for sensible cooling. In cool, dry weather, the ventilation system can be deactivated, allowing its functions to be performed by operable windows.

12. Consider using carbon dioxide sensors to vary the amount of ventilation air delivered to spaces.

13. Consider the use of direct outside air delivery to isolated assembly spaces.

14. Use HVAC delivery systems that condition the people rather than condition the space; for example, control the cooling in an atrium to maintain a microclimate at only the occupied level (up to 10 or 15 ft), but not above.

15. Capitalize on stratification in higher-than-normal spaces, using displacement ventilation and radiant cooling systems. Properly utilized, stratification allows the lower, occupied area of a space to be conditioned while ignoring heat gains higher in the space.

16. For spaces that will have only transient occupancy, provide controls that can extend the occupancy conditions beyond the sedentary comfort range.

17. Size systems and equipment based on a well-thought-out long-term plan for the building, rather than strictly on current occupancy.

18. Provide variable-speed drives for all major prime movers in the system. Utilize control schemes that permit reduction of flow for heat transfer fluids during part-load operation.

19. Consider new ways of piping multiunit central plants. One may save energy by decreasing pumping costs.

20. Consider using units of varying sizes in a multiunit central chiller plant, so that any level of operating load can be met efficiently.

21. Exploit the capabilities of digital controls. Through new sensors and programmable controllers, an HVAC system can be controlled to deliver exactly the right conditioning at the highest efficiency.

SYSTEMS FOR A SUCCESSFUL FUTURE

Whether or not the client wants to incorporate any features of smart buildings or green engineering into the project, a huge number of mechanical, electrical, and plumbing options must be considered in the design of today's office building. Before design can advance beyond the most basic conceptual sketch, an MEP professional must be on board to assess the client's needs and project their implications for the building's architecture.

Throughout the process MEP provisions must go beyond mere numbers of watts or square feet to ensure reliability, ease of maintenance, and backup capacity for contingencies. Considering the variability of current and future office interior demands—with concepts such as hoteling potentially increasing occupancy per square foot—all building systems must be adaptable to increased and changing demands. What makes corporate or developer office space "Class A" at any point in its history is the performance of its internal systems, so that the building designed today is not soon outclassed in the office marketplace.

VERTICAL TRANSPORTATION

JOHN VAN DEUSEN *Van Deusen & Associates*

Ever since the first passenger elevator was developed by Elisha Otis in 1857, engineers and architects have been trying to make elevators larger, faster, and more elaborate.

This chapter will break down the design and application of vertical transportation equipment in office buildings into manageable segments.

ELEVATOR EQUIPMENT

Elevators are divided into three basic groups: hydraulics (low-rise), geared traction (low- to mid-rise), and gearless (high-rise).

Hydraulic Elevators

Hydraulic elevators now come in many forms. The traditional application is the direct-acting in-ground piston type. This application originally used water as a pressure medium and was utilized in buildings of 15–20 stories with speeds as high as 700 ft per minute (fpm). Water hydraulics are still used in New York City but are rapidly being replaced with more efficient traction designs. Because water was not a good driving medium, oil was introduced for lower-rise units and remains in use today.

In the last 10–15 years, the industry has developed a number of different hydraulic applications that do not require the traditional in-ground piston to raise and lower the elevator. These are known as "holeless" hydraulics, which generally fall into two categories:

1. For light-duty holeless applications (low capacity, low speed, low-rise—two or three floors) a single piston, mounted to the side or rear of the platform, lifts the elevator in a manner similar to a forklift operation.

2. Heavier-duty holeless applications with capacities up to 4000 lb, speeds of 125–150 fpm and traveling up to 70 ft, use a roped system known as a 1:2 elevator. This means that for every 1 ft the piston rises, the elevator actually travels 2 ft. This application, originally developed in Europe, was brought to the United States in the late 1980s.

Because codes addressing persons with disabilities mandate vertical access to and within buildings—often for short vertical distances—the use of hydraulic elevators has increased dramatically. Moreover, with the current attention to the environment, the use of holeless hydraulics (no oil pressure vessel in the ground) has grown. In-ground piston hydraulics are still used for larger-capacity freight and truck lifts, but the pressure units and in-ground protection now available eliminate the threat of oil contamination.

Geared Elevators

The term *geared elevator* describes a driving unit that has a horizontal worm (screw) attached to a motor that meshes with an upright gear. The gear is attached to a traction sheave over which hoist ropes are run. The elevator cab structure is attached to one end of the hoist ropes, and a counterweight is attached to the other end.

Geared elevators have been used in apartment houses up to 30 stories for years. They are also very effective in low-rise suburban office buildings of 8 to 12 stories.

▶ *Cantilevered holeless hydraulic elevator, plan and elevation drawings.*

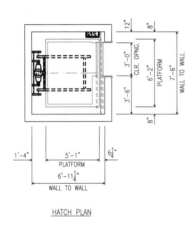

HATCH PLAN

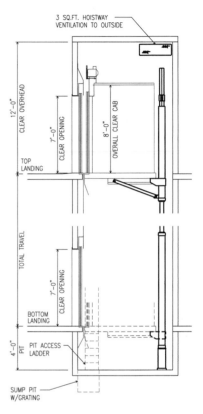

ELEVATIONAL SECTION

Modern geared elevators can generate speeds up to 500 fpm, which equals the low range of gearless units. However, geared elevators should be used in office buildings with caution because they are less efficient than gearless units, can require more maintenance, and do not run quite as smoothly as gearless units.

Special geared elevator applications

Over the years, geared elevators have been used in special ways to solve specific problems. With the advent of hydraulic elevators, specifically holeless hydraulic units, these special applications are no longer used much but are mentioned here as possible options.

Basement traction

The basic traction application simply takes the geared traction drive equipment from the top of the elevator shaft and locates it to the side or rear of the hoistway and somewhere below the top landing (usually, but not necessarily, at the lowest landing, called the "basement" for convenience in elevator terminology).

The reason for using this application is that it reduces the overhead dimension (clearance above the top cab position) from about 24 or 25 ft for straight overhead applications to 18 or 19 ft. For buildings in which future vertical expansion is desired, it makes elevator expansion quite easy.

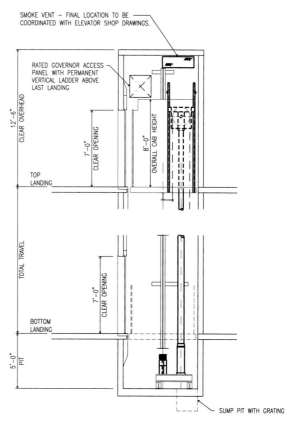

SMOKE VENT – FINAL LOCATION TO BE COORDINATED WITH ELEVATOR SHOP DRAWINGS.

RATED GOVERNOR ACCESS PANEL WITH PERMANENT VERTICAL LADDER ABOVE LAST LANDING

CLEAR OVERHEAD 12'-6"

CLEAR OPENING 7'-0"

OVERALL CAB HEIGHT 8'-0"

TOP LANDING

TOTAL TRAVEL

CLEAR OPENING 7'-0"

BOTTOM LANDING

PIT 5'-0"

SUMP PIT WITH GRATING

ELEVATIONAL SECTION

▶ Roped holeless 1:2 hydraulic elevator, plan and elevation drawings.

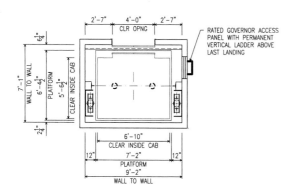

2'-7"   4'-0"   2'-7"
CLR OPNG

RATED GOVERNOR ACCESS PANEL WITH PERMANENT VERTICAL LADDER ABOVE LAST LANDING

WALL TO WALL 7'-1"
PLATFORM 6'-4½"
CLEAR INSIDE CAB 5'-6½"
6¼"
2¼"

6'-10"
CLEAR INSIDE CAB
12"   7'-2"   12"
PLATFORM
9'-2"
WALL TO WALL

HATCH PLAN

The drawbacks of this application include the following:

- An expanded machine room must be located somewhere below the roof, requiring more area than needed with an overhead application.
- The structural overhead loads are doubled.
- There are "basement" up-pull structural loads to be dealt with.
- Price increases about 5 percent because of added equipment.

Basement underslung

The basement underslung application was used (on a limited basis) before the advent of the holeless hydraulic. The underslung application used a "basement" machine location to the side or rear of the cab and, with the overhead sheaves positioned outside the area of the cab, allowed the elevator to be lifted from below, up to a clear overhead. With the speed limited to 200 fpm, the elevator could be installed in 13–14 ft clear from the last landing.

An underslung application was used when it was not possible to "pierce" the slabs above the last stop.

The drawbacks of this application include the following:

- Wider than normal hoistway in order to keep the lifting sheaves outside the area of the cabs

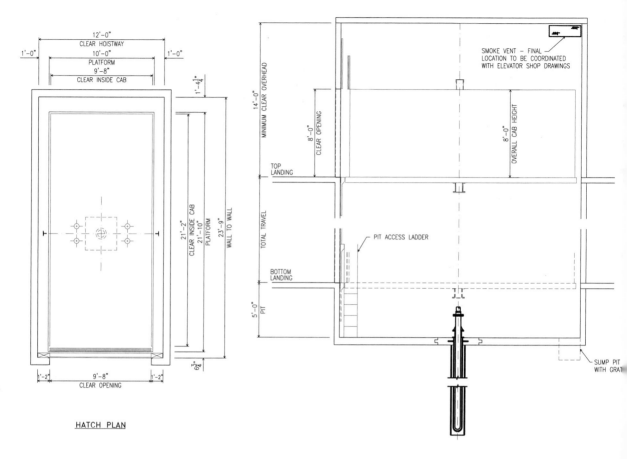

HATCH PLAN

▲ *Direct acting hydraulic freight elevator, plan and elevation drawings.*

- Heavy structural loads
- A 10 percent increase in price because of the difficulty in construction
- Deeper than normal pit, because the "underslung" sheaves are under the platform

The holeless hydraulic has done away with this application except where speed is critical (up to 200 fpm, whereas holeless roped hydraulics are generally limited to 150 fpm).

Gearless Elevators

Gearless elevators are the top-of-the-line high-speed hoisting equipment. The original gearless elevator was designed around a DC motor with a traction sheave attached. The hoist cables go over the traction sheave, with one side attached to the cab structure and the other ends attached to the counterweight, similarly to the geared traction application. DC machines were originally used because DC power was easier to control during the acceleration, deceleration, and landing patterns.

The newer gearless applications are designed around AC motors. With the new technology/microprocessors, AC power is more manageable than DC, and it is cleaner (no carbon brushes on the commutator). The new machines are extremely efficient and are a major part of the "green" building. All major manufacturers are providing AC gearless machines now, and speeds of 2000 fpm or greater can be obtained.

Controls

Each elevator has two control elements: motor control and signal control. Motor control refers to devices that convert and/or apply power to the hoist machines. The older equipment received AC power at one end of the control and converted it to DC power, which was then used to drive a DC motor on a geared or gearless machine. Motor generators or silicon control rectifiers (SCRs) are the primary devices used for this conversion to apply power to the older DC machines. SCRs will continue to be used as a new power source when the DC machines are re-used.

In the newer controls, AC power is applied directly to the motor control, where it is run through a microprocessor that applies it directly to the AC motors on the hoisting machines.

The rate of acceleration is a very important part of motor control. Acceleration rate is the feeling a person has as an elevator starts from rest and gets up to contract speed. A machine's rate of acceleration in the new gearless equipment in the United States is about is 4 fps/s. This means that a 500 fpm elevator gets up to speed in 19 ft, whereas it takes a 1600 fpm elevator about 105 ft to get up to speed. The current thinking is to reduce the acceleration rate to about 3.5 fps/s. At this rate, it takes a few tenths of a second longer to go floor to floor, but the ride is more comfortable.

Signal controls are used to manage the car and corridor pushbutton actuations. The older systems have a dispatcher for a system (two or more cars) and a controller for each car. The corridor pushbutton signal goes to the dispatcher, where it is assigned to a car to answer. The individual car controller accepts the dispatcher's signals and directs the assigned car to respond. The determination of this assignment is based on which car is closest in distance to the corridor call.

The newer microprocessor systems have a combination controller/dispatcher for each elevator. These units process the information many times a second and will assign an elevator to answer a corridor call based on the quickest time to arrive rather than the distance.

Another benefit of the newer microprocessor systems is that if one car is shut down, the other cars can continue to operate as a group. If the older system loses the dispatcher, elevator operation is severely curtailed.

ELEVATOR TRAFFIC ANALYSIS

Elevator trafic analysis is an important phase of office building design because it establishes how efficient a building will be as compared with industry standards for good elevator design. In determining the size of the elevator core, this phase will also strongly affect the efficiency of the building in terms of percentage of floor area available for offices and related functions.

Determining the number, capacity, and speed of elevators in a system depends on many variables:

- Potential number of floors in the building
- Floor-to-floor heights

- Shape of the floor plate
- External access points to the main lobby
- External influences such as subways, trains, and parking structures
- Location of cafeterias, conference centers, etc.
- Type of building, i.e., single or multiple occupancy

As a general rule, allowing one elevator per 40,000 GSF is a good start in determining the potential number of elevators required. Another rule of thumb is that one elevator should be provided for every 200–225 building occupants. For two- to three-story buildings, the elevator demand may be considerably lower, assuming that many users find it convenient to use stairs.

Once a building's potential size and shape are developed, it is important to calculate the population, which is based on the usable or "carpetable" area. The architect can develop the carpetable area, but lacking that, 75–85 percent of gross area will generate usable area. In a more detailed consideration of tall buildings, the usable area of higher floors will be at the high end of the range, as the core will get smaller as elevators drop off.

The question then arises, what is a realistic square footage per person to use based on the net usable area? Throughout the years this figure has varied considerably. The ultimate answer lies with the owner/developer and his or her potential "exit strategy." Recently, we have been using 150–165 sq ft per person (based on net usable or carpetable area), which is considered conservative. However, special levels such as trading floors can double the aforementioned densities, reducing the usable square footage per person to 65–70 ft.

Once the population is determined, the analysis can start. The challenge is, what is the optimum number, speed, and capacity of the elevators in the system?

The interval and the five-minute handling capacity of the elevators are calculated to develop the system's efficiencies.

The *interval* is the theoretical longest waiting time, calculated by developing the round-trip time of one elevator. A theoretical round-trip time takes into consideration probable stops and is based on the number of potential stops and the number of passengers in the car. For example, if an elevator is loaded with 18 passengers (realistic maximum for a U.S. 3500-lb-capacity cab) and has 12 potential stops, there would be 9.5 probable stops. There is a door open, door close, passenger entrance or transfer, acceleration, deceleration, and running time associated with each probable stop. When the theoretical elevator makes its run up and down the building, it completes a round-trip. Divide the round-trip by the number of elevators in a group to arrive at the interval.

Note that the "average waiting time" is about 60 percent of the interval. This is because one person may push the corridor push button and wait the full "interval," while another passenger may arrive and enter the elevator as its doors are opening, which gives that person a wait time of "0." Intervals for major Class A office buildings should be less than 30 sec.

The five-minute handling capacity is calculated after the interval is determined and the population is known or calculated. It is expressed as a percentage of the population that is served by the elevator group. The formula is as follows:

$$\frac{\text{No. of passengers in the cab} \times 300 \text{ (sec in 5 min)}}{\text{interval}} = \text{no. of passengers moved in 5 min}$$

$$\frac{\text{No. of passengers moved in 5 min} \times 100}{\text{Population of building}} = \text{percentage of population carried in 5 min (handling capacity)}$$

Multiple-tenant office buildings should have a minimum handling capacity of 12–13 percent, and single-tenant office buildings should have a minimum of 13 percent handling capacity.

The same calculation is used for hotels, apartments, hospitals, and other buildings, but different minimum or maximum efficiency values are assigned:

Apartments
50–70 sec intervals
7–9 percent handling capacity

Hotels
30–40 sec intervals
12 percent handling capacity

Hospitals
35–45 sec intervals
12–13 percent handling capacity

This calculation is also applied to existing buildings to determine the existing elevator efficiencies. If the efficiencies are above or below the standards shown for Class A office buildings, they may be classified as B or C buildings. These lower classifications are not necessarily bad, they simply reflect the quality of elevator service that can be expected.

Equipment layout and sizing

Performing a traffic analysis assumes certain speeds and capacities of the elevators, as well as the number of floors served, especially in multibank office buildings. Several analyses are usually performed to optimize speeds, capacities, and floors served.

In large office buildings, the industry usually applies 3500 or 4000 lb capacity cars, depending on the efficiency desired. The standard 4000 lb car is 1'0" wider than a 3500 lb car and therefore uses more core space; that is, reduces usable area.

Larger-capacity cars are effective in the event that one elevator is out of service. The remaining cars will have capacity to carry the passengers, albeit with a little more crowding.

Lower-rise suburban multitenant office buildings can usually sustain lower-capacity cars (2500–3500 lb), because the entering and exiting rate of pedestrian traffic is somewhat reduced and therefore there is no determinable peak that would require larger-capacity elevators.

An elevator group should not be more than four cars wide, so as to facilitate passenger movement to an elevator (from the corridor push button to the entrance of an arriving car). The best layout of a four-car group would be two cars opposite two other cars. An elevator group should not exceed eight cars (four opposite four).

Corridor widths are very important in the layout of cores. With smaller cores (two opposite two) that have access from either end, 8'0" corridors are sufficient. The worst condition would be an eight-car group (four opposite four) of 4000 lb capacity cars with one end closed. The corridor width for this arrangement should be a minimum of 11'0" to facilitate movement of passengers at the main lobby.

▶ *Plans of possible elevator groups, showing recommended corridor widths. Widths shown assume 3,500-pound capacity cars. For cars of 4,000-pound capacity or more, increase corridors by at least 1 ft.*

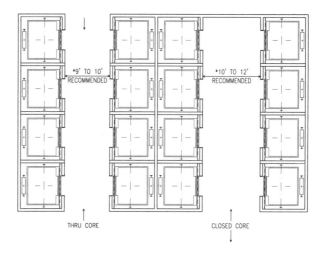

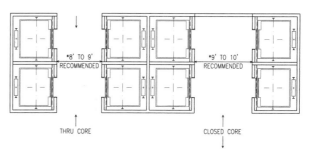

FIGURE 4

* – IF THE CAPACITY OF THE ELEVATORS IS 4000# OR GREATER, INCREASE THE CORRIDOR BY AT LEASE 12"

The number of floors served by an elevator group will vary, depending on the population, square footage and/or total elevator travel. This is also determined during traffic analysis. As a rule of thumb, an eight-car group of 4000 lb cars will support 350,000–400,000 GSF of space in the lower part of a building and 300,000–350,000 GSF at the top.

Alternative Elevator Applications

So far, we have discussed relatively standard applications of elevators for low-mid- or high-rise structures. With the introduction of super-high-rise buildings in the 100-story range, concepts using sky lobbies and/or double-deck elevatoring were also introduced. Any time a building of more than 50–60 floors is proposed for development, the use of sky lobbies or double-deck elevators has to be considered.

Double-deck elevators

The double-deck concept simply uses two elevator cabs in one hoistway. The two cabs are connected together in a common sling, with safety devices on the top and underneath the sling.

In a double-deck application, one deck serves the even-numbered floors and the other serves the odd-numbered floors.

The main lobby has two levels, usually connected by escalators, with one level designated to load passengers going to odd floors and the other loading those going to even floors.

During a peak-time trip, the potential for coincidental calls is great. This means that the elevator will make one stop, with passengers discharged at both an "odd" *and* an "even" floor. At stops where only one deck is discharging passengers, there will be a sign in the other cab that illuminates "Other Deck Operating" and the doors will not open.

The concept of double-deck elevatoring was originally developed to generate handling capacity in a building that was being designed with a requirement to move 20–25 percent of the population in a five min period. The concept was further developed with the introduction of large buildings that would require very large, inefficient cores if standard single-deck elevators were used. With the use of double-decks, the number of hoistways and elevator banks was reduced, thereby making the core (and the building) economically efficient.

Although the concept remains valid, the actual application of double-decks is used as an alternative for shuttle elevators to sky lobbies, and only for very tall buildings (more than 100 floors) is it considered for the local elevator application.

Because the capacity of the elevators is essentially doubled, the hoisting machines must be quite large. Most elevator companies have used their largest DC-drive machines for this application to generate duties (speed and capacity) of over 3000 lb capacity at 1200 fpm. With the development of new AC-drive machines, higher duties can be expected.

Double-deck elevators require the floor-to-floor heights to be exact because of the fixed dimension between cab sills. This necessitates some additional effort in the general construction. The fixed dimension requirement precludes the use of different floor heights commonly used today for trading floors and the like.

The cost of double-deck cars can also be a prohibitive factor, with individual cars costing up to $1,000,000 for high-rise, high-speed applications.

Sky lobbies

The sky lobby concept was used in New York's World Trade Center, where in effect three 35-story standard elevatored buildings were stacked on top of each other. The "main lobbies" of the second and third buildings were served by large (10,000 lb capacity) shuttle elevators that carried each building's population from the ground level up to its sky lobby.

By stacking cores on top of each other, separated by mechanical rooms and sky lobbies, very tall buildings can be developed.

The most effective use of shuttle elevators is a front and rear entrance application whereby passengers enter the shuttle car on one side at the ground and exit at the opposite side at the sky lobby. New bigger hoisting machines will allow the use of double-deck shuttles, which can lead to two-level sky lobbies, making the cores more efficient.

Other Applications

A major elevator manufacturer has developed a control system that requires passengers to register their floor destination at the main lobby *before* they enter an elevator. The registration panel will then direct them to an elevator. The system is designed so that any one elevator in a group will usually serve only a few consecutive floors on a given trip, reducing the number of potential stops produced in a conventional system. The theory is that the system reduces the total travel time or "destination time," thereby making it more efficient. A number of these systems have been installed internationally and are now being evaluated as to their effectiveness in the United States.

Another major manufacturer has developed a new compact AC hoisting machine that is mounted in the elevator hoistway for low-rise, low-speed applications or can be mounted in a reduced-space overhead machine room for higher speed, larger capacity applications.

Many of these units have been installed in Japan under a licensing agreement, and they are being used extensively in Europe as well. We expect their use in the United States to increase and eventually replace the hydraulic elevator as a low-rise hoisting medium because of their compact design.

Service elevators

Service elevators should not be confused with freight elevators. Service cars can carry passengers and are designed around passenger elevator requirements. Freight cars do not carry passengers and generally have lighter capacities for the same square footage.

We usually specify a separate service for every 500,000 GSF of space in a building. For buildings of less than 500,000 sq ft, a "swing" passenger/service car in the group will be used during off-hours as a service car.

Service elevators in office buildings should normally be deeper than they are wide and should have an entrance that will accept the largest piece of equipment (broken down) in the building. The entrances are 4'0" wide minimum, 4'6" wide as a standard. In addition, high entrances (8'0") and high cabs (10'0" minimum, 12'0" desirable) should be considered.

ENTRANCES, FIXTURES, AND CAB DESIGN

The design and finish of elevator entrances is a very important part of any building. We suggest that any "statement" that is to be made be done at the main lobby, with manufacturers' standard fixtures and/or entrances used for the typical floors.

Entrances

The entrances discussed in this section refer to those in the hoistway or corridor side. They are operated by and in conjunction with the elevator cab entrances.

Whether they are single-speed-side-slide, two-speed-side-slide, single-speed-center-opening, or two-speed center-opening, consideration should be given to the design and finish of the frames, door panel(s), and sill or saddle. The shape of the entrance frame can be configured to just about any design. The manufacturers' standards reflect a rectangular design, but rounded or bullnose shapes are readily available.

Entrances can be made as a unit or can be the knockdown (KD) type, coming in pieces and bolted together in the field. The unit type is more expensive than the KD frame, but it does not affect the operation. Therefore, unit frames may be used at the main lobby and KD frames above.

The entrance sill has a slot that keeps the door panel from swinging into the hoistway. Such sills can be manufactured from a number of different materials, including bronze (yellow Muntz metal), aluminum, nickel silver (has a yellow tinge), and stainless steel. Note that there is a sill at the corridor side and one on the cab, which should be coordinated where possible.

It is recommended to use nickel silver sills on service cars (car and hoistway) because of its hardness. Aluminum is too soft and will bend over time with heavy use. If you do not specify the material, aluminum will be estimated.

Panel and frame finishes range from painted to decorative metal to stone. On large projects with multiple finishing contractors, we recommend that the typical floor entrances be provided in prime paint and finished in the field by the painting contractor. This is done because no matter how well entrances are protected, they will be scratched during installation and field refinishing will never match a factory paint job.

Consider entrance heights during the building design. Standard entrance heights are 7'0". Standard sheet metal or decorative metal panels come in 4' × 8' sheets. Any entrances more than 8'0" in height require special panel sizes that are expensive.

Fixtures

Fixtures (such as corridor push buttons, car operating panels, hall lanterns, etc.) are part of the base elevator contractor's contract, even though they may be shown in the cab. Therefore, they should be thought through and included with the base specification.

As with the entrances, we suggest that any "statement" be made at the main lobby and standard items used at typical floors. Note that if you do not show or specify a design and simply describe a function, a manufacturer's standard unit will be provided.

Be careful of special push-button designs. We have found that they can jam. Rather, select from standard push buttons provided by a manufacturer and apply a decorative cover plate.

The standard cover plates are stainless steel. Be careful of yellow metal push-button plates, because they must be lacquered to keep their color (this is true with natural or oxidized plates). Unfortunately, the lacquer wears off with constant touching, which causes unsightly discoloration.

The Americans with Disabilities Act (ADA) requirements for elevator fixtures are very exacting and should be followed. Be aware that many cities have their own requirements for accommodating disabled persons (such as ASME 117.1 Code), which initially take precedent over ADA requirements, especially for the final city certificates. A blend of both codes should be adopted, with the more stringent prevailing.

Cabs

The design of elevator cabs in major office buildings can often become too detailed. The elevator cab fabricator, whether it be the elevator manufacturer (such as Otis, Schindler, or Thyssen) or an independent cab company, will tend to add to the price because of too much detailing. We therefore suggest that time and thought be given only to materials and intricate interfaces that are important, rather than detailing every last connection.

Consideration should be given to airflow through a cab. This requires air inlet vents near the base and a free path to the exhaust fan.

The use of swing-front return panels (the panels on either side of center-parting cab doors) rather than separate surface-mounted car station panels is relatively easy for cab companies and does not increase the cost dramatically.

Weight is a very important factor in cab design. If the design calls for stone floors and/or wainscoting and/or woven wire mesh panels, the base specifications must alert the bidder to this fact so that he or she may increase the size of the hoisting equipment, if required.

COST ESTIMATES AND LEAD TIMES

Cost estimates vary with the economy. During the boom times of the late 1990s, most companies, both manufacturers and contractors, became very busy, and consequently lead times and prices increased. The following information is quite general and should be used only for rough budgeting. More accurate pricing and lead times are usually developed after an outline specification is completed.

Cost Estimates

Hydraulic passenger elevators are the least expensive units. A two-stop elevator, 2000 lb capacity, at 100 fpm, 12 ft rise, with a standard cab, entrances, and fixtures should cost $40,000–60,000.*

Geared traction elevators have speed variables from 100 fpm up to 500 fpm. A ten-stop, 2000 lb capacity, at 350 fpm, car with standard equipment should cost $140,000–175,000.*

Gearless traction equipment has the greatest variation in price. Office building gearless cars in New York City with ratings of 3500 lb capacity at 500 fpm serving 12 stops may cost $300,000 each. Large service elevators, 6000 lb capacity at 700 fpm serving 45 floors, can cost $1,000,000 each.

Escalators with rises up to 20 ft should be budgeted for $100,000–125,000.* These figures include solid or glass balustrades and either 600 mm or 1000 mm wide units. Escalators for higher-rises and/or transit applications can be anywhere from twice to eight times as expensive.

Lead Times

After a project is awarded, manufacturing lead times, including shop drawings, can extend from 14 to 16 weeks for hydraulics or escalators, up to 26 weeks or more for gearless equipment.

Installation time depends on the building progress, but can be from 8 to 10 weeks for a simple hydraulic to 30 to 40 weeks for high-speed gearless equipment.

Special consideration should be given to the lead time for elevator cabs. When designs are elaborate, shop drawings may take 8 to 10 weeks, with another 16 weeks for fabrication. Designers often leave the cabs to the last minute, and these can actually be the "long lead" items that make or break the schedule.

MODERNIZATION

The term *modernization* may be interchanged with *upgrading*. The process takes an existing elevator system and replaces all or some of the major devices with new modern ones that will perform faster or better.

In the United States, modernization of

*Depends on the area of the country. As speeds, capacity, and travel increase, cost goes up accordingly.

an old group-supervisory system includes the installation of a new microprocessor-signal control system and perhaps the replacement of the power drive system with silicon controlled rectifiers (SCRs) instead of keeping AC-DC motor generators. More than likely the car and corridor fixtures are replaced to be compatible with the new microprocessor system. Finally, the cab interior is upgraded to reflect a modern feeling along with a new master car door operator.

Equipment such as DC gearless or geared-drive machines may be retained along with car and counterweight rails, platforms, slings, buffers, compensation equipment, and perhaps the hoistway entrance tracks, hangers and interlocks, door panels, and frames.

Special care must be taken to do the following:

- Make sure the AC main power feed is suitably sized for any new power drives.
- Make sure the new installation meets all current codes, such as ADA or Firemen's Service.
- Be cautious about adding too much weight to the new cab interior. The ASME Code is very definite in its requirements as to how much weight can be added. How any added weight affects the existing hoisting machine should also be explored.

The amount of equipment that is reused depends on its condition and the ability of local contractors to modify it to accept new equipment. For example, in New York City it is not uncommon to remove a DC motor from a geared machine and fit it with a new AC motor, then apply the latest state-of-the-art variable voltage variable frequency

(VVVF) drive, along with a microprocessor signal control system. However, in other parts of the United States and in other countries, the entire machine would be replaced along with many other devices, making a "modernization" job more like new construction.

Modernizations are done for many reasons: Equipment is worn out, the owner of the building wants to reposition it for a new market, or a new tenant requires an upgrade as a lease issue. In any event, when a five- or six-car elevator group serving 12–14 floors using old relay logic controls is modernized with the latest microprocessor technology, one can expect a 15–20 percent increase in efficiency, which is equivalent to adding one elevator.

MAINTENANCE

An ongoing comprehensive preventive maintenance contract on an elevator system is the key to a properly running system.

The process begins when a job (either new or modernized) is designed and put out for bid. A detailed maintenance specification should be developed and issued with the base equipment specification. The maintenance requirements/specifications should be negotiated with the contractor as seriously as the base equipment specification. It is not unusual for a contractor with a low base equipment specification to be more expensive when his or her monthly maintenance price is projected over a five-year period.

The maintenance specification/proposal can be specifically developed for a client, or the operating/performance requirements of the project can be specified and the contractor's specification/proposal can be accepted, evaluated, and negotiated.

The important aspect of this "drill" is to

have the owner or end payor of the lease involved in the negotiations so that the monthly maintenance cost (for the next five years) is not a surprise after construction.

The following areas should be addressed in a comprehensive maintenance contract:

- Performance requirements, including floor-to-floor times, door open–door close times, dwell times (time the door stays open at a floor in response to a car or corridor call), etc.

- Maximum callback (arrival) times for a shutdown; 30 min during the day, 60 min after hours

- The number of shutdowns per unit, per month, that will be acceptable

- Penalties for shutdowns that exceed those stipulated

- Maximum annual/monthly increase in the contract price that will be acceptable

ESCALATORS

Escalators are the ultimate mass movers of people for one to three floors. The design of escalators has not changed dramatically over the years. A constant-speed AC motor drives a chain to which step units are attached, running on a continuous track, along with a moving handrail that is synchronously attached to the motor control.

Escalators come in three widths: 32 in. (600 mm), 40 in. (800 mm), and 48 in. (1000 mm). Designers should realize that the inch dimension represents an old code designation that was actually measured horizontally 27 in. (700 mm) above the step tread. The actual step widths are now represented by metric designation:

Nominal width	Tread width
32 in.	600 mm (24 in.)
40 in.	800 mm (32 in.)
48 in.	1000 mm (40 in.)

All escalators made in the United States have a 30-degree angle of inclination. In Europe and the Far East, the angles of inclination can be more than 30 degrees for certain applications. The speed of all U.S. escalators is currently 100 fpm. The European and Far East units can have higher speeds.

Realistic carrying capacities of the escalators are as follows:

600 mm	=	250 persons/5 min
800 mm	=	350 persons/5 min
1000 mm	=	450 persons/5 min

The carrying capacities may seem modest, but they can cause passengers to accumulate in a hurry, and adequate queuing space must be assigned in a building to accommodate this passenger accumulation.

Required flat steps at the top and bottom of an escalator vary from country to country. The United States requires two flat steps (up from an early one and a half). European countries generally permit automatic starting (passenger-activated) escalators, which are not allowed in the United States. One company, Mitsubishi, offers curved escalators, dramatic installations that can cost in excess of $600,000 each.

QUEUING CONCERNS

Queuing relates to the number of people who enter a space within a given time. This space can be fixed, as inside an elevator cab, or a traveling space such as the exiting area of an escalator.

A person standing still requires about

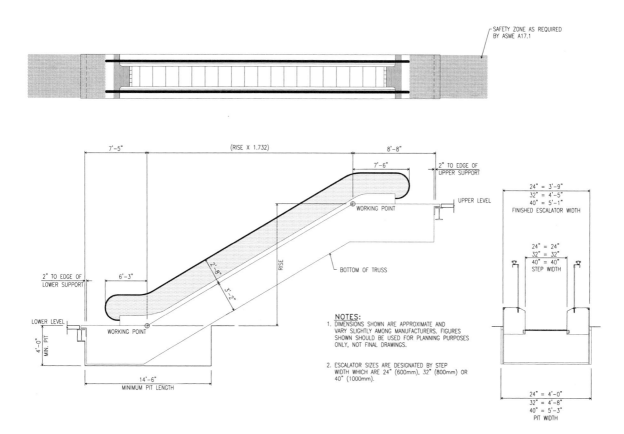

NOTES:
1. DIMENSIONS SHOWN ARE APPROXIMATE AND VARY SLIGHTLY AMONG MANUFACTURERS. FIGURES SHOWN SHOULD BE USED FOR PLANNING PURPOSES ONLY, NOT FINAL DRAWINGS.

2. ESCALATOR SIZES ARE DESIGNATED BY STEP WIDTH WHICH ARE 24" (600mm), 32" (800mm) OR 40" (1000mm).

3.4 sq ft of space without touching someone else. This requirement applies primarily to elevators. Elevator traffic studies assume up to 17 or 18 persons in a 3500 lb capacity car. The inside area of a 3,500 lb capacity car is 35.5 sq ft. If you divide 3 sq ft per person into this area, you arrive at a maximum comfortable capacity of 12 persons.

A person walking at a slow rate will require 5–7 sq ft of (moving) space. This is important when you consider the space required to accept escalator traffic moving from one escalator to another. A 1000 mm wide escalator can "push" 450 persons in five minutes into a space. If these passengers have to move to another escalator for service, they must be provided with

adequate queuing space of about 450–630 sq ft (90 persons per minute × 5–7 sq ft of space per minute).

This concept gets more involved with different situations. A good book on the subject is *Pedestrian Planning and Design,* by John J. Fruin (Elevator World, Inc., Educational Services Division).

INTERNATIONAL DESIGN

In this age of computers, high-speed faxes, web sites and CAD design, it is very easy for a designer in New Jersey to converse with another in London, Paris, or Hong Kong with very little loss of design time. In working with "lifts," as elevators are called in many countries, it is important to understand and have a

▲ Diagram of escalator design requirements, showing key dimensions, which vary with specific equipment selected. Table shows actual dimensions for some frequently used equipment.

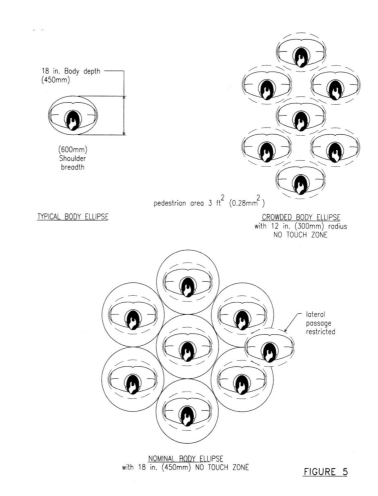

▶ Standard "body ellipses" used in planning vertical circulation.

good working knowledge of the EN81 Code. This code, with minor modifications, controls the design of vertical trans-portation equipment outside North America.

The following are some of the major differences:

1. Very specific requirements for fire service elevators

2. Escalators that can have different angles (more than the 30 degrees allowed by the ASME Code)

3. Allowable use of ½-hour rated hoistway entrances vs. 1½-hour requirements in the United States.

In addition, a number of different types of units that have been introduced in Europe are just being introduced in the United States. This slow introduction process is caused primarily by the conservative (not necessarily wrong) approach of the ASME Code committee.

Many of the breakthroughs that we are now experiencing, such as roped holeless hydraulics and AC variable voltage variable frequency (VVVF) drives, were developed and operating in Europe and East Asia well ahead of their U.S. prototypes.

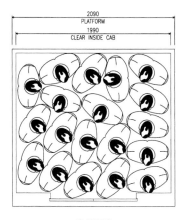

2090
PLATFORM
1990
CLEAR INSIDE CAB

19 PERSONS

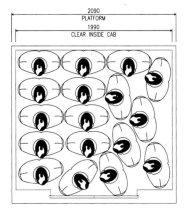

2090
PLATFORM
1990
CLEAR INSIDE CAB

17 PERSONS

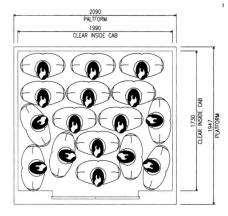

2090
PALTFORM
1990
CLEAR INSIDE CAB

1730 CLEAR INSIDE CAB
1947 PLATFORM

16 PERSONS

CONCLUSIONS

There is no end to the vertical transportation conveyance cycle. What starts as a new construction project will eventually be modernized and eventually torn down to start the process again.

The key steps are as follows:

1. Evaluate your needs conservatively (allow for a good "exit strategy").

2. Design and provide good quality equipment using "judicious overdesign."

3. Install and turn over a product that is running as designed.

4. Provide ongoing maintenance that will keep the system operating as it was originally designed.

▲ *Illustrative arrangements of passengers in elevator of nominal 24-passenger capacity.*

CHAPTER 7
CURTAIN WALLS

JOE KHOURY *ALT Philippines*

With advances in technology, it is becoming possible to design, engineer, and fabricate ever more complex curtain walls. The challenges of curtain wall design, however, remain formidable, as they fulfill a wide variety of crucial functions. Moreover, owners and architects are continually demanding more from curtain walls, in terms of energy efficiency, environmental sensitivity, versatility, low maintenance, and longevity.

Until the late 1980s, curtain wall manufacturers, particularly in the U.S., produced 75–80 percent of the components of these walls and were constantly engaged in research and development of the materials and assemblies before releasing them on the market. As a result of recent economic downturns, downsizing of producing companies, and fast-track construction, much of that research and development has disappeared.

No longer curtain wall innovators, today's contractors and manufacturers act as brokers, coordinators, and assembly plants for components from different sources. Warranties and guarantees are passed on from suppliers directly to owners individually, rather than the curtain wall contractor providing the overall coverage.

Curtain wall contractors and manufacturers alike are disappearing at an alarming rate because of deteriorating profit margin, leaving the industry with less and less experience. The fabrication and installation of curtain walls are left largely to newcomers gaining experience in a costly learning process.

Owners and developers are thus becoming more reliant on architects,

consultants, and specification writers for advice and direction, so adequate knowledge of curtain walls is essential for all of them. Unfortunately, curtain wall standards, philosophy, and expertise vary widely around the world, and there are no known handbooks that integrate the subjects of curtain wall design and technical performance.

This chapter attempts to explain the principles of curtain wall design, providing definitions, methods, new concepts, and particulars on how to achieve a result that meets a project's objectives.

CURTAIN WALL DEFINED

A curtain wall is a self-supporting and continuous cladding system—inherently different from infill elements such as window walls or masonry cladding. It must protect the structure from the weather, separate indoor air from outdoor conditions, control light, afford views, and move with the structure to criteria set for it, as the structure is affected by thermal movements, live loads, dead loads, wind, and seismic events.

Fire-rated curtain walls may be necessary, depending on code requirements. In such cases, the wall design and the materials must meet specified standards in case of exposure to fire.

High-rise curtain wall designs normally incorporate special safety features to accommodate window washing. For the typical system of gondolas suspended from above, a curtain wall must incorporate a safety tieback system.

Curtain wall systems are divided into two basic categories: stick walls and unitized walls.

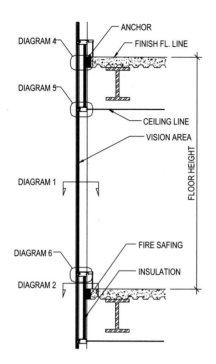

DIAGRAM 4 — ANCHOR

— FINISH FL. LINE

DIAGRAM 5

— CEILING LINE

— VISION AREA

DIAGRAM 1

FLOOR HEIGHT

DIAGRAM 6 — FIRE SAFING

— INSULATION

DIAGRAM 2

▶ *Floor-to-floor section of stick curtain wall system, showing locations of diagrams 1, 2, 4, 5, and 6.*

Stick Wall Systems

Stick wall systems are available in either standard designs or custom designs, but the same basic principles apply. Stick walls are composed of individual components shipped in knockdown form to the site, where they are assembled and installed.

Systems of this type require highly skilled laborers on-site to carry out combined assembly and installation work and enough space to store loose components. The many prominent buildings completed this way worldwide include the Sears Tower in Chicago and the World Trade Center in New York City.

Structurally, this kind of curtain wall is based on the principle of simulated continuous beam, distributing the load evenly along the building perimeter. Vertical mullions are anchored at the floor slabs, with splices or sleeve connections

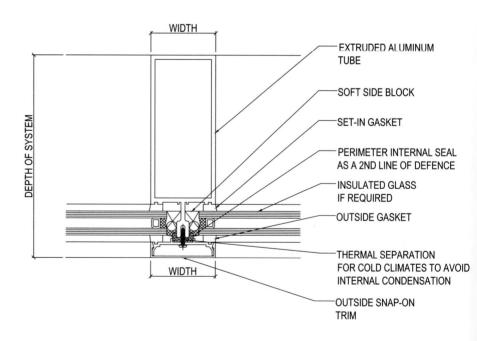

WIDTH

— EXTRUDED ALUMINUM TUBE

— SOFT SIDE BLOCK

— SET-IN GASKET

— PERIMETER INTERNAL SEAL AS A 2ND LINE OF DEFENCE

— INSULATED GLASS IF REQUIRED

— OUTSIDE GASKET

DEPTH OF SYSTEM

— THERMAL SEPARATION FOR COLD CLIMATES TO AVOID INTERNAL CONDENSATION

WIDTH

— OUTSIDE SNAP-ON TRIM

▶ *Diagram 1: Plan detail of stick curtain wall system showing vertical mullion, at vision glass level.*

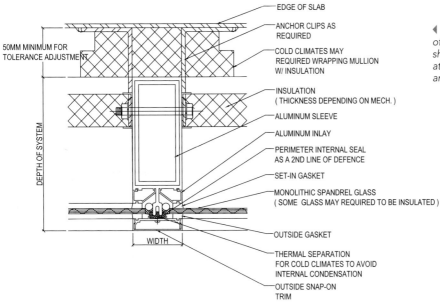

EDGE OF SLAB

ANCHOR CLIPS AS REQUIRED

COLD CLIMATES MAY REQUIRED WRAPPING MULLION W/ INSULATION

INSULATION (THICKNESS DEPENDING ON MECH.)

ALUMINUM SLEEVE

ALUMINUM INLAY

PERIMETER INTERNAL SEAL AS A 2ND LINE OF DEFENCE

SET-IN GASKET

MONOLITHIC SPANDREL GLASS (SOME GLASS MAY REQUIRED TO BE INSULATED)

OUTSIDE GASKET

THERMAL SEPARATION FOR COLD CLIMATES TO AVOID INTERNAL CONDENSATION

OUTSIDE SNAP-ON TRIM

50MM MINIMUM FOR TOLERANCE ADJUSTMENT

DEPTH OF SYSTEM

WIDTH

◀ *Diagram 2: Plan detail of stick curtain wall system showing vertical mullion, at spandrel level, showing anchor.*

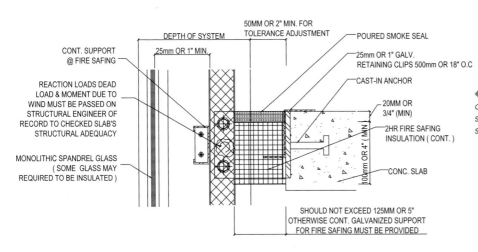

DEPTH OF SYSTEM

50MM OR 2" MIN. FOR TOLERANCE ADJUSTMENT

25mm OR 1" MIN.

CONT. SUPPORT @ FIRE SAFING

POURED SMOKE SEAL

25mm OR 1" GALV. RETAINING CLIPS 500mm OR 18" O.C

CAST-IN ANCHOR

REACTION LOADS DEAD LOAD & MOMENT DUE TO WIND MUST BE PASSED ON STRUCTURAL ENGINEER OF RECORD TO CHECKED SLAB'S STRUCTURAL ADEQUACY

20MM OR 3/4" (MIN)

2HR FIRE SAFING INSULATION (CONT.)

MONOLITHIC SPANDREL GLASS (SOME GLASS MAY REQUIRED TO BE INSULATED)

CONC. SLAB

100mm OR 4" (MIN)

SHOULD NOT EXCEED 125MM OR 5" OTHERWISE CONT. GALVANIZED SUPPORT FOR FIRE SAFING MUST BE PROVIDED

◀ *Diagram 4: Detail section of stick curtain wall system, showing anchor and fire safing.*

preferably located above the floor at a dimension of 1/5–1/4 of the vertical span, thus giving the mullions the optimum structural integrity.

The depth of the system is determined by several considerations: the wind load, the aesthetic objectives, and the performance requirements for controlling deflection and stresses, as established in national and/or industry standards.

The accompanying drawings demonstrate the basic requirements.

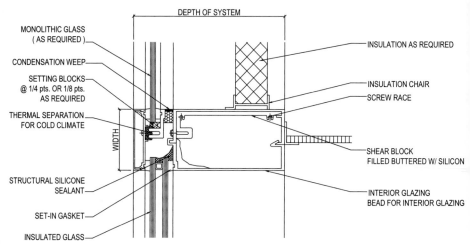

> Diagram 5: Detail section of stick curtain wall at head of vision glass.

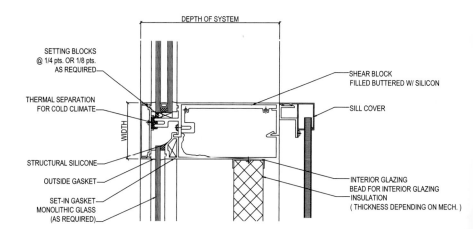

> Diagram 6: Detail section of stick curtain wall at sill of vision glass.

Unitized Wall Systems

The use of unitized walls is becoming the most effective and the preferred method for creating curtain walls in the construction industry. The popularity of such systems is attributable to the off-site control of the component assembly, especially structural silicone application, and the elimination of site damage to loose material.

Unitized wall systems require fewer skilled workers for shop assembly, but with a high degree of in-plant quality control. They do, however, require skilled installation crews at the site to protect anchors and set the units in place.

The structural design of unitized walls is identical in principle to that of the stick wall. The main difference is that the mullions have sections composed of open

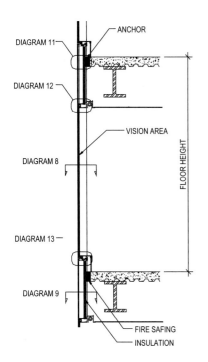

DIAGRAM 11

ANCHOR

DIAGRAM 12

VISION AREA

FLOOR HEIGHT

DIAGRAM 8

DIAGRAM 13

DIAGRAM 9

FIRE SAFING

INSULATION

▲ *Floor-to-floor section of unitized curtain wall system, showing locations of diagrams 8, 9, 11, 12, and 13.*

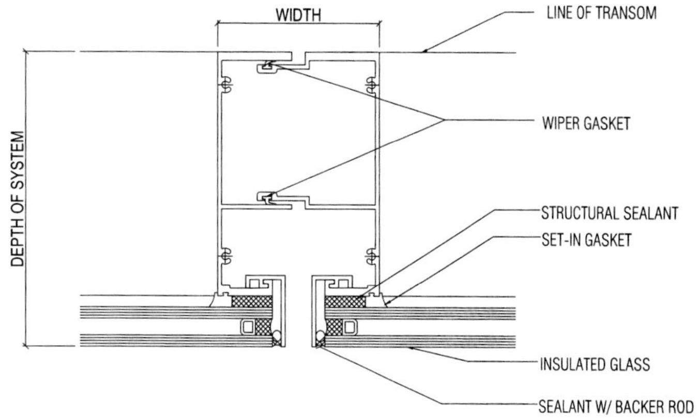

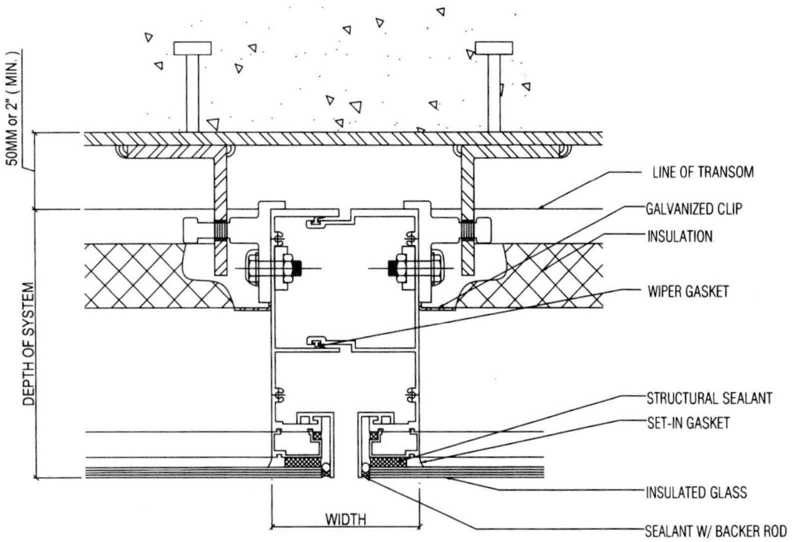

▶ *Diagram 9: Plan detail of unitized curtain wall system at spandrel level, showing anchorage.*

▼ *Diagram 8: Plan detail showing split vertical mullion of unitized curtain wall system at vision glass level.*

WIDTH

LINE OF TRANSOM

DEPTH OF SYSTEM

WIPER GASKET

STRUCTURAL SEALANT

SET-IN GASKET

INSULATED GLASS

SEALANT W/ BACKER ROD

50MM or 2" (MIN.)

DEPTH OF SYSTEM

LINE OF TRANSOM

GALVANIZED CLIP

INSULATION

WIPER GASKET

STRUCTURAL SEALANT

SET-IN GASKET

INSULATED GLASS

SEALANT W/ BACKER ROD

WIDTH

shapes that are joined to share the load, hence the mullion size may be larger in width and depth as compared with that of a stick system.

As with stick wall systems, the depth, width, and/or shape of the unitized system depend on performance and aesthetic requirements. The accompanying diagrams demonstrate the basic and minimum requirements.

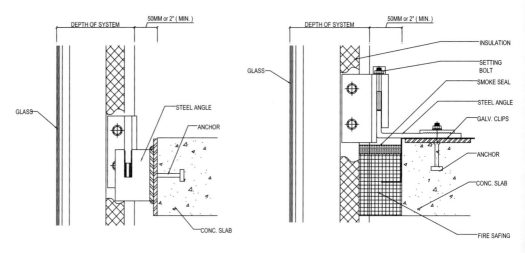

▲ Diagram 11A: Detail section showing anchorage of unitized curtain wall system.

▲ Diagram 11B: Detail section showing anchorage with fire safing.

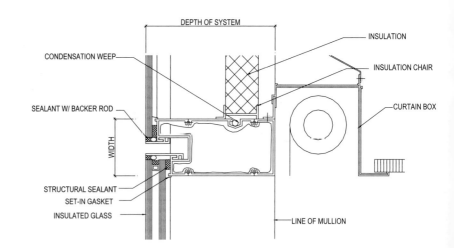

▶ Diagram 12: Detail section of unitized curtain wall system at head of vision glass.

LOW-MAINTENANCE WALLS

To avoid staining and continuous maintenance on exterior cladding, architects and manufacturers alike are adopting open-joint systems. These minimize or eliminate exposed sealant at the face of the wall, adopting the concept of a rain screen pressure-equalized cavity wall, allowing water in cavities to escape.

Pressure equalization is based on enabling the spandrel cavity to adjust instantly to changes in the atmospheric pressure. This can be achieved only by designing the rain screen with large vents, allowing air pressure to become equalized between the exterior and the cavity. It is important that the internal barrier be sealed tight to avoid suction due to pressure differences.

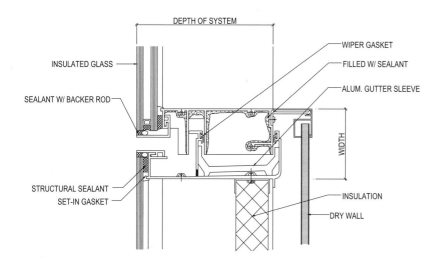

INSULATED GLASS

SEALANT W/ BACKER ROD

STRUCTURAL SEALANT
SET-IN GASKET

DEPTH OF SYSTEM

WIPER GASKET

FILLED W/ SEALANT

ALUM. GUTTER SLEEVE

WIDTH

INSULATION

DRY WALL

◀ Diagram 13: Detail section of unitized curtain wall system showing split rail at sill level.

Pressure equalization is best achieved in a unitized wall in which the seals can be shop-applied. Most of the open-joint systems can be applied to granite, aluminum panels, or any solid material. They are not recommended for glass because of the detrimental effects of internally retained moisture on glass.

A pressure-equalized cavity wall offers structural advantages for the wall's face materials. Wind loads on the outer surface may be reduced up to 40 percent because of pressure equalization, thus reducing material thickness, stiffening, and the like. Internal barriers, however, must be reinforced to absorb 100 percent of the wind loads.

ENERGY-EFFICIENT WALLS
There are two types of energy-efficient walls: cavity walls (or double walls), which have long been popular in Europe, and thermally broken walls with high-performance glass, which are predominant in North America, Asia, and the Middle East.

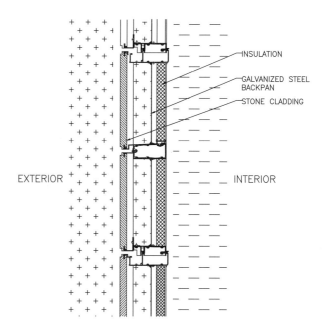

EXTERIOR

INTERIOR

INSULATION

GALVANIZED STEEL BACKPAN

STONE CLADDING

▲ Section of open joint wall system, indicating atmospheric pressure in the cavity equal to that of exterior.

Double Walls/Cavity Walls

Double walls have been created for two principal reasons, one of which is to provide light control with maximum transparency—that is, with clear glass, with no coating or tint. The other reason is to reduce heating and cooling loads by creating a lower U-value than is possible to achieve with insulated glass. Walls of this type are also used where there are high acoustical isolation requirements.

In some instances, winter heating may be virtually eliminated by utilizing heat from lighting and human occupation, and summer cooling can be achieved through natural ventilation if air pollution is not a problem. Because of pollution, the more popular application involves heating via transmission through the heated cavity and cooling by venting the cavity, using shading devices to help reduce internal cooling loads. Shading devices also eliminate direct sunlight and glare for occupants.

There are several theories and methods for achieving double walls, as indicated in the following paragraphs.

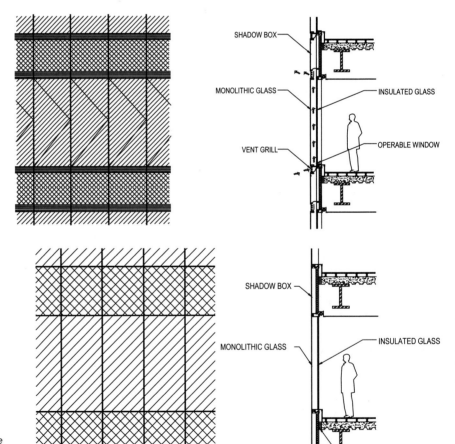

▶ Section of double wall, type 1, showing summer ventilation of cavity induced by heating of air.

▶ Section of double wall, type 2, with sealed cavity through which dry air is pumped.

SHADOW BOX

MONOLITHIC GLASS

INSULATED GLASS

VENT GRILL

OPERABLE WINDOW

SHADOW BOX

MONOLITHIC GLASS

INSULATED GLASS

FIRE SAFING INSULATION

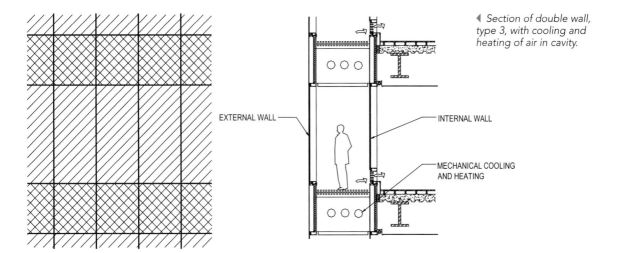

◀ Section of double wall, type 3, with cooling and heating of air in cavity.

EXTERNAL WALL

INTERNAL WALL

MECHANICAL COOLING
AND HEATING

Double wall, type 1. In winter the type 1 (vented) double wall is not vented and heat is trapped and transmitted to the interior. In summer the cavity is vented and air circulates, cooling the cavity. With shading devices lowered, thus eliminating direct heat and glare, it will reduce the required cooling load. This wall type will require interior doors for access to the cavity for cleaning and maintenance.

Double wall, type 2. The type 2 double wall (with pressurization) is a nonactive wall creating a low U-value, with a continuous volume of dry air pumped through the cavity to prevent condensation. It is similar in concept to wall type 1, but requires less maintenance because of the sealed cavities.

Double wall, type 3. The type 3 double wall (with internal mechanical heating and cooling) utilizes cool and warm water to control cavity temperature and adjust for exterior atmospheric fluctuations. This type of wall is easier to maintain

than the other two wall types. However, it is also the costliest.

The major difficulties with types 1 and 3 are keeping them clean and free of moisture, such as condensation, and the maintenance of mechanical parts such as the vent doors and shading devices, which may be operated either mechanically or electronically.

Cost is also a major factor. Therefore, a study must be conducted to determine the difference in operating expenses of the mechanical system related to the costs of the different wall systems. Of all three wall types, type 2 is the most economical because of lower maintenance demands and fewer operable parts.

COMPONENTS
Glass

Glass is the most extensively used product in curtain walls. It is economical, versatile, and available tempered or annealed, in a multitude of colors, and in various thicknesses and numbers of layers. A variety of coatings, including frits, are available.

ENVIRONMENTAL VALUE OF GLASS TYPES	
Type	**Environmental value**
Clear	No significant value
Tinted	Slightly better
Coated glass	Better
Insulated	Good/depending on makeup
Insulated with coatings	Good
Insulated with glass and coating	Excellent

For detailed information regarding glass, refer to the industry standards listed at the end of this chapter. However, the following are guidelines for general use.

Glass thicknesses for curtain walls are usually at least 6 mm (about ¼ in.) and are readily available up to 19 mm (about ¾ in.). The glass is also heat treated, depending on strength and thermal stress requirements. Glass manufacturers provide technical data in their brochures and further assistance upon request.

Glass can and should be specified primarily for the following properties.

Strength, that is, resistance to wind load. ASTM 1300 should be followed as a guideline for design purposes. Manufacturers' literature includes charts and tables for quick reference for actual conditions, but manufacturers should be requested to calculate the exact thickness and heat treatment required.

Thermal stress, which depends on the curtain wall design. The glass may be overstressed because of heat absorption, entrapment, or partial shadowing of the glass. The specific designs are usually reviewed and calculated by the manufacturers. When the glass is heat treated, it is usually not necessary to perform an additional thermal stress analysis.

Maximum size available. Glass size limitations vary with each type of glass and product. Architects and designers must verify with manufacturers the availability and suitability of the proposed sizes. Size limitations are dependent on the types of glass, such as monolithic, coated, laminated, and heat treated.

Heat treatment. Glass is produced in the annealed form, which has the least strength, but can be heat treated after fabrication and coating. The most common heat treatment of glass is heat strengthening, which is recommended for most curtain wall applications but is not a safety requirement. For doors and store-fronts, which are in contact with pedestrians, and railings, infills, full-height glass, and so forth, full tempering is usually required. Tempering will provide high strength and a breakage pattern that is less likely to cause injury to people. Laminated glass, with an inner layer of transparent plastic, can also be utilized in lieu of tempered glass, depending on conditions; it is used mainly for overhead glazing such as skylights.

Environmental performance. Glass performance values are critical to the energy efficiency of buildings. All glass manufacturers publish data on their glass products that are useful in the design of custom glass curtain walls.

MANUFACTURER'S GLASS PERFORMANCE CATEGORIES									
Transmittance			**Reflectance**			**ASHRAE U-value**		**Shading Coefficient**	**Relative Heat Gain**	**European U-value**
Visible	Solar	UV	Vis Out	Vis In	Solar	Winter	Summer			
						BTU/HR-sq ft-°F	BTU/HR-sq ft-°F			
%	%	<1	%	%	%			.00	W/sq m	W/sq m

Glass coatings

With the current available coating machinery, combination coatings and double coatings can produce very high performing glass. Glass coating is available in two basic forms.

The pyrolitic form of coating, which embeds the performance coating during the float glass process. The glass can be fabricated and heat treated postproduction. The color and variety of coatings are limited. This type of product is typically used in economical construction, where monolithic glass is preferred. Because of the integral coating, scratches and other damages are minimized.

The other form of coating is sputter or vacuum deposited, referred to as "soft," coating, and is available in a multitude of colors and types. The glass must be fabricated and heat treated prior to coating. This glass is frequently used in insulated units (double glazed) to achieve higher performance, with the coating on a surface inside the unit to eliminate possible scratches and damage.

Most manufacturers publish data for their glass, as shown in the table at bottom left.

Glass performance measures

The following terms are in common use:

Visible light transmittance. Percentage of visible light transmitted through glass.

Solar transmittance. Percentage of ultraviolet, visible, and near infrared energy transmitted through glass.

Visible light reflectance. Percentage of visible reflectance observed from either inside or outside.

ASHRAE U-value. A measure of heat gain or loss through glass due to differences between indoor and outdoor temperatures. These are center pane values based on ASHRAE standard winter nighttime and summer daytime conditions.

Shading coefficient. The ratio of solar heat gain through a specific type of glass that is relative to solar heat gain through a ⅛ in. (3 mm) ply of clear glass under identical conditions. As the shading coefficient number decreases, heat gain is reduced, which means a better-performing product.

Relative heat gain. The amount of heat gained through glass taking into consideration the U-value and the shading coefficient using the ASHRAE standard.

Solar heat gain coefficient (SHGC). The portion, directly transmitted and absorbed, of solar energy that enters into a building's interior. The higher the SHGC, the higher the heat gain.

European U-value. Based on ISO-DP10292 draft standard conditions.

Stone

Stone is a natural product that is quarried and generally classified in the following categories:

Granite. Strong and uniform, best suited for exterior application and thin-wall cladding.

Limestone. Inconsistent, although some limestone is strong and can be used in curtain walls, but at greater thickness than granite.

Sandstone. Inconsistent; although some sandstone is strong and can be used for exteriors, it is rarely used in curtain walls.

Marble. Weak and also inconsistent, not recommended for thin-wall exterior application.

Testing

Stone requires extensive testing; refer to standards at the end of this chapter. Some

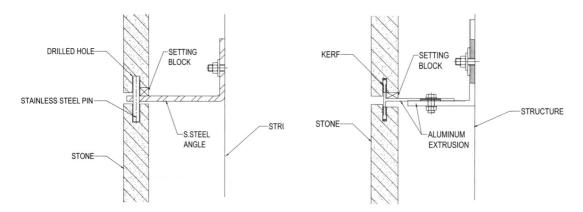

DRILLED HOLE
SETTING BLOCK
STAINLESS STEEL PIN
STONE
S.STEEL ANGLE
STRL

KERF
SETTING BLOCK
STONE
ALUMINUM EXTRUSION
STRUCTURE

▲ Anchoring stone to wall using continuous kerf (slot) cut in tops and bottoms of stone cladding units.

◥ Anchoring stone to wall using pins in holes drilled in stone cladding units.

granite has been tested and verified and is consistent. Published data on frequently used stone is available from quarries and fabricators. Extra care should be exercised in the selection of the stone for exterior application. Test data should be requested prior to final selection to determine suitability for application.

The following standard tests will determine the strength and durability of the stone. Designers, architects, specifiers, and consultants should be aware that stone is a long-lead-time item; hence, testing should commence at the earliest possible date.

C97 *Absorption and bulk specific gravity of stone.* This test is to determine stone durability in alternating wet and dry conditions.

C170 *Compressive strength of stone.* This test is to determine the crushing stone strength and is not critical for curtain wall application.

C99 *Modulus of rupture of stone.* This test is to determine the stone's breaking load when tested parallel and perpendicular to its rift. This is helpful in predicting its capacities under wind load and at anchor point engagements.

C880 *Flexural strength of stone.* This test is to determine tensile strength in bending, which can predict safe

distances between anchorages for thin stone in curtain wall application.

Stone anchorage design

Anchoring stone to a curtain wall can be achieved in two ways: hand setting, or preinstalling on unitized walls.

Anchorage of stone to the supporting system can be achieved with a continuous kerf, which is a slot cut in the stone along its edge, usually top and bottom, depending on the requirements, or with stainless steel clips or pins, again depending on the requirements.

Stone anchorages should be designed to allow for easy replacement. There are many stone-fixing methods available, ranging from simple proprietary methods to custom-designed systems. Depending on design requirements and cost, the choices should be evaluated on a job-by-job basis. For more detailed information, refer to the available standards and books relating to stone.

Aluminum

Aluminum, in most cases, is the main supporting material for a curtain wall. The American Architectural Metals Manufacturers Association (AAMA) and the Aluminum Association publish data on the alloys that are most frequently used architecturally. The Aluminum Association also publishes data on the mechanics and workability of alloys, which are applicable to extrusions and aluminum sheets.

The most frequently used alloys are the following:

Extrusions   6063 T5 and T6

Aluminum sheet 3003 – H 14

Architectural extruders must be qualified and experienced, thus making it crucial during the bidding (tendering) process for architects, specifiers, and/or consultants to carry out due diligence on extruders.

Designers must also be aware that the sizes and shapes of extrusions are very critical to the cost and availability. For example, most extruders can produce only 8–9 in. shapes, although 10 in., 12 in., and even larger sizes are available from limited sources.

The designing of complex shapes and large profiles should be studied carefully to avoid unsightly joints, deformation, or lines. It is advisable to consult extruders and request performance data.

The key element in architectural panels is flatness. To meet this requirement, design of the panels is critical with regard to the thickness of the material, bending of edges, use of stiffener attachments, and allowance for movement due to thermal expansion and contraction.

A popular selection has been sandwich panels produced with two-face sheets laminated to a honeycomb core, because of the flatness and color consistency that can be obtained. If longevity and durability are more important considerations, however, the use of monolithic sheet is more suitable, but requires careful selection and design. It is important that the manufacturer of solid panels is experienced, with an excellent track record, to avoid the risk of unacceptable design and workmanship in claddings.

Aluminum sheet is available in standard 3'0", 4'0" widths. Larger widths are also available, but must be ordered in advance. Available thicknesses of aluminum for monolithic panels include 0.125 in. (3.2 mm), 0.187 in. (4.8 mm), and 0.25 in. (6 mm). Lesser thickness can be used, such as 3/32 in. (2 mm), but panel sizes for such thicknesses must be limited to maintain flatness and minimize bow.

The advantages of thinner material such as the 3/32 in. (2 mm) is that it can be coil-coated at the mill. Depending on the architectural requirements, this can save cost and ensure color matching. Thinner material such as .060 in. (1.5 mm) or less is usually used in laminated panel products such as honeycomb, compressive, and sandwich panels.

STAINLESS STEEL

Stainless steel is available in bar and sheet stock, the choice depending on the desired finishes and other requirements.

The most frequently used alloys are 304 and 306. Because of harsh environments in some regions of the world, however, 316 is becoming more popular for its resistance to rust, but it is costly. There are also higher grades available, but at prohibitive costs.

Stainless steel sheet is available mainly in 3 ft and 4 ft widths; 5 ft sheets are very difficult to obtain. Thicknesses usually available include 1.2 mm (.05 in.), 1.5 mm (.06 in.), and 2 mm (.078 in.).

Stainless steel is becoming very popular for curtain walls because it is available in several surface finishes and embossed patterns. Selection of finishes should be carefully considered, however, in relation to other requirements. Some finishes, for example, can be applied after fabrication.

Stainless steel sheet is formed and fabricated in a similar manner to aluminum, and hence careful consideration must be given to bending, stiffening, welding, surface finishing, and special fabrication (for example, back cuts at corners to achieve sharp edges). Stainless steel storefronts made of formed sheet are not easily made leakproof. Formed sheet is also more difficult to align and match as compared with aluminum extrusions.

Basic finishes

All hot- and cold-rolled material is heat treated and given a basic finish by the rolling mill. The basic mill finishes may be sufficient for the required use or may be the basis for further finishing, either by the stainless steel producer, by a polisher, or during fabrication.

- The basic finish for hot-rolled plate products is heat-treated and pickled.
- The equivalent basic finish for cold-rolled material is cold-rolled, heat-treated, and pickled. This gives a uniform matte finish with some susceptibility to finger marking. This finish is often used for industrial applications.
- A smoother surface, with a brighter, semilustrous appearance is produced with an additional final light rolling process using polished rollers. It is commonly used for industrial cladding and roofing, and is the basis for many other finishes.
- Highly polished surfaces are also produced on a large scale using heat treatment in a controlled atmosphere and cold rolled with polished rollers.

Scratches on this material can be removed by skilled polishing. It is used in areas where damage is unlikely once it is installed.

Patterned finishes

Embossed, three-dimensional patterns may be rolled into a strip by cold rolling, either by steel producers in the course of manufacture—such finishes are often referred to as "special mill finishes"—or by specialist finishers. Patterned or textured rolls are used to impart surface features to one or both sides of the strips.

Mechanically polished
and brushed finishes

A wide range of mechanically polished finishes are available. Cutting or polishing of surfaces is performed with an abrasive medium or a sequence of media, using belts, wheels, or brushes. Such a finish may be applied to any starting surface, as a pre- or postproduction finish, in the steel plant or by specialist polishers or fabricators. The same general principles apply to postfabrication work on components or installations.

The major categories of these finishes are the following:

- Coarse
- Smooth, with controlled cutting action
- Mechanically polished (nondirectional)

Major steel producers have established standard finishes, but all finishes may be varied depending on the requirements agreed upon by the manufacturer and the purchaser, such as grade of grit, polishing sequence, and surface roughness.

Bead-blasted surfaces

Nondirectional, matte surface finishes can be developed by the impact of a hard, inert medium on the steel surface. The technique can be used in the shop and under site conditions. The surface texture created by bead blasting is dependent on the medium used, as indicated in the following list:

Medium	Surface finish
Sand	Dark, coarse
Glass bead	Light, smooth
Silicon carbide	Very dark, coarse
Stainless steel shot	Honed
Ground quartz	Shiny, coarse

Electropolished surfaces

Electropolishing is used to enhance the reflectivity of stainless steel and to provide smooth surface finishes. It is commonly used for intricate components that are difficult to polish by mechanical techniques, including textured surfaces such as checker plate flooring.

Colored and special decorative finishes

Stainless steel can be colored either by the application of paint or by chemical treatments. Both types of finish are durable in normal service. But damage can be difficult to repair, especially in finishes produced by chemical treatment. Special decorative finishes can be produced by acid etching, masking, the silk screen process, and the photo resist process.

Applied finishes

Applied finishes or coatings are critical elements of many curtain walls, adding color and providing protection to cladding materials such as aluminum and steel. Finishes are categorized by performance, durability, and cost. Available finishes include anodic coatings and painted finishes (or organic coatings).

Anodic coatings

For architectural purposes, anodic finishes for aluminum are available in two basic classes:

Class I anodic coatings for exterior surfaces requiring little or no maintenance

Class II anodic coatings for interior and maintained exterior surfaces

Anodic coatings, especially clear coatings, are very appealing because of their luster. But they may yield variations in color, depending on the alloy and the chemical content of the aluminum. Careful consideration must be given to the selection of the alloy and the process. AAMA describes the process, quality control, testing, and methods of achieving consistency in color and texture. Designers and specifiers should be cognizant of the requirements and insist that certain procedures be followed to achieve high performance and color matching.

Anodic finishes are available in a multitude of colors, and if applied properly can and should perform satisfactorily. However, because of the corrosive atmosphere found in large cities, including air pollution, acid rain, and the like, anodic coating applications are being specified less often for these situations.

Painted finishes (organic compounds)

Organic coatings have been popular and maintain their desirability because of the multitude of colors and textures available, and some finishes are extremely effective and durable. They are available at a wide variety of performance levels.

- *Acrylic paint.* Medium performance poor for exterior, excellent for interior.
- *Silicone modified polyester.* Medium

performance for exterior, good for interior.

- *Power coating.* Now available for exteriors and interiors (environment-friendly) Excellent performer for interior finish for metal because of its hard surface. For exterior use, this new product has been tested for only three years and has not matched the durability of PVDF coatings such as Kynar 500, Valspar, Hylar, Lumiflon, or any 70 percent resin paint.

- *Polyvinylidene fluoride (PVDF) coatings.* Based on Kynar 500 fluoro-polymer 70 percent resin. This product has proven superior for exterior applications. It is not recommended for interior surfaces of metal because of its ease of brazing and damage.

As with anodic finishes, paint must adhere to AAMA requirements and be applied properly. Careful inspections of paint and licensed facilities must be carried out to ensure proper treatment and application.

The cost of a paint finish will depend on the type of finish, color, and texture. The most costly—and durable—are the PVDF coatings, especially the metallic finishes that require three or four coats.

All of the coatings discussed here are factory applied, but there are fairly new products available for aluminum and steel that are site applied with similar performances and warrantees. According to paint manufacturers, a base primer application is the key to achieving good site application.

Gaskets

Gasket systems such as molded gaskets, weather strips, and zipper gaskets are becoming increasingly desirable as an alternative to sealants for sealing curtain walls.

Of the many available gasket materials, the most frequently used are neoprene, EPDM, and silicone. All components and materials used should adhere to the standards of the American Society for Testing and Materials (ASTM) and conform to the minimum requirements. Silicone gaskets are the only gaskets that can be produced in custom color, and they are the most costly.

The appropriate hardness of gaskets is determined by the design of the curtain wall and the location. The specified hardness is very critical, because gaskets are often the primary lines of defense and must also allow for movements.

Specifiers, designers, architects, and consultants must insist on compatibility and adhesion tests for all sealants used in the same wall with gaskets. This is critical to the life of the wall, as the effect of an incompatible sealant on the gaskets may adversely affect the performance of the curtain wall.

Sealants

Many compounds are available as sealants. Depending on the application, silicones and polyurethanes are the most commonly used. Silicones are by far the most desirable because of their ease of application and availability.

Sealant costs are very small as a percentage of the curtain wall cost, but sealants are the most critical components and should be attended to and reviewed carefully.

Sealants basically have two functions:

1. To seal and maintain water tightness

2. Structural application

In weather seal applications, tests must be performed to ensure proper adhesion and compatibility with the substrates with which they are in contact. This is critical for long-term performance. All sealant manufacturers perform free reviews of shop drawings and testing of materials for the architects. The sealant manufacturer will usually recommend the method of cleaning and application. This is critical, especially where glass is structurally adhered to aluminum frames, using silicone as the only means of attachment.

Nonstaining silicone sealants are available. Tests can be conducted on panels and stone to determine whether a sealant stains the cladding materials.

Extensive and ongoing testing during the application should be conducted to eliminate any chance of failure. It is recommended that structural silicone application be carried out in the factory.

Miscellaneous Components

Curtain walls contain a multitude of miscellaneous components that are equally important for performance and safety.

Insulation

There are special insulation materials used in curtain walls, with specific density and performance values. In certain applications, they must also be fire rated.

Insulation in cold climates will require an attached vapor barrier, whereas in warm and subtropical locations it may not be necessary. In any location, a perforated reinforced aluminum foil is recommended to protect the insulation from rainwater during installation.

Fire-Safing

Fire-safing is critical at floor slabs and compartmentalized zones to seal and prevent the spread of fire. This is usually a two-hour fire-rated insulation with a specific density of 100 mm (4 in.) thickness, placed in the cavities between the curtain wall and the structural support.

Smoke seals

Liquid-applied smoke seals are frequently used on top of the fire-safing to eliminate possible smoke penetration from one space to the other.

Hardware

Hardware for operable units, doors, windows, and vents should be researched to ensure accurate specification. For the operable parts, the use of stainless steel or nonferrous parts is recommended to avoid deterioration over time. Tests and certifications of products should be obtained to ensure conformance and proper performance.

Fasteners

Nuts, bolts, and screws, in most applications exposed to weathering, should be specified as 316 stainless steel. All other fasteners should be 304 stainless steel to avoid any corrosion or embrittlement.

Self-drilling fasteners are used in many applications, but for the most part, their material specifications are ignored. There are several manufacturers that provide a superior product with 300 series stainless steel shanks, fused hardened steel drill tips, and corrosion-protective coating.

Miscellaneous steel

Steel supports and anchors should be properly specified, with a special coating for corrosion protection, such as hot-dipped galvanized for exterior applications and wet areas, and for interior purposes, two coats of zinc-rich primer.

Embedments

Curtain wall anchors are attached to embedments placed at the edge of the slab. These may be made of miscellaneous steel plates or angles with headed studs to support anchor loads when cast in concrete, or channels with bolts allowing for adjustment.

COST

The cost of curtain walls varies from job to job, but a good rule of thumb is 10–20 percent of the total building construction cost.

Curtain wall cost is too often ignored until bid or tender time. Architects should be considering cost implications and alternative means to save costs during the design and preparation of drawings so as to avoid cost-cutting sessions by the owner, the contractor, or others, that may lead to design compromises.

The cost of the wall is divided into two categories: labor and materials. Depending on the region or country, percentages may vary drastically. For example, in North America and Europe 45 percent labor, 55 percent material is common, although this may vary by 5 percent or so depending on the location. In Asia and the Middle East, labor is usually 25–30 percent, with the material amounting to 70–75 percent.

The costs of materials and labor are typically divided as shown in the table below.

Glass

Monolithic clear is the least costly, with added cost for tint, insulated units, and coating, the most expensive including gas within the insulated cavity. The cost of glass is also influenced by the quantity of typical and nontypical sizes.

Aluminum Extrusions

For aluminum extrusions, costs are affected by a number of factors:

Size of extrusions. The size of extrusions other than supporting members—essential decorative features—should be minimized if possible.

Tonnage of metal, which is increased by large frame extrusion and exterior profile.

Number of shapes, contributing to the number of dies required.

Types of finishes (anodized, painted, PVDF coated; metallic).

Cladding Material

Stone

Cost is affected by the following factors:

Size of stone

Thickness

TYPICAL MATERIAL AND LABOR COSTS			
Materials	**Cost (percent of total)**	**Labor**	**Cost (percent of total)**
Glass	12	Fabrication	15
Aluminum extrusions	25	Assembly	30
Cladding material — stone/aluminum panels or other cladding	25	Shipping/transportation	5
Insulation/fire-safing	3	Installation	45
Hardware	35	Cleaning	5

High and low volume, i.e., number of different sizes

Exotic or standard materials or units

Special fabrication

Finish (polished, thermal, honed)

Aluminum

Cost is affected by the following factors:

Size of panels

Thickness

Fabrication—bent or sheared

Finish—standard or metallic; the number of coats of finish can be crucial.

Additional cost will be incurred by the use of less common materials such as stainless steel, titanium, and the like.

Other Material Categories

- *Insulation and fire-safing:* No impact.

- *Hardware:* Some impact if custom made.

- *Miscellaneous material:* Almost constant.

- *Testing:* Depending on how many mock-ups required; each mock-up usually costs $200,000–350,000.

- *Engineering design and management:* Varies from 10–16 percent, depending on complexity.

Labor costs can be affected by certain factors:

- *Fabrication:* Depends on complexity and production, i.e., typical parts

- *Assembly cost:* Usually constant unless there are many types of units

- *Shipping:* Almost constant

- *Installation:* Usually constant unless building is unusual shape with special areas

- *Cleaning:* Usually constant

The most critical factors for cost savings are almost always materials and finishes. Labor savings can also play a key role, depending on complexity and scheduling.

CODE AND DESIGN REQUIREMENTS

National codes and local requirements may play key roles in the design of curtain walls. Particular attention should be given to fire regulations and municipal requirements.

Wind Loading

Wind loading can be determined by local code or by wind tunnel test. Most local building authorities will accept wind tunnel results.

A rule of thumb: If a structure is of more than 18 stories and is located in a high wind load area—that is, an area subject to typhoons or hurricanes—it is essential to carry out a wind tunnel test.

A wind tunnel test can predict hot spots on a façade that cannot be detected through calculations or codes. The test can accurately determine the typical loads on the façade, for which the code is usually conservative. There may be a cost saving, or if loads in some areas of the building exceed code, that safety issue can be addressed.

Seismic Loads

Seismic loads for curtain walls can be calculated easily and, depending on the wind load, may or may not be important. The movements generated by the seismic load may be critical to the curtain wall and should be accounted for.

Movements

Allowance for movements of the structure due to wind load, dead load, live load, and creep are critical in the design of a curtain wall, especially in determining the joint sizes.

Test Requirements During Construction

Tests should be conducted on an ongoing basis during the job, as follows:

Mock-up performance test

Mock-up tests are conducted on specific areas of the curtain wall to prove that the system will perform to specifications. Air- and watertightness, structural soundness, and ability to absorb movements are among the key test requirements.

Component and assembly tests

The following tests are important to assure a long-lasting curtain wall.

- *Deglazing tests:* Conducted to prove silicone adhesion to the metal and glass.

- *Compatibility and adhesion test of sealant:* To ensure proper method and application of sealant.

- *Aluminum alloy and temper test:* Should be conducted on production material to ensure proper strength. This can be done in a laboratory or with a simple apparatus in the factory.

- *Paint adhesion and film thickness test.*

- *Conformance testing of production material,* such as glass/gaskets and fasteners.

- *Thermal tests:* For condensation and thermal transmittance.

ALTERNATIVE WORKPLACE SOLUTIONS

FRANKLIN BECKER, PH.D. *Cornell University*

Evolving technology, mergers and acqui-sitions, changing workforce demographics, constantly shifting organizational strategies, new ways of working, global competition: All of these factors place a premium on facilities management that can adapt to changing requirements.

For almost ten years I have been closely identified with what has been known as "alternative officing." Much of that has involved some form of nonterritorial office in which the individual employee had access to a workstation or closed office when in the company's facility, but did not "own" the workstation in the sense of its being exclusively assigned to one individual.

During that time I have argued for the value of providing employees with a robust array of workplace settings through what I called the "cafeteria"-style office. Giving up ownership of a Dilbert-like cube seemed to me ten years ago, as today, a pretty good deal *if* two conditions are met. One is that in place of remaining in the small, standardized cube, people can work wherever they feel they will be most productive, inside or outside the office. The second is that when employees do come into the office, the work environment will be very pleasant, full of distinctive settings in which they can choose to work, depending on what work they are doing, whom they need to be working with, and so on. The goal is a win-win situation: The organi-zation will reduce or contain costs, and the employee will have a better place to work.

The model, for me, was found in offices like those of Digital Equipment Corpor-ation in Finland. These were delightful places to be. From swing sets and leather recliner chairs to the sound of water splashing in decorative fountains, brightly painted murals, plants, and free food, the features of these offices were wonderful. And they really worked. Sales and perfor-mance exceeded expec-tations, media attention was lavish and positive, and bright people wanted to work there.

Offices like these bear scant resem-blance to the kind of standardized hoteling designs that have proliferated over the past decade, driven less by an interest in how people work or what will attract and retain them than by a desire to reduce real estate costs. Fortunately, the concept of "good office design" continues to evolve, driven by a combi-nation of dot.com/New Economy-inspired competition and unparalleled organizational uncertainty.

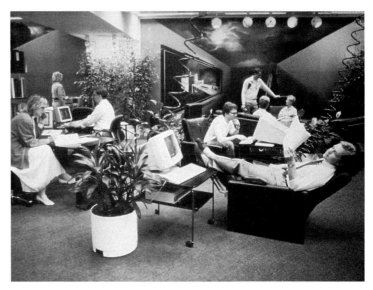

▼ *Digital Equipment Corporation offices in Finland represent evolving office design concepts by offering a variety of work settings.*

ZERO-TIME SPACE

A consulting firm obtains a major project that will involve 30 consultants working on-site for a period of six months. The project begins in a week's time, but there is no space in the client's offices for the consultants to work, and conventional leasing and fit-out of space would take several weeks to complete and involve a two-year lease commitment, much longer than needed.

Zero-time space borrows from the concept of "acting in zero time" in an agile organization. It is space that can be procured and/or constructed and is ready for use in as short a period of time (as close to zero) as possible. Zero-time space can be achieved physically, by new approaches to construction; organizationally, by new approaches to procurement; technologically, by exploiting the potential of information technology to enable remote work; and operationally, by new policies for allocating and using space. The challenge, as noted earlier, is to meet the organizational need for speed, low cost, and flexibility while meeting the employees' expectations for a desirable and productive work environment, particularly when the supply of labor exceeds demand, as it does today.

Policy Approaches

Nonterritorial space

Some forms of alternative offices, notably nonterritorial offices, are in fact forms of zero-time space. Conventional office allocation, in which each person is assigned an office or workstation, means that any growth in employee population requires physically adding new workstations or offices. Nonterritorial space accommodates such growth seamlessly (within limits) simply by changing the ratio of workers to office spaces. This strategy can accommodate organizational changes at a far faster and less disruptive rate than virtually any other zero-time space approach. Done right, as Digital Equipment Corporation did it in Finland, such approaches provide a wide range of work "niches" that employees occupy as they choose where to work, both inside and outside the office.

ZERO-TIME SPACE STRATEGIES

Policy

Nonterritorial offices
Time- vs. event-paced planning
Shelling or "dark" space
"Copy exactly" design
Telework
Mix of highly standard and customized
   solutions

Construction

Preengineered structures
   Mobile
   Modular
   Tensile

Procurement

Fully serviced offices
Excess capacity space
Shared resources
Design
Anticipation of future uses; design for
   conversion
Modular (kit-of-parts) and freestanding
   systems
Raised access floors
Mobile and easily reconfigured furniture
Software-based programmable HVAC
   systems
High-bay and clear-span structures
Flexible and fixed zones; service spines

Shelling or "dark" space

One of the most typical forms of zero-time space policies is "shelling." This is the policy of constructing the base building shell, without interior fit-out, in advance of needing the space. When the space is actually needed, the time to occupy is much shorter because fit-out can be done quickly. At Sears corporate headquarters outside Chicago the shelling concept has been refined to accommodate the fact that exactly where in a building or complex more space will be needed is often not known. Sears addressed this issue by leaving some space in each building or floor (rather than in a single building or on a few contiguous floors) "dark" so that it can be allocated intelligently as the need arises. Here, the employee benefit is being more proximate to one's own work group or corporate customers.

Time-paced versus event-paced construction

Intel, the world's largest computer chip maker, builds new fabrication facilities every nine months, before the chip to be manufactured in that facility has been designed. Its strategy is time-paced as opposed to event-paced. Most organizations wait until a need has arisen, then start to consider how to house it. Intel's facility is waiting, ready for use, when the need arises. For Intel, the benefit of having space available when needed (and the impact on revenue flow and market share) outweighs the downside of building space that may not be needed. The key is that the *probability of not needing* the space is much lower than the probability of needing it. That risk profile drives the decision process.

Contingent (fully serviced) space

Regus and other companies provide fully serviced or "turnkey" office space—that is, space that comes fully ready to use, including everything from furniture, computers, and telephones to a receptionist. Originally, such turnkey space served primarily very small professional firms (e.g., legal, accounting, marketing) and start-ups.

In recent years, large companies like AT&T, Andersen Consulting, and Hewlett-Packard have formed alliances and special relationships with such providers on a national basis to help provide zero-time space to their mobile workers. Companies launching a new business venture in a foreign country have also exploited the turnkey approach to occupy and exit space quickly, depending on the success of the venture. The fully serviced office industry is now estimated to exceed $2 billion in revenue annually.

Excess capacity space

Wineries and breweries routinely contract to use excess manufacturing capacity in a competitor's facility. Using the same principle, Digital Equipment Corporation (before being acquired by Compaq) sold its building on the outskirts of Newmarket, England, and renovated and moved into what had been a warehouse space less than two miles away. When its group grew, the company forged a deal with an alliance partner located nearby to occupy some of its surplus space at below-market rates. Both firms benefited. Space was available immediately at below-market rates for Digital Equipment, and its alliance partner reduced its fixed space costs and gained a prestigious co-tenant.

In California, Pacific Telesis sent 20–30-person sales teams to communities for three or four months each year to sell Yellow Pages advertising. The sales staff would live in a local hotel, drawing per diem living expenses, and lease and fit out office space in the community, often acquiring a lease that was for longer than needed. In a pilot project, Pacific Telesis contracted with a Marriott Suites Hotel to provide all employees with accommodations. They also obtained exclusive use of its conference rooms for use as a sales campaign headquarters. As a result, Pacific Telesis's real estate costs were limited to information technology, office furniture, and reduced room rates. It paid only for what it wanted when it needed it.

Construction Approaches

Mobile, modular, and tensile structures are three types of preengineered building construction approaches that have the common value of being transportable and reusable. What makes them preengineered is that they start their lives in a factory, from which they are transported to the site and erected. Most people think of modular, mobile, and tensile structures as being of poor quality or just downright ugly. The reality is more complex.

What makes tensile, modular, and mobile structures viable is that when developed with care and imagination, they are accepted and liked by a broad cross-section of employees. None of these approaches, by themselves, will suffice for large organizations. Their strength lies in how they complement more conventional ways of procuring office space.

Mobile structures

Since at least the 1940s, mobile office units have been used as field offices for contractors and builders on construction sites. This zero-time space solution allows a construction team to be housed on the project site as soon as construction starts and to leave as soon as the project is completed.

Intel applies the same principle to trailers. They are used (1) when occupancy is short term, (2) to avoid the costs of compressing office size to increase density, (3) to improve synergy by closer on-campus adjacency to existing buildings than would be possible if the only alternative was leasing available office space. Cost is not the primary consideration. Time and flexibility are.

Intel attaches trailer modules to form an open bay structure to which rest rooms, conference rooms, access ramps/stairs, lighting, an overhead sprinkler system, and open-plan-system furniture are added. All utilities (electricity, voice/data, water, and sewer) are brought to the trailer site underground and distributed within the modules. The time from construction to occupancy is typically about three months. The primary benefit, in addition to speed, is the ability to keep the design engineers on the same site in close proximity to those with whom they need to interact frequently.

Modular units

Three years ago the ABN/AMRO bank found itself needing space for 600–700 people, in about six months time, with no such space available to lease in or near its southeast Amsterdam headquarters. Today the bank occupies 100,000 sq ft of Class A corporate office space, constructed from prefabricated modular units. In its final form the building consists of four floors with a total gross area of about 115,000 sq ft (11,500 sq m).

The building was constructed using 675 prefabricated modules to create 710 work spaces that are a mixture of cellular, group, and open-plan offices. The floors are made of concrete, and the ceiling height is about 9 ft (2.70 m). The data infrastructure is state-of-the-art. The building includes an entrance, reception area, meeting rooms, computer room, restaurant, kitchen, and coffee corners.

The contract is structured as a sale and guaranteed sell-back. The manufacturer, De Meeuw, will buy back and remove the building after five years should the bank want to sell it. (The modules can actually be dismantled and returned to the factory for refurbishment.) The building is designed to last anywhere from 10 to 25 years or more with proper maintenance. The total project costs were 31 percent lower than leasing conventional office space (including rent and refurbishing). Completed and fitted out, the structure was essentially indistinguishable, from the employees' perspective, from a well-built conventional office building.

Tensile structures

Like that of some of their more modest portable building brethren, the impermanence of tensile structures provides a form of zero-time space that can be used in a variety of sophisticated ways when permanence is unnecessary.

As in other life sciences companies, the nature of the research being done at Monsanto has been transformed over the last decade. In this context Monsanto wanted to launch a new bioinformatics group of 30–40 researchers. The company wanted the group operational in less than three months, but had no available space in existing buildings. Furthermore, it was not clear how long, beyond one year, the

new group would exist.

The solution selected was "the Bridge," a 7200-gross-square-foot (GSF) temporary, translucent, bubblelike tensile structure using high-technology tenting material stretched over a steel frame. The structure had to meet all the same building codes as a permanent structure. Rising from snow-covered ground to being fully operational took 25 days. Somewhat to Monsanto's surprise, the research scientists occupying the building

▲▲ *Mobile office units being fabricated in factory for ABN/AMRO bank offices near Amsterdam.*

▲ *ABN/AMRO bank's 115,000 sq ft structure, assembled of mobile office units, was occupied six months from start of design.*

▲▲ *Translucent, tensile 25,000 sq ft structure erected in 25 days for Monsanto research team.*

▲ *Interior of Monsanto tensile structure.*

for companies that cannot predict the activities and types of work that will be done in a building over time.

Manufacturing sophisticated bearings/bushings and industrial chains, IGUS, located in Cologne, Germany, wanted a building shell that could house anything from a factory to a supermarket. The interior had to accommodate any kind of reorganization of space, even if that meant having office workers sitting where bearings had been manufactured a few days before.

The solution was a clear-span structural system designed by the Nicholas Grimshaw Partnership. Tensile cables connected to structural columns (masts) in courtyards allow for totally open floor areas where almost any function can be located or relocated. Panels can be quickly and easily changed from a solid panel barrier, to a window, to a door, simply by removing bolts. "Pods," self-contained mezzanine-level rooms within the building shell, are not easy to move, but easy to add. Exposed building systems, including HVAC, water, plumbing, and power/data, which is organized in easily accessible cable trays and "drops," make it possible to locate services anywhere in the building without restriction.

Modular systems (furniture and interior panels, as well as interior and exterior cladding) use exposed bolts that minimize the need for special tools or labor. The furniture is freestanding, and the walls are demountable. High-bay space makes it possible to erect buildings within buildings to create multilevel space within the same building shell.

The building construction took nine months. An exterior polyester-coated aluminum panel, simply bolted on, can be removed in ten minutes; an

liked working in a "tent" and thought it was as good as, if not better than, working in a conventional office building.

Warehouse space
Most white-collar workers find the idea of working in a warehouse or factory as appealing as an ice storm. Yet such structures have potential to provide a special kind of zero-time space solution

interior panel takes from one to two hours. It took two weekends to change the tooling department, with all its machines, into offices. The bearing department, growing 40–60 percent each year, has completely moved locations five times in five years. Employees working in the factory/office characterized their space as "energizing" and felt it improved morale and communication.

Learning from New Economy Companies

Cornell University's International Workplace Studies Program (IWSP) is currently examining strategies such as those discussed earlier. Not surprisingly, it has found that start-up workplaces do not look much like those found in large organizations. In comparison to large organizations, such firms typically deemphasize status, have higher employee density levels, make minimal renovations to new space, spend less money on standard furniture elements, and exhibit much higher degrees of what might, in biological terms, be called self-organizing principles.

At DesignGraphics (a pseudonym for a small start-up software development company), for example, virtually no renovations were made to the firm's leased office space. All the senior managers occupy what was once a conference room; developers' "workstations" are the kind of folding tables hotels use in their meeting spaces; the conference room is a couch and white board in a supply room; folding divider screens come from Pier I Imports, not the major contract office furniture manufacturers. In place of standard vending machines or a corporate cafeteria, a vendor arrives in the space every morning with a cart from

▲ Warehouselike structure for IGUS offices in Cologne, intended for easy conversion to retail or industrial use as needs change.

◀ Interior of IGUS offices, showing adaptation of warehouselike structure.

which he dispenses every conceivable specialty coffee.

Is this space perfectly comfortable? No. Does it convey a unified corporate image? Yes. It just happens to be messy vitality rather than what is too often the ordered banality of "good corporate design." Is it

▲ At DesignGraphics (pseudonym for a startup company), existing space was occupied with virtually no renovation.

large organizations without necessarily adopting the visible form of its workplaces? This might mean, for example, that one leaves a hung ceiling in leased space rather than spending hundreds of thousands of dollars to remove it in order to create an industrial aesthetic. The dot.com principle is to make creative use of what exists, not to spend money for a highly designed image, even if that image is the industrial aesthetic of many dot.coms. The message is that they are in renovated light industrial space, not Class A office space.

The Pattern Counts

Each workplace solution described in this chapter has advantages and disadvantages. Modular structures are quick to construct, but they have less residual value than conventional construction. Tensile and modular structures can be disassembled and relocated, but the permitting process may require much extra time and effort. Fully serviced offices make immediate occupancy and exit possible, but are often not located exactly where the company wants space. The high density of a dot.com makes informal communication impossible to avoid, but can make concentration difficult. The deliberately noncorporate look and feel of New Economy offices helps attract the kinds of employees required to get that type of work done, but may repel older employees accustomed to conventional office design.

inexpensive? Yes. Can it be easily reconfigured? Yes, within the spaces defined by the existing walls. Does it require a lot of bureaucracy to make changes to the environment? No.

Obviously, the employee population served by independent and corporate start-up initiatives is young. But these are the kind of people whom increasingly technocentric companies must attract and retain to survive in today's marketplace. These young people are not energized by occupying standard Class A office space, sitting in a cubicle, and imagining how in ten years they can move up the hierarchy to occupy a small closed office. The focus is on doing work that is challenging and getting it done fast, not using corporate resources to generate symbols of status and rank.

Not every large company has to look like a dot.com start-up. Rather, the challenge is how to expand the corporation's workplace gene pool to embrace the diversity of young, technocentric employees in key parts of the organization. Can some of the New Economy workplace strategy *principles* be transferred to

The objective is not for every company to build a tensile structure, or to sign a contract with Regus for fully serviced offices, or to allocate 15 percent of its next new building to "dark" space. Nor, however, is it to rely on a limited array of familiar workplace solutions unlikely to help a company use its scarce resources to best advantage in an uncertain world. The goal is to create real options that preserve flexibility at a cost that recognizes the value of flexibility. Robust, adaptive strategies willingly sacrifice the apparent certainty that traditional strategies imply for the sake of flexibility and a higher probability of success *over time.*

SAFETY AND SECURITY

JOHN W. McCORMICK, PE *Code Consultants, Inc.*

Providing for the safety of building occupants is a complex design challenge, which is frequently overlooked in the training of architects and engineers but becomes a distinct reality in the design of buildings. This challenge has been further complicated by the overt acts of terrorists. Codes already provide for fire protection and life safety from "accidental" fires and other damaging events. Designers must now also consider the potential destruction of a building through the introduction of explosive devices, incendiary materials, and projectiles.

This chapter presents the basic principles of building safety and then examines specific building features related to the implementation of those principles. Finally, it discusses special methods or tools that have been developed to accommodate the design objectives of a structure without jeopardizing the safety of building occupants.

MAJOR FIRE PROTECTION AND LIFE SAFETY ISSUES
Applicable Codes

The design and construction of all structures are controlled by the provisions of building codes, which most major metropolitan areas of the world have adopted to specify features of construction necessary for fire protection and life safety of building occupants.

In the United States these codes are usually based on a model building code that has been promulgated by a code-setting body, such as the Building Officials Conference of America (BOCA National Building Code), the International Conference of Building Officials (Uniform Building Code), or the Southern Building Code Congress (Standard Building Code). Beginning in 2000, these three building code groups joined to produce a single model building code known as the International Building Code.

Outside the United States many building codes are based on British standards and regulations. In general, the construction requirements for fire protection and life safety found abroad are more stringent than those in United States.

The National Fire Protection Association (NFPA) publishes a Life Safety Code, which provides for life safety of building occupants without making provisions for building construction features. The Life Safety Code is usually adopted by fire prevention bureaus on the local or state level. The NFPA plans to publish a new model building code, which will establish the requirements for all building construction features. The NFPA building code was scheduled for publication in 2001. As a result, the United States will have two model building codes for "authorities having jurisdiction" (AHJ) to choose from for adoption.

In addition to building codes, there are fire codes, usually enforced by fire department organizations within a jurisdiction, adopted primarily to establish the requirements for fire protection and life safety features in a building after it is constructed. However, certain fire codes (the Uniform Fire Code) establish requirements for new buildings, such as those for fire alarm systems.

Most, if not all, jurisdictions will publish local amendments to these codes in their process of adopting the model building code. For example, a local jurisdiction may wish to be more restrictive than certain requirements of the model code. The model building codes are not applicable until they have been adopted by a governmental jurisdiction.

Authority Having Jurisdiction

The primary authority having jurisdiction (AHJ) is the building department of the municipality or local jurisdiction. If a building code and fire code have been adopted by the local jurisdiction, the local authorities will also have established the means for enforcing them. It is with the approval of these local jurisdictions that, based on the submittal of documents, a builder is issued a permit to begin construction.

The local building department will inspect the construction, and when satisfied with the completion of the work, will issue a certificate of occupancy, which will allow the building to be used by the owners and tenants. In most jurisdictions, the fire department, typically the fire marshal's office, will participate in the review of building code construction documents and will be specifically interested in implementing those provisions of the code that relate to fire protection systems and the ability of the fire department to fight a fire in the building. In some large municipalities, state agencies may also become involved in approving the construction of a building, particularly if it is a state-sponsored (funded) structure.

Compliance with established building and fire codes is overseen by state and local authorities, depending on the laws in the particular jurisdiction. At the beginning of each project, it is imperative that these requirements and relationships

be established to avoid surprises during or at the completion of the design process or, worse yet, during the construction phase. Many horror stories can be told by architects and engineers about the changes that were made to buildings after they were constructed in order to comply with the codes and standards of a jurisdiction.

It is a basic rule that if, in spite of the issuance of a permit by a local authority, a code compliance mistake has been made, it is the responsibility of the owner and designer to correct it. Such a mistake will not be accepted simply because it was missed by the local authority during the plan review and permit process.

All jurisdictions have provisions in their codes to allow variances for alternative means and methods. When such a variance is processed in accordance with these provisions, it becomes an official change to the code, and the completion of the project in accordance with such a variance constitutes code compliance. However, if mistaken departures from codes are made, and the local authority is not willing to issue such a variance at a late stage in the construction, the result will be a painful memory of changing construction to achieve compliance.

Building Security

The provisions of a local code provide safety for occupants and for the building to mitigate the consequences of an accidental fire or other devastating event. These codes and standards do not specifically address the type of incident that is planned by terrorists or other activists intent on doing damage.

Measures taken to counteract these intentional acts are beyond the scope of the local building and fire codes. On significant projects it is necessary to consider the security strategy in the building design to reduce the possibility that such attempts will be successful. Security can take the form of active entrance restrictions and visitor screening, as well as measures to avert the effects of explosions that occur on the exterior of the building.

These measures may consist of hardening the building against an exterior blast through the design and the type of materials used in the exterior walls. In addressing interior explosions, consideration can be given to upgrading the materials used for certain safety features; for example, exit stair and elevator hoistway enclosures can be constructed of reinforced concrete instead of masony units or gypsum shaft wall.

Countering such acts is an extremely difficult design challenge. In spite of the best efforts of the designers and engineers, the consequences of an event that is unanticipated and unpredicted will exceed the planned countermeasures. For example, the events leading to the collapse of the World Trade Center towers were not predicted, and as a result, countermeasures to prevent their collapse were not in place. Although it may be possible in the future to design tall buildings to withstand such an attack, such projects may not be economically feasible.

Most terrorist attacks produce significantly lower levels of damage to a building. Effective countermeasures can be incorporated into the design of a building to mitigate the effects of such attacks. It is unrealistic to think one can design buildings to withstand all possible events. If a building is designed to withstand the impact of one large airplane, a terrorist will find a way to attack the building with two such airplanes.

Occupancy

In order to establish the basic fire protection and life safety requirements for a building, the uses of buildings are classified into roughly a dozen specific occupancies. When the occupancy is established for a building, the provisions of the applicable codes can then indicate the required type of construction of the building and the allowable height and area.

The occupancy classifications identify buildings by the amount of fuel load and the degree to which occupants are exposed to danger. Typically, offices have a low fuel load as compared with factories or warehouses. As a result, the building code regulates these structures differently. Similarly, additional safety measures are required for the occupants of a theater because of the potential for the loss of a great many lives. Because of the nonambulatory nature of hospital occupants and the restrictions imposed on occupants of jails and prisons, specific code requirements must be incorporated into the design of these facilities. Such measures include installing automatic sprinkler systems and fire alarm and detection systems and constructing compartments in the building to restrict the movement of fire and create areas of refuge.

The basic occupancies include Assembly, Business, Institution, Industrial, Storage, Education, High-hazard, and Residential. Most large projects include a combination of many of these uses. The provisions of the applicable codes will address how these different occupancies are intermingled, so that one occupancy does not decrease the level of safety of an adjacent occupancy. Frequently, a fire-rated occupancy separation wall is required between two different kinds of occupancies.

However, most codes have provisions to allow unseparated occupancies (no fire-rated separation walls) when the code provisions for the most restrictive occupancy are applied to the entire building. Thus, the less hazardous occupancies are encumbered by the more restrictive provisions, and in such a case it is not necessary to construct fire-rated walls to separate one from the other.

Construction Type

Building construction types are divided into two basic categories: noncombustible and combustible. In the category of noncombustible construction, a further subdivision occurs: (1) buildings whose elements are considered to be fire-resistive with the application of fire-resistive coatings to maintain structural integrity in a fire, and (2) buildings with unprotected elements that have no fire-resistive protection. Most large building projects use noncombustible fire-resistive types of construction.

In the case of noncombustible materials, buildings of fire-resistive construction are permitted to be of unlimited height and unlimited area. In noncombustible buildings, the applicable codes do permit the introduction of certain combustible materials that are attached to the noncombustible elements, but the basic core construction is noncombustible.

Most high-rise buildings are permitted to be of "unlimited" height and area, based on the use of fire-resistive materials to protect the structural elements (framework). This includes the application of fireproofing materials on columns, beams, girders, and floor slabs, and the construction of fire-rated interior enclosures for

exit stairs, elevator hoistways, and utility shafts.

Noncombustible materials that have been tested to withstand the effects of a fire are applied to structural steel components. Masonry construction has an intrinsic fire resistance, depending on the type and thickness of the materials.

Fire-resistance ratings used in high-rise buildings are usually established at 3 or 4 hours for the structural frame and 2 or 3 hours for floors. Vertical enclosures typically have a 2-hour fire-resistive rating. These fire ratings are provided to ensure that the building structure will resist the effects of a fire and will not collapse.

Many interior building walls must have a fire-resistive rating. Such walls include those required to enclose vertical openings (exit stairs, elevator hoistways, and utility shafts) for 2 hours; walls of public corridors used for access to exits from the floor for 1 hour; walls enclosing large storage areas for 1 or 2 hours; and walls separating one occupancy type from another, such as offices from assembly areas, for 1–4 hours.

Combustible/Noncombustible

Materials classified as noncombustible are subjected to specific tests, which essentially determine that they will not maintain combustion when a flame is applied and removed from them. This is an extremely demanding criterion for a material. For example, steel materials and masonry materials are regarded as noncombustible materials. However, gypsum wallboard materials, because of the paper face, do not comply with the provisions for the category of noncombustible. Yet most building codes will allow gypsum wallboard as a specific exception to the very demanding requirements for noncombustible construction, regarding it as "limited-combustible" material.

Interior Finishes

Interior finishes in a building are limited by the applicable codes. These requirements limit the ability of a fire to travel through various parts of a building based on the continuity of the interior finishes. Classes A, B, and C wall and ceiling finishes are specifically limited in the code. The determination of such classifications is based on standard tests that have been developed by the applicable industry codes.

Similarly, specific requirements have been developed for interior *floor* finishes. These are distinguished from the interior finish requirements for walls and ceilings because floors behave differently in a fire. As a result, different tests are conducted to properly evaluate floor finishes. However, a fire in an interior building space primarily involves the burning of walls and ceiling materials. The involvement of floor materials is seldom a factor in the burning of a building.

The applicable codes establish requirements for exterior finishes and veneers of a building. Frequently, such finishes may be of combustible materials, even when the building is regarded as a noncombustible building.

Protection from Exposure to Fires

Roof coverings are typically composed of combustible materials. They are attached to the noncombustible roof decks, which are supported by noncombustible elements. The requirements for roof coverings (Classifications A, B, and C) are related to the susceptibility of the covering to ignition from exterior sources,

known as flying brands, which emanate from nearby fires involving other buildings.

The exterior walls of buildings may have fire-resistive ratings, depending on how close a wall is to a property line. This concern is usually waived for those sides of a building that face a street. However, for the other sides of the building, the fire-resistive rating is intended to prevent a fire in one building from advancing to a second building.

Most large cities have suffered conflagrations prior to the twentieth century. As building codes evolved, one of their primary goals involved the mitigation of fires advancing from building to building. Today this concern is reflected in the requirements for exterior walls and their proximity to lot lines.

Combustible Materials in Noncombustible Buildings

The applicable codes specifically address the use of plastic insulation materials and exterior finish materials. Plastics are very susceptible to combustion, and fires involving them burn vigorously, giving off large quantities of smoke. The code has established requirements to mitigate the effects of such fires, particularly in noncombustible buildings.

In the construction of noncombustible buildings, it is often necessary to use combustible materials, such as wood for blocking and furring used for the attachment of building materials to the basic structure. The use of these materials is very limited, and they are frequently required to be treated with a fire retardant. Fire-retardant-treated wood is not regarded as a noncombustible material. It is a combustible material that resists ignition and burning for specific periods of time. Ultimately, it will be consumed by a fire.

Life Safety

For all buildings, life safety egress construction features are provided to allow for the safe and efficient evacuation of building occupants. The basic concept established in the code is that from any point on any floor of a building, an occupant will be able to choose between two different paths of egress. The code establishes this as a basic tenet and only rarely allows the provision of a single exit from a floor of a building, with some accepted modifications for single-access travel. Single exits are permitted from small rooms having fewer than 50 occupants when the travel distance within the room is limited to 75 ft.

The number and capacity of the exits described here are based on the occupant load of the building. The building and fire codes establish the basic parameters for determining this occupant load, based on traditional uses of spaces. If a building is programmed to be occupied by a number of persons greater than that determined by the parameters of the building code, the number of exits and the sizes of the exits must be designed for the larger number of occupants.

The capacity of the exits is a direct function of their widths. The wider an exit, such as a stair, the greater the number of persons that can be accommodated by that stair. The basic requirements of the code for capacity of exits is designed to allow for egress of a space within a 4- to 5-minute period of time. These requirements have the greatest impact on a building design, and they are the most highly scrutinized by the local building and fire officials.

Accessible Egress

In the 1980s and 1990s, provisions were established in the code to provide access to buildings for disabled persons. In turn, provisions have been established for the accessible egress of such persons from a building. In essence, it is required that disabled persons have the same opportunities for building safety as ambulatory occupants.

Specific requirements have been established both in the applicable building codes and in the Americans with Disabilities Act that delineate the requirements for "areas of rescue assistance" or "areas of refuge" for disabled persons. The use of elevators is broadly discouraged in an emergency. Attempts have been made to establish elevators as safe means of egress, but these are permitted only under specific circumstances.

Accessible egress from the upper stories of a building is established by providing enclosed areas where disabled people can gather and communicate with emergency crews. These occupants are made safe by the enclosure while awaiting assistance from emergency personnel, who can evacuate them from the upper floors.

The most effective means of providing safety for disabled persons is the installation of automatic sprinkler systems throughout the building. See the following discussion regarding this predominant feature of building safety.

Fire Protection Systems

Many building code requirements relate to "passive" fire protection measures, such as the construction of fire-resistive-rated walls and fire doors and windows. Fire protection systems are the "active" mode of protection for a building. They include automatic sprinkler systems, fire standpipe systems, fire alarm systems, smoke management systems, emergency power systems, and fire detection systems.

Automatic sprinkler systems have been determined to be the most effective means of providing occupant life safety and construction safety. An automatic sprinkler system is designed to control the effects of a fire and sometimes extinguish the fire.

Automatic sprinkler systems have an excellent record of protecting the lives of building occupants. Unless an occupant has set him- or herself on fire, the record shows that it is rare for a person to die from a fire in a building protected by an operating automatic sprinkler system.

As a result of the effectiveness of these systems, the requirements for interior finish materials may be relaxed somewhat, exit access travel distances may be increased, and the ratings of building elements such as exit corridor enclosures may be reduced, to name a few such trade-offs.

All new high-rise buildings require the installation of an automatic sprinkler system. In fact, some cities in the United States, such as New York, Philadelphia, Boston, and Los Angeles, have required the retroactive installation of sprinkler systems into existing buildings at the expense of the building owners.

In concert with the automatic sprinkler system are the provisions for fire alarm systems, which transmit the discovery of a fire to the fire department and sound the alarm in the building to alert building occupants.

Fire standpipe systems are specifically designed for use by the fire department to attack a fire in a structure. In a building protected by automatic sprinklers, this will be a much smaller operation than

may occur in a building not protected by automatic sprinklers.

Emergency power systems are provided in buildings to serve in the event that the normal power is interrupted. Emergency power, which must be provided within 10 seconds of a loss of power, is typically required for emergency exit lighting and exit signage.

Standby emergency power systems are provided to supply electrical power to emergency equipment, such as smoke management system fans, elevators, and fire pumps. Standby power systems must be in operation within 60 seconds of the loss of normal power.

Special Features

The building codes address special design features with specific requirements. Such special features include the construction of a building as a high-rise, the incorporation of an atrium connecting multiple floors of a building, the construction of covered malls typical of shopping centers, and the development of institutional occupancies requiring a higher level of safety for persons who are infirm or are in detention (such as jails). Other special provisions address garages, large places of assembly, and buildings that house hazardous materials.

HVAC

Heating, ventilation, and air-conditioning systems (HVAC) are designed to prevent the migration or transmission of products of combustion from a fire in one area of a building to other areas of the building. Such systems are compartmentalized through the use of fire-rated design and building construction features.

In addition, HVAC systems can be used for smoke management in large buildings.

Typically, in high-rise buildings, a smoke management system may be used to control the transmission of products of combustion from one floor to other floors. The purpose of this protection is to limit the migration of smoke to other areas of the building and thereby avoid endangering additional occupants.

The use of exit facilities as HVAC air plenums is specifically prohibited. For example, exit corridors are not permitted to convey supply or return air. The intent of this provision is to prevent the transmission of smoke from an occupied area to exit corridors.

FIRE PROTECTION AND LIFE SAFETY FEATURES

The preceding paragraphs discussed fire protection and life safety measures broadly. This section addresses the specific application of those measures to selected features of the building. The features selected are those for which the omission of protection has resulted in many design/construction corrections.

Means of Egress

The means of egress from a building is one of the primary considerations that will affect how a building is designed and constructed. The first factor to consider is the occupant load for various areas of the building, prescribed by the building code based on the building's uses. For example, a restaurant seating area is typically determined to have an occupant load of one person for each 15 sq ft of seating area. For a business occupancy, a factor of one person per 100 sq ft of area is used. In any event, when these calculations are performed, if the expected occupant load of a space exceeds these figures, then the larger number must be used to establish the occupant load for the space.

Once the occupant load is determined, the exits must have the capacity to allow emergency egress by persons from each level of the building. Typically, such capacity factors are based on an egress time of 3 to 4 minutes. The capacity of egress from the space is expressed in the number of inches per person. For example, in a space having an occupant load of 200 persons, a door may be required to have 0.2 in. per person or to be 40 in. in clear width. For a stair, the capacity factor is 0.3 in. per person, so that for 200 persons a clear width of 60 in. is required.

Next, one must determine the required number of exits from a space, which is based on the total occupant load for the space. Where fewer than 500 persons are calculated to occupy a space, two exits are required. Where 500–1000 persons occupy a space, three exits are required, and where more than 1000 persons occupy a space, four exits must be provided. These exits must be separated from each other, so that a single fire will not block more than one exit.

From the upper level of a building, when a person egresses from a floor, he or she enters an exit stair enclosure that must have a 2-hour fire-resistive rating. After someone enters the enclosure, that person is considered to be in a "safe" space and can exit from the building. The stair must be wide enough for the occupant load for a single floor, and the exit stair must be continuous to the exterior of the building.

Such exit stair enclosures must usually connect to an exit passageway (having the same degree of fire resistance as the exit stair), which then connects to the exterior of the building. Some codes will allow the discharge of up to 50 percent of the exit stair enclosures to the building's lobby areas. The other 50 percent of the exit enclosures must discharge either directly to the outside or into exit passageways.

On a specific floor, exit corridors may be required to have a fire-resistive rating. Typically, in a building protected by automatic sprinklers, such corridors are not required to have a fire-resistive rating. However, in unsprinklered buildings, the exit access corridors are required to be enclosed by construction having a fire-resistance rating of up to 1 hour.

A specific feature of all codes is to allow areas of refuge on a floor to provide additional egress capacity. Such exits are referred to as horizontal exits. Horizontal exits are established by the construction of a 2-hour fire-resistive-rated wall that extends from exterior wall to exterior wall. Openings in this wall are required to have a 1½-hour fire-resistive rating. This horizontal exit allows persons on one side of the wall to exit to a refuge on the other side of the wall, which is separated by the 2-hour fire-resistive-rated construction from the point of a fire's origin. Credit is given in calculating exit capacity for providing such walls on a given floor.

Fire Resistance

Fire-resistance-rated assemblies are evaluated on the ability of the protection materials to prevent the failure of specific structural elements or structural barriers (walls or floors) due to heat exposure. The requirements can be prescriptive or performance-based.

Prescriptive methods for determining fire resistance are usually developed by laboratories such as Underwriters Laboratories, Factory Mutual Research Corporation, and Warnock-Hersey, which use standardized tests of the American Society for Testing and Materials (ASTM) to evaluate the fire resistance of structural assemblies. In addition, several resources are available that present the fire-resistance ratings for archaic construction. All of these methods for determining fire resistance are based on specific test results.

There are, as well, methods that have been developed to evaluate the fire resistance of assemblies based on performance criteria. These methods use analytical techniques to calculate the estimated fire resistance of assemblies based on the known properties of materials. The basic information that has resulted from fire tests and the fire modeling evaluations that establish the fire-resistance ratings is available in the technical literature.

Typically, fire-resistant materials are applied to structural elements such as columns, beams, and girders, to structural wall assemblies, to floor assemblies, and to roof assemblies. When a building is established as a fire-resistive building, it uses assemblies that have been either tested on a prescriptive basis or evaluated on a performance basis.

Fire-Rated Walls

The applicable codes establish the requirements for construction of various types of walls used to subdivide a building into compartments so that a fire originating in one compartment will not advance to other compartments. Fire-rated walls are also used to enclose vertical shafts to prevent the advance of fire from floor to floor. Examples of such shafts are exit stairways, elevator hoistways, and utility enclosures.

A structure known as a fire wall is used to divide a building in two, or to separate buildings on a property line. A fire wall is intended to be structurally stable so that the collapse of construction on either side of the wall will not result in a reduction in the fire resistance it is required to provide. The structural independence is such that a fire wall may be a single freestanding wall, or it may consist of two walls, each of which is tied to an adjacent structure, so that if a structure were to collapse, pulling down one of the walls, the other wall would remain standing. Such fire walls may have a fire resistive rating as high as 4 hours.

Lesser fire-rated walls are used to subdivide a building into compartments to provide for enclosure of vertical shafts, enclosure of corridors, subdivision of a building into smoke compartments, or separation of occupancies. These walls are not structurally independent, in that if the construction on one side of the wall were to collapse, the wall itself would be destroyed. Such fire separation walls are divided into categories according to many codes, which stipulate varying fire-resistive ratings and degrees of smoketightness.

For example, smoke barrier walls are used to subdivide hospital floors into compartments so that a fire occurring in one will not convey products of combustion, such as smoke, to an adjacent one. Such walls must provide for continuous separation so that a fire on a given floor will not do an end run around the wall. As a result, these walls typically extend from exterior wall to exterior wall within the enclosure, or they serve a complete enclosure such as that required for an exit stair.

Whenever a fire-rated wall, like other fire-resistive construction, is established, it must be supported by fire-rated construction equal to the rating of the wall. For example, for a 2-hour fire-resistive-rated wall that is provided on an upper floor of a building, the construction of the floor and the elements supporting that wall must have a 2-hour fire-resistive rating.

Fire-Rated Floors/Roofs

The floors that subdivide a building and the roofs of the building are typically required to have a fire-resistive rating of 2 or 3 hours in fire-resistive structures. Where openings occur in these floors, they must be protected to prevent the advance of fire from one floor to another.

For a fire-resistive-rated roof, when all portions of the structural support for the roof (the roof structure) are 15 or 20 ft or more above the floor below, the fire-resistive rating for the roof may be omitted. This determination is based on the "safe" height of the structural elements above a floor where the fuel load is located.

Structural Frame

The structural frame of a fire-resistive building has a required rating of 3 or 4 hours. This includes the columns, beams, and girders that support the building. Meeting this requirement involves discret protection such as the use of a rated enclosure or spray-on fireproofing for a beam or girder.

All elements of the structure that contribute to the stability of a building are required to be fire-resistive rated. Questions frequently arise as to the extent of the structural frame. If structural supports are used to attach a curtain wall to the structural frame, typically the curtain wall is not required to have a fire-resistive rating. However, if X-bracing is used to withstand wind loading, this element is usually required to have a fire-resistive rating.

Tests are frequently conducted on certain types of floor/roof ceiling assemblies, which consist of a composite of a ceiling membrane, floor support structure, and the floor itself. In this case, the ceiling membrane, which may be a suspended ceiling, may be used to provide fire resistance for the structural elements above. Such assemblies are usually specifically tested on a prescriptive basis by laboratories such as Underwriters Laboratories.

Shafts

A major objective of a building code is to prevent a fire from traveling from one floor to another. But in many instances the code allows openings between two floors. For high-rise buildings, the vertical penetrations of the building must be enclosed in 2-hour fire-resistive-rated construction. Such openings include egress stairs, elevator hoistways, utility ducting systems, and utility pipe/conduit systems. For stairs enclosed in 2-hour fire-resistive walls, doors must have a 1½-hour fire rating.

For elevator hoistways, a 2-hour fire-resistive-rated enclosure is typically required, and elevator doors themselves must have a 1½-hour fire-resistive rating. Utility duct shafts have a 2-hour fire-resistive-rated enclosure, and where HVAC ducts penetrate a shaft to serve adjacent floors, fire dampers are usually installed at the penetration of the shaft wall to prevent fire from entering or leaving the shaft.

In utility chases, pipes and conduits may run from floor to floor in a shaft enclosure, as long as the piping or conduit is sealed with fire-rated materials where it penetrates the enclosure. If the pipe or conduit that travels from floor to floor is sealed at the floor penetration, then the enclosure wall is not required to have a fire-resistive rating, because the barrier is maintained at the floor line.

Opening Protectives

Fire separation walls and fire walls of all types must have protected accessways. The protected openings may consist of fire doors, which have a variety of ratings associated with the wall construction, fire windows, fire dampers, and conveyor protection systems. In all instances, if you have a fire-rated wall and you need access through the wall, the opening protective for this access must have a fire-resistive rating.

Penetrations of Fire-Rated Construction

Where other elements of the building construction, such as piping and conduits, penetrate a floor or wall, the opening must be protected to prevent fire from advancing from one side to the other. The material of the construction that is penetrating the wall, whether metallic or nonmetallic, is important in determining the protection system to be used. Certain elements for piping, conduits, wiring, and HVAC ducts have been tested as special "through-penetration" systems by laboratories in very demanding fire tests.

At the perimeter of a floor, attention must be given to the opening that occurs where it adjoins a curtain wall. If the opening is very small, it can be easily sealed between the edge of the floor and the curtain wall elements. However, this opening frequently varies in width, and special perimeter protection systems have been developed to prevent the advance of fire at such openings.

For the exterior of the building, the code may require fire-resistive-rated spandrels at each floor. They are typically of 1-hour fire-rated construction and usually 3 ft in height. The intent is to prevent a fire that breaks through the exterior glazing of a building from advancing up the side of the building, attacking the glazing on the floor above, and entering it at that point.

Special Engineering Tools

It is often necessary to evaluate fire protection systems and the limitations of the applicable codes by using special engineering tools.

Fire models have been developed that will evaluate the fire protection of a building based on a fire that produces smoke and heat in a specific configuration. Such fire models can assess variances from the code at a level that is acceptable to the authorities.

Special systems of automatic sprinklers and glazed assemblies have been developed to meet fire-resistance requirements. Typically, a fire-resistant-rated wall is of solid construction, usually gypsum board and steel studs, that does not allow one to see through it. The use of glazed walls is highly desirable, and interior walls and systems using specially designed automatic sprinklers located in the vicinity of the glazing can be used to provide a fire-resistance rating of 1 or 2 hours.

Quick-Response Sprinklers

Special automatic sprinklers have been developed that are known as quick-response sprinklers. Such sprinklers have a life-saving capability that exceeds that provided by standard sprinklers.

A relatively new technology developed to save occupants of the room of fire origin in residential buildings, quick-response sprinklers activate faster in all fire conditions than conventional sprinklers. A comparison of quick-response sprinklers and conventional sprinklers has been studied by the Factory Mutual Research Corporation.

A Factory Mutual technical report prepared for the Federal Emergency Management Agency indicates that the time for conventional sprinkler activation in a given test fire was 1 min, 50 sec. A quick-response sprinkler, under identical test fire conditions, activated in 1 min, 25 sec—*22 per-cent faster* than the conventional sprinkler.

TRENDS AND EXPECTATIONS
Public Buildings

The dominant trend in improving the safety of buildings today is to require the installation of automatic sprinklers in nearly all buildings. This will lead to a significant reduction in life and property loss in public buildings. (Even today, nearly all the loss of life due to fire in the United States occurs in one- and two-family dwellings.)

Performance-Based Designs

A recent movement in the fire safety industry is to use performance-based approaches to providing building safety. For example, rather than specifying the maximum allowable distance of exit travel, the code would state that a "safe" distance of exit travel must be provided. This leaves it to the designer to prove that a safe exit travel distance is provided, based on a fire protection engineering analysis. Such an analysis would employ fire models and engineering evaluations, weighing the potential threat of a fire in an area and the ability of the building occupants to escape.

Until recently, variances in the code requirements were developed for alternative approaches to building fire safety. The trend now is to incorporate such alternative methods into the codes, deriving them from performance-based analyses.

▲ IBM World Headquarters, Armonk, New York, 1997, by Kohn Pedersen Fox Associates. The low, angular forms of the building, nestled into its wooded setting, reflect company goals of a smaller, less hierarchical management structure. © Peter Aaron/Esto.

◀ Aid Association for Lutherans, Appleton, Wisconsin, 1974, by John Carl Warnecke & Associates. Comprising largely one-story, skylighted work spaces laid out around a circular court, this building was the first collaborative effort among the three architects who later established Kohn Pedersen Fox Associates. © KPF/Elliot Fine.

▶ *Gannett/USA Today headquarters, McLean, Virginia, by Kohn Pedersen Fox Associates, Lehman-Smith + McLeish. Portion of curtain wall, with glass fins. © Michael Dersin.*

▼ *Pond at entrance to Gannett/USA Today headquarters, with lobby at left, elevator tower at center. © Timothy Hursley.*

▲ Stair to second floor in lobby of Gannett/USA Today headquarters. © Timothy Hursley.

◀ Rooftop view of Gannett/USA Today headquarters, with office blocks to either side, entrance court at center, landscaped grounds beyond. © Timothy Hursley.

▲ Thames Court, London, by Kohn Pedersen Fox Associates, seen as a glass-enclosed lantern at river's edge. © H.G. Esch.

◀ One Raffles Link, Singapore, by Kohn Pedersen Fox Associates, LPT Architects Singapore. Underground passage link to transit lines and other buildings, showing installation of colored lighting. © John Marshall/Wordsearch.

▶ Tour CBX, Paris, by Kohn Pedersen Fox Associates, Saubot Rouit Associés. Rendering as seen from east, showing existing neighboring buildings and pedestrian walks passing under portions of building. Courtesy KPF.

◀ 11 Chater Road, Hong Kong, by Kohn Pedersen Fox Associates, LPT Architects. Night rendering, showing lantern effect of corner turret. Courtesy KPF.

▲ Ernst & Young Building, New York City, by Kohn Pedersen Fox Associates. Detail of attached signage. Courtesy KPF/DBOX.

◀ Ernst & Young Building in New York's Times Square had to meet requirements for lighted signs and pass design review that favored angular, fragmented architectural forms. Courtesy KPF/DBOX.

▶ *Espirito Santo Plaza, Miami, Florida, by Kohn Pedersen Fox Associates, Plunkett & Associates. View north along Miami's Biscayne Boulevard. Courtesy KPF.*

▼ *View out to Biscayne Bay from hotel/apartment atrium of Espirito Santo Plaza. Courtesy KPF.*

PART III
CASE STUDIES

© H.G. Esch.

▲ Gannett/USA Today headquarters,
McLean, Virginia, nearing completion.
Photo © Michael Dersin.

GANNETT/USA TODAY CORPORATE HEADQUARTERS

MCLEAN, VIRGINIA *Kohn Pedersen Fox, Lehman-Smith + McLeish*

FOCUS POINTS

High-visibility suburban site

Height restrictions

Special workspace needs

Exceptional amenities

No "exit strategy"

This project is documented more fully than others in the book because it represents a thorough restudy of an office building. Every aspect of the office environment was critically reconsidered, from the individual workstation to the exterior form and cladding of the complex to the ecology of the site. The building has been tailored entirely to the needs of Gannett/USA Today, because the corporation did not request any "exit strategy"—that is, adaptability to the needs of a different future owner.

The resulting complex follows no familiar precedents. It is neither high-rise nor low-rise, provides consciously varied work settings, and looks unlike any other corporate headquarters.

The client and occupant of this project is a two-part corporate entity, encompassing

Basics

Client: Gannett Co., Inc.

Development manager: Hines

Architects: Kohn Pedersen Fox Associates (master plan and base building); Lehman-Smith + McLeish (programming and interiors)

Principal consultants: TOLK, Inc., mechanical/electrical/plumbing engineering; CBM Engineers, Inc., structural engineering; Michael Vergason Landscape Architects, land planning and landscape architecture; DVI Communications, communications; Persohn/Hahn Associates, Inc., vertical transportation; HMA Consulting, Inc., security; Shen Milsom & Wilke, acoustics; R. A. Heintges Architects, curtain walls; Fisher Marantz Renfro Stone, lighting

Schedule: development manager hired 4/97; completion 12/01. 12 months for design through construction drawings; 24 months for construction

Site: 30 acres at intersection of two major expressways; variation of about 90 ft in elevation from knoll at southeast end of site to storm water management pond at center; northwest end of site previously used as borrow pit and spoils site for development work in area

Floor areas: total 700,000 sq ft

Height: 9 and 12 stories

Occupancy: Gannett corporate offices and companywide news services; USA Today offices and newsrooms; 1,800 employees

Workspaces: large floor plates on two floors for both news functions; small mid-rise floors for management offices

Auxiliary facilities: conference center (215 seats); auditorium (299 seats); food service (two areas, with 400 and 278 seats); health center (20,000 sq ft); credit union; bank branch; concierge service

Circulation: two banks of six elevators each serving the two mid-rise blocks;

one shuttle elevator from the 11th floor to the 12th floor board room suite; one elevator in the garage

Zoning/codes: site preapproved for 1.3 million sq ft; height limited by sky plain at 14-degree angle from edge of residential area north of Dulles Toll Road

Structural system: concrete flat slab; steel for angled roof and lobby framing

Energy/environment: see page 195

Mechanical systems: see page 195

Envelope/materials: all-glass curtain wall, most of it with 10-inch glass vertical fins on exterior

Landscaping: reworking of landscape around building and pond; some restoration of woods to southeast; jogging/walking trail system, softball field, volleyball courts

Cost: About $150 million, or $92 per sq ft for base building, $36 per sq ft. for garage

the Gannett Company, owner of 99 daily newspapers and 22 television stations, and the offices of *USA Today,* the company's national newspaper. From these headquarters, the corporation manages a worldwide staff of some 40,000 and publishes *USA Weekend,* which is distributed in 534 Sunday papers. And

here *USA Today* is written and edited for more than 2.2 million daily readers.

The two-pronged operation had outgrown its 550,000 sq ft of rental space in two high-rise buildings in a dense urban neighborhood of Rosslyn, Virginia, within sight of Washington's monumental core. Leases in both buildings extended through

▶ *Five stacking diagrams illustrating alternative ways of organizing programmed areas in the proposed building. Courtesy KPF.*

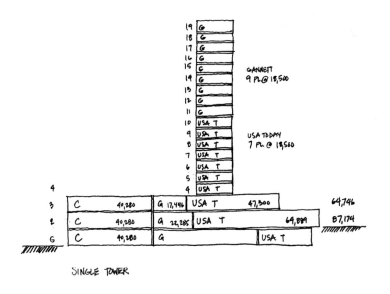

OVERALL AREA SUMMARY:

OFFICES, GANNETT & USA TODAY	303,027	45.9%
HIGH-CEILING SPACES	151,920	23.0%
COMMON AREAS	120,841	18.3%
BELOW GRADE (COMBINED)	83,813	12.7%
	659,601	100%

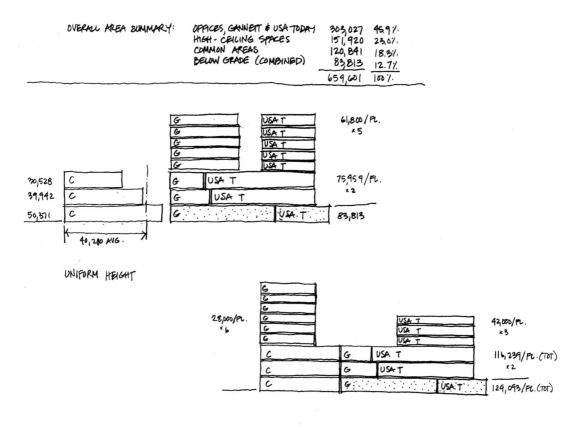

UNIFORM HEIGHT

LOW RISE + MID-RISE

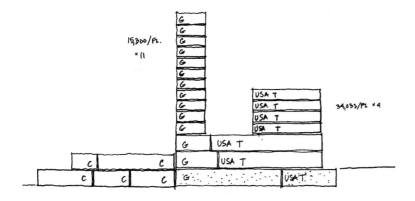

MID-RISE & HIGH-RISE
(2-STORY COMMON AREAS)

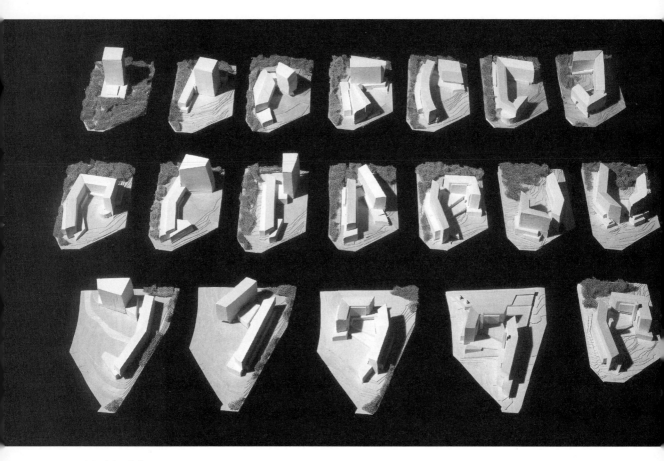

▲ *Models of alternatives developed by the architects for the massing of proposed building. © Jack Pottle.*

December 2001. This project stems from Gannett's decision to build a larger, owner-occupied complex on a highly accessible and visible suburban site. Among the objectives were the integration into the workplace of the most modern electronic technologies and the provision of exceptional employee amenities.

The 700,000 sq ft building is situated at the intersection of two regional arteries, the Beltway and the Dulles Toll Road. It consists of two mid-rise structures for Gannett and USA Today spiraling up from a base of shared facilities that wraps around an exterior "town square" at the main entrance. The single-loaded corridor system used on all floors hugs the glazed walls of the courtyard, making interior circulation visible and fostering a sense of community. Cladding is composed of glass for spandrels as well as vision glass, with closely spaced vertical glass exterior fins that modulate the appearance of the walls as one moves around the structure.

The three functional components of the headquarters are:

- Newsroom and production areas, which work best with large floor plates and the fewest possible floors—in this case the building's second and third stories—and flexible space, with high ceilings in keeping with their extensive areas

- Typical office floors for management functions, narrow to provide maximum daylight and views

- Common facilities, including an auditorium and conference center, dining facilities, a health club, convenience retail, an on-site jogging trail, and parking for 2000 cars

The Design Process

A site search evaluated 51 possible locations. The selected 30-acre site rated high for accessibility to employees and was approved for 1.3 million sq ft of construction, but it had some daunting peculiarities. The bow-shaped tract, following the boundary of the highway interchange, drops in elevation toward a pond at the center and rises toward both ends. The previously negotiated zoning envelope allowed for a tall tower at the southeast end of the site. Building height on the northwest portion was limited by a "sky exposure plane" (a zoning limit above which no building could extend) that rises at an angle from the edge of a residential neighborhood to the north.

After site acquisition, a design team was assembled. While Gannett had an internal real estate group to handle ongoing needs, it was decided not to expand that group for this one-time effort, but to bring in a development management company to oversee the project, in close coordination with Gannett management. From a short list of national companies, Gannett chose one on the basis of experience, staff, strong local office, and competitive fee proposal, awarding the contract to Hines in April 1997. The company had a long history as an investment developer of high-quality speculative buildings, but in the 1990s it had broadened its scope to include fee-based management of building projects for corporate clients. Hines was at the time working on new headquarters buildings for Swiss Bank (Stamford, Conn.) and Owen-Corning (Toledo, Ohio). Hines's project officer, Gregory Spivey, sums up the distinction between investment and corporate office buildings by saying that while efficiency is the only valid measure of spec buildings, the ultimate measure for corporate buildings is "whether people want to be there."

The design team was assembled in a somewhat unconventional sequence:

- Establishment of preliminary project schedule and budget with project manager.

- Selection of an interior architect, who would prepare the program, then go on to design the building's interiors.

- Selection of a base building architect, who would draw up a master plan and building design based on the program.

- Selection of major subconsultants.

The interior and base building architects would be separate firms, for the sake of the project schedule and the quality of the result. Today, everyone involved agrees that the building benefited from the participation of two firms working as equals. The architects and some consultants worked under contract directly with Hines, on Gannett's behalf. Other consultants worked for one or the other of the architecture firms. Gannett may also contract for a firm to operate the building after completion—possibly Hines.

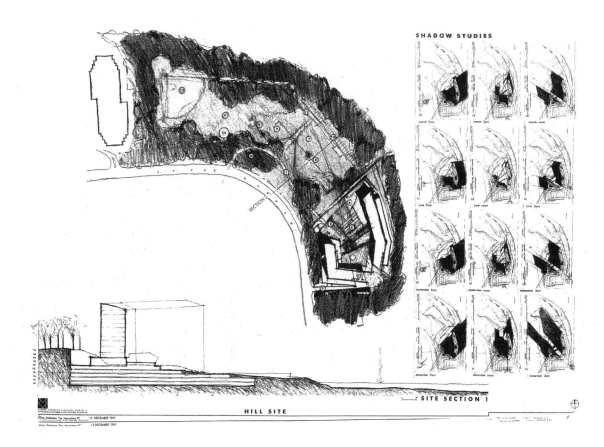

SHADOW STUDIES

SITE SECTION 1

HILL SITE

▲ *Proposed site plan with building at southeast end. Courtesy KPF.*

Gannett entrusted its day-to-day decisions to one full-time employee, Nancy Hauser, who had a working knowledge of design and construction, and was assured direct access to top executives for major decisions.

The project schedule, drawn up when Hines took on the job in April 1997, called for occupancy in the fall of 2001. It allocated three months for master planning, 12 months for completion of construction documents, and 24 months for construction, allowing six-month contingencies.

Selection criteria for the interior architects were:

- Strong local (D.C. area) office
- Programming experience relevant to this project
- Design experience relevant to this project
- Depth of organization
- Strong design aesthetic
- Ability to collaborate with base building architect
- Competitive fee proposal

From a short list of firms that included RTKL, Gensler, Skidmore Owings & Merrill (SOM), and Lehman-Smith + MacLeish (L-SM), L-SM was chosen in May 1997.

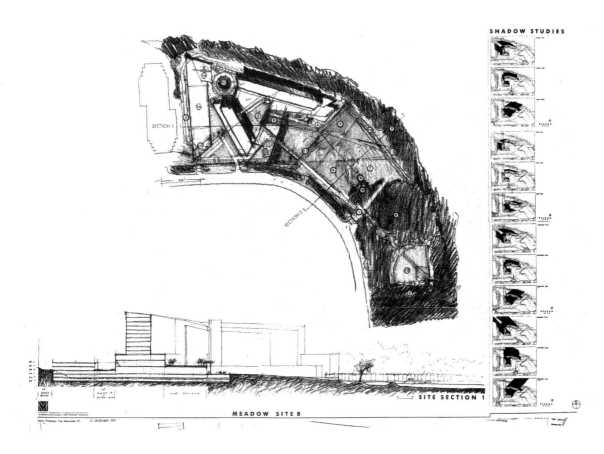

▲ *Proposed site plan with building at northwest end.*

For the base building architects, criteria were:

- National recognition
- Strong corporate headquarters experience
- Strong, clear design aesthetic
- Experienced project team
- Depth of organization
- Ability to work on equal basis with an interior architect
- Competitive fee proposal

The list of firms invited to compete included some that Hines had worked with repeatedly. In order not to unduly limit the field, design architects who would team up with production architects were considered. After presenting their qualifications to Hines, six firms were invited to informal meetings with the top Gannett executives. They were: DMJM/Keating, Kohn Pedersen Fox Associates, Pei Cobb Freed, Roche Dinkeloo, Skidmore Owings & Merrill, and Robert A.M. Stern Architects. KPF was awarded the commission in July 1997.

Shaping the Building

Before the design team went to work, the assumption had been that the

191

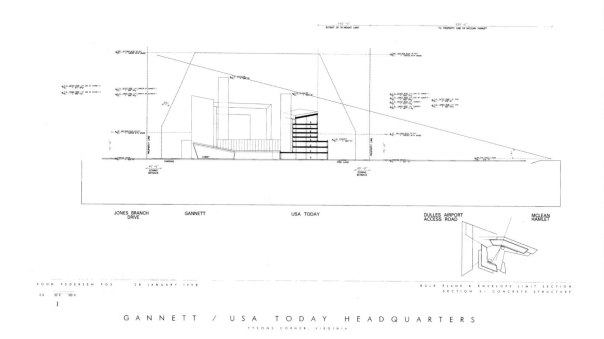

GANNETT / USA TODAY HEADQUARTERS
TYSONS CORNER, VIRGINIA

▲ *Study of building profile in relation to "sky exposure plane" established by zoning regulation to minimize impact of buildings on this site upon nearby residential area. Courtesy KPF.*

corporation would erect a highly visible tower at the southeast end of the property. It became clear as programming proceeded, however, that about half of the building's space would not be conventional office space, but newsrooms, a cafeteria, an auditorium, conference and training suites, and amenities such as a health club and on-site retail, all of which could best be housed on a few large floors.

Lehman-Smith + McLeish's 185 meetings with Gannett executives and staff made it clear that, among other things, dividing news operations among several small floors was inconvenient and required wasteful duplication of services. Discussions ranged from desired amenities to the fine points of workstation configurations. The resulting program recommendations took effect only after department heads signed off on them.

Due to the move from an urban location to outer suburbs, the program included amenities such as a bank, a credit union, an employee health club (with a one-mile jogging track on the property), in-house food service, coffee kiosks, and concierge service for errands and shopping. The company was also able to include an auditorium and conference center, neither of which it had previously. The final program calls for fewer square feet per person than the rental space, even including the additional facilities, since considerable redundancy in circulation and services space was eliminated.

In the stacking diagrams based on L-SM's programming, it was clear that a low, broad podium would be needed to house a substantial portion of the complex. If a single tower were to rise from such a podium, only one half of the dual operation would get the higher floors. Instead, KPF studied 19 distinct

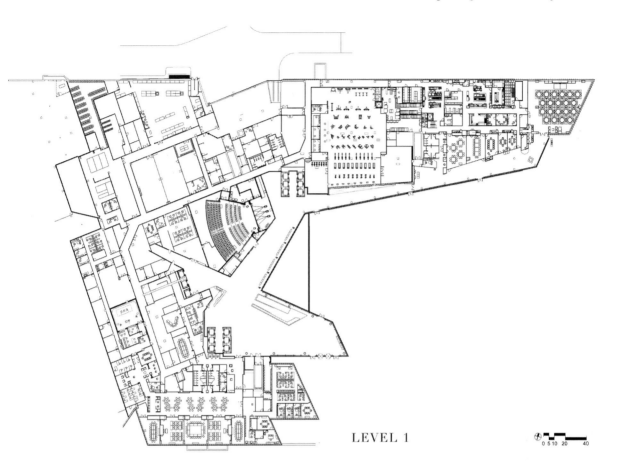

LEVEL 1

0 5 10 20   40

building configurations to arrive at a scheme with two mid-rise volumes rising from a shared podium, giving each of the two functions its own identity in an integrated composition. With the complex shaped into a loose U plan, the space between the two higher blocks could become a shared-entry courtyard.

William Pedersen of KPF speaks of the need to draw clients into a discussion of alternatives. If the client is not convinced through this process that the architect's preferred scheme is best, then it must be faulty, he says, and has to be reconsidered.

The building was initially expected to be located on the southeast portion of the

site—the highest area, with the most attractive landscape and without a height limitation. But the broad-based building concept would have wiped out most of the woods there, while the treeless northwest end—which had been excavated previously—would have needed considerable relandscaping to make it attractive when seen from upper floors. The northwest portion of the site turned out to be ideal for the U-shaped building, with the entry court facing southeast capturing desirable sunshine while shielded from the coldest winds, as well as highway noise. The two mid-rise towers could just be fitted within the

▲ *Plans of floors 1, 2, 3, 4, and 12, showing principal shared facilities on lower floors and special meeting room suite at top of building. Coutresy Lehman-Smith + Mcleish.*

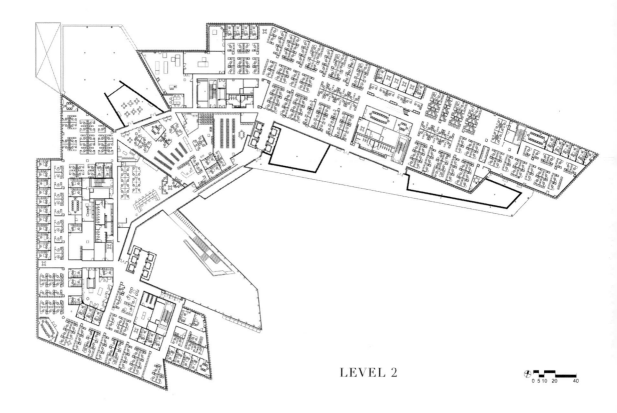

LEVEL 2

limiting zoning plane. The site's southeast corner forms an attractive setting for a softball field, playing fields, picnic areas, and trails for walking or running.

As the design evolved, other opportunities followed. Running glazed corridors along the edges of the central courtyard provided desirable views into and out of them, with the least interruption of the open office floors. Pulling the elevators outside of the building volume and enclosing them in glass adds to the sense of activity as seen from both corridors and courtyard, while it reduces the obstruction of floor layouts that elevators typically entail.

The lobby is a high space connecting the two elevator towers, with a reception desk from which both elevator banks can be observed. It can be used as a break-out space for the 299-seat auditorium and the meeting rooms on this floor, and its 20,000 sq ft area can be a setting for receptions and dinners. A stair of yacht-rigged construction swoops up to a balcony with access to the company's library and other amenities. A corridor extending east from the lobby leads past various employee facilities to a dining room at the end of the wing overlooking the site's pond.

Given the architects' development of an angular footprint and the angular plane of the height restriction, the building took on

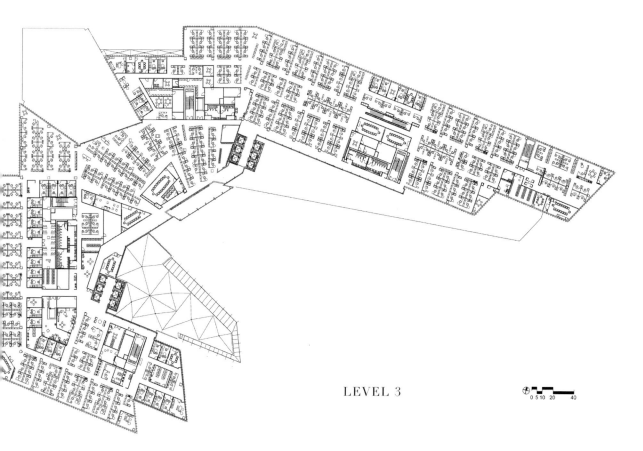

LEVEL 3

0 5 10 20 40

the form of a cluster of volumes recalling mineral crystals. The roofs rise from a low point of 119 ft above grade on the USA Today side to 180 ft on the Gannett portion, over the boardroom. Top-floor executive offices in both towers include some exceptionally tall interiors under sloping roofs. The elevator towers for the two blocks rise to 188 and 224 ft above grade. On each tower, mechanical equipment is located under the roof slopes; areaways and intakes are hidden through integration into perimeter gutters.

Mechanical Systems
Because of the newsrooms' 24-hour, 7-day operation, air-conditioning had to be designed for continuous, failsafe operation, and exceptional provisions had to be made for emergency power. The general approach was to install equipment of a very high standard of performance and durability — for instance, custom air-handling units that are double-walled, hence more durable, with lower sound transmission, and interior surfaces that are easy to clean for the sake of interior air quality. Electrical switching equipment is of a type that can be serviced without interrupting power. Equipment that was "exotic" — with unfamiliar operation and maintenance procedures — was avoided. Redundancy was built in; for example, only three of

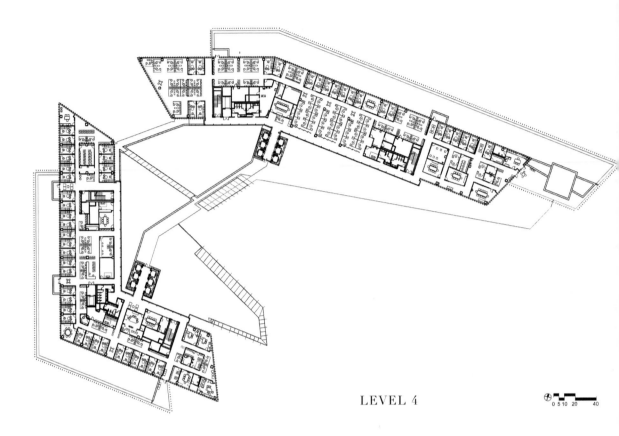

LEVEL 4

0 5 10 20   40

the four central chilled water plants are needed at any time.

Air is delivered to occupied spaces at constant volume (and varying temperature), so that air movement is maintained even when no change in temperature is called for. There is no direct temperature control by occupants, which could lead to uneven conditions. Electronic air filters clean entering outside air with a minimum drop in pressure and minimum need for maintenance (i.e., no filters).

Emergency electrical power can provide two-thirds of the full electrical power

delivered to the site. Equipment, lighting, and air conditioning for the newsrooms, elevators, and other key facilities can be maintained even under extreme climatic conditions, and the building can operate fully under most conditions. A battery-based system provides totally uninterrupted power while emergency generators get up to speed.

Among the features that result in energy savings:

- Heat exchangers that eliminate the need for mechanical refrigeration much of the year.

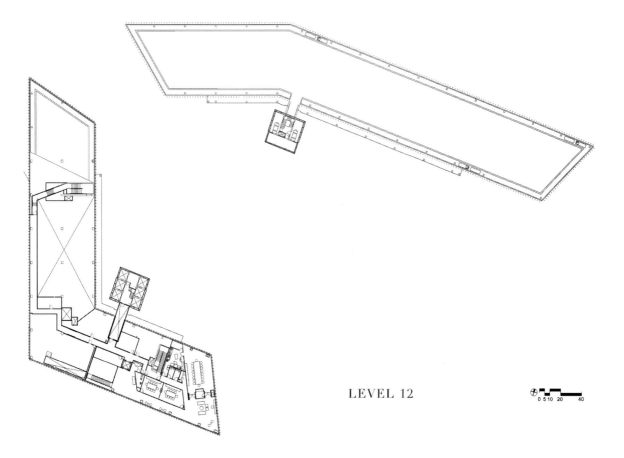

LEVEL 12

- Optimized HVAC air and water temperature differentials that reduce fan and pump power requirements.

- Electrical resistance heating in the few perimeter spaces that need it part of the year, eliminating the need for a heating boiler.

- Insulated HVAC ductwork.

- Night setback controls.

- High-efficiency lighting with energy-saving ballasts and lamps.

- Positive air pressure maintained in entire building to minimize air infiltration through walls or doorways.

- Interior air pressure relieved through the tops of the elevator shafts, heating and cooling them adequately as a by-product.

Communications

Communications systems were shaped by the client's need for uninterrupted contact within the building and with offices worldwide. Fiber optics connects all floors and the satellite dishes in a self-healing configuration, in which any interruption instantaneously switches service to an alternative cable. There is a central switching room for each of the

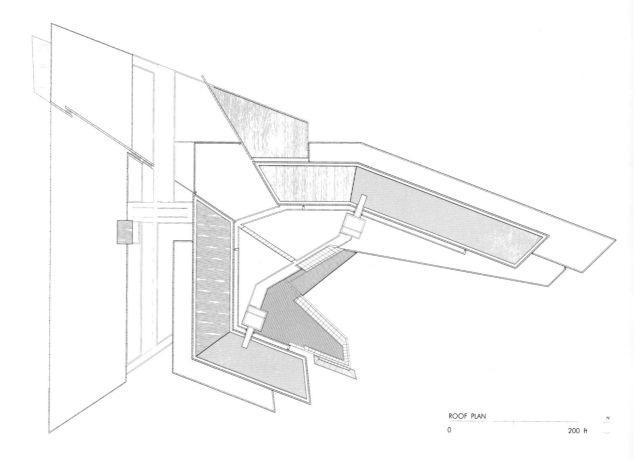

ROOF PLAN

0   200 ft

N

▲ *Roof plan, showing layout of angular roof planes. Courtesy KPF.*

two towers, either of which is capable of serving the entire building. On each floor, individual workstations are connected by high-performance copper cable, at savings of 50 percent compared to fiber optics (not because of the cable cost, but because of the electronic equipment that cable requires at individual stations). The technology for wireless communication to work stations was not considered well enough developed for use at this time. Security of communication is handled, where required, by encryption, rather than shielding the building against electronic interception; such shielding inconveniences all users

by blocking wireless devices such as cellular phones.

Structural Systems
Concrete flat slab construction was selected as the primary structural system for several reasons:

- With the thinnest structural section for any given span, flat slabs yielded the minimum floor-to-floor height for a building with a fixed height restriction.

- Small cantilevers beyond structural supports, which occur at several points, were most easily executed in concrete.

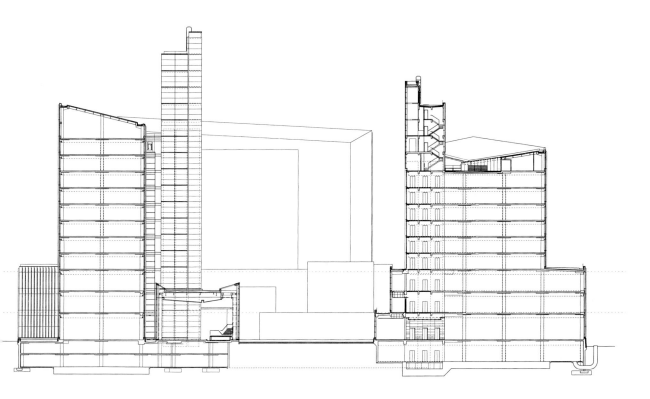

▲ Cross-section of proposed building. Courtesy KPF.

- For the garage under part of the building, a concrete slab provided an acceptable ceiling at minimum cost.

- In the Washington area, the concrete construction industry is well developed, with an ample experienced labor supply.

This job was large enough to warrant an on-site batching plant, thus reducing the coordination problems of trucking concrete to the site.

Steel framing was introduced in those areas where it was most effective, for the roof and for the framing of the lobby space. In both areas, the exceptional height of the spaces being spanned would have required elaborate scaffolding for concrete, and steel framing is particularly compatible with the standing-seam metal roofs used here.

Exterior Surfaces

The roof material is lead-coated copper over steel framing and metal deck.

For the exterior walls, the architects considered a variety of possibilities: brick walls with punched openings, horizontal bands of glazing with metal spandrels, and finally the all-glass vocabulary that was adopted. The homogeneous appearance of the glass cladding was the most adaptable to wall surfaces cut at angles. To make the vision and spandrel look essentially the same, a glass with the minimum reflectivity acceptable to energy codes (20 percent) was used.

(continued on page 203)

▶ *Section through typical floor, including curtain wall on outer face of horseshoe-shaped building. Courtesy KPF.*

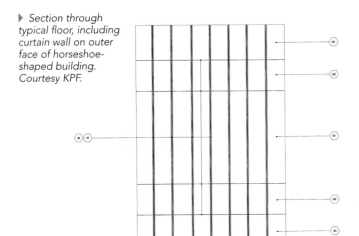

ELEVATION – WALL TYPE 2

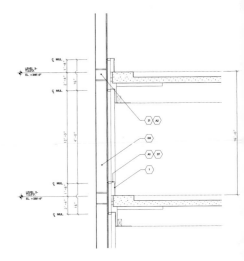

SECTION – WALL TYPE 2

Gannett/USA TODAY Headquarters Project

▶ *Details of curtain walls for outer faces of building.*

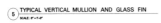

5 TYPICAL VERTICAL MULLION AND GLASS FIN
SCALE: 6"=1'-0"

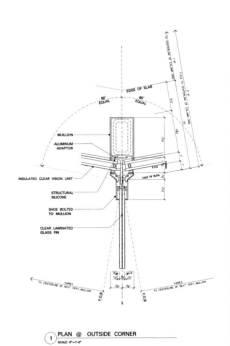

1 PLAN @ OUTSIDE CORNER
SCALE: 6"=1'-0"

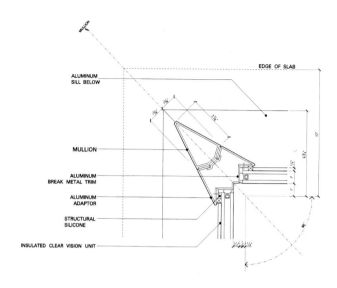

ALUMINUM
SILL BELOW

MULLION

ALUMINUM
BREAK METAL TRIM

ALUMINUM
ADAPTOR

STRUCTURAL
SILICONE

INSULATED CLEAR VISION UNIT

EDGE OF SLAB

◀▲ *Detail of glass fins attached to curtain walls on outer faces of building.*

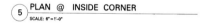

5 **PLAN @ INSIDE CORNER**
SCALE: 6" = 1'-0"

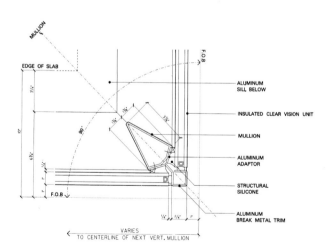

EDGE OF SLAB

ALUMINUM
SILL BELOW

INSULATED CLEAR VISION UNIT

MULLION

ALUMINUM
ADAPTOR

STRUCTURAL
SILICONE

ALUMINUM
BREAK METAL TRIM

VARIES
TO CENTERLINE OF NEXT VERT. MULLION

4 **PLAN @ OUTSIDE CORNER**
SCALE: 6" = 1'-0"

CASE STUDIES

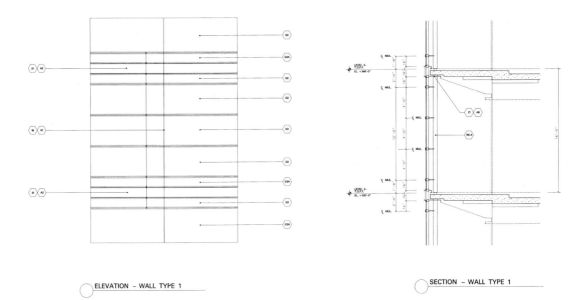

ELEVATION – WALL TYPE 1

SECTION – WALL TYPE 1

**Gannett/USA TODAY
Headquarters Project**

▲ Section through
typical floor, including
curtain wall on inner
(entry court) face of
horseshoe-shaped
building. Courtesy KPF.

▶ Study model of
curtain wall for inner
face of building.
© Jock Pottle.

(continued from page 199)
The desired energy performance and
acoustical isolation from highway noise
were achievable with a 1" insulating glass
assembly.

In order to "activate" the otherwise flat
wall, to generate variations in appearance
with different angles of view, the architects considered a variety of vertical fin
schemes. Metal fins, when spaced closely
enough to work visually on the exterior,
produced a prisonlike image from the
inside. The glass fins that were used

produce a pleasing mix of transparency
and reflection, and occasional rainbow-
like refractions from light striking their
edges. Fins 10" deep, spaced at 2'6" intervals, produce the desired degree of surface
animation, leave comfortably scaled vision
openings, and are compatible with the
5'0" interior planning module.

The fins increased the cost of the walls
by only about $5 per sq ft, to a moderate
$66. The two basic types were mocked
up and tested for their physical performance under design wind loads and

▲ *Perspective drawing of office interior. © LSM.*

columns to support the much higher floor-to-ceiling dimension.

The glass enclosures of the elevator shafts are also assembled of horizontal panels and have a fritted pattern of narrow horizontal silver bands. The double glazing comes in two varieties: clear glazing for the second layer on exterior surfaces; textured glass on sides facing another elevator shaft.

Parking

Parking consists of one level under the building and a six-level ramped garage of precast concrete just to the west, separated by a landscaped area (which doubles as fire truck access). The roof of the garage accommodates tennis and basketball courts, as well as a helicopter pad and a satellite dish farm.

Landscaping

The entry courtyard was developed with elements scaled to the individual. There is a lotus pond along the building edge and, in the center of the space, an iris-lined stream running down toward the pond. A number of fieldstone walls negotiate the change in grade and divide the space into zones. Southeast of the pond, an area that had already been partially regraded was made into a softball field. Volleyball courts were constructed, and the wooded knoll was restored. A system of trails offers a roughly half-mile circuit for joggers and connects the playing fields, benches, and picnic tables along the way.

ability to shed water. Fins do not, of course, facilitate window washing, which will be handled by cherry picker for the lower floors, and by bo's'n's chairs suspended from the roof for the higher stories.

For other parts of the buildings, different curtain walls were developed. For the glazed corridors surrounding the entry courtyard, maximum transparency, uninterrupted by fins, was desired. Clear, low-e glass and horizontal mullions are used, supported by interior pipe columns at 10'0" intervals. For the main lobby, a similar wall was designed, but with larger

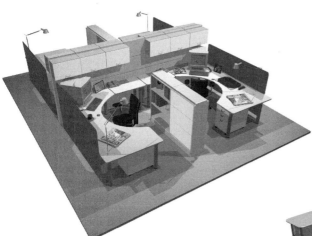

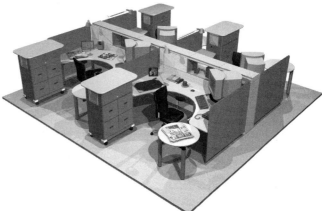

▲ ▶ Drawings of typical workstations. Courtesy Vitra.

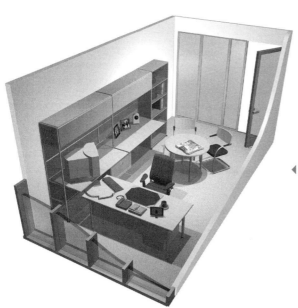

◀ Drawing of typical private office.

▲ Gannett/USA Today lobby.
Photo © Timothy Hursley.

◀ First-floor corridor in
Gannett/USA Today headquarters,
overlooking landscaped entrance
court. Photo © Timothy Hursley.

CHAGRIN HIGHLANDS BUILDING ONE

CLEVELAND, OHIO *Kohn Pedersen Fox Associates*

FOCUS POINTS

- Low-rise investment building
- Suburban office park site
- Distinction from competing buildings

For the first building in a new office park, one that would be prominently visible from a major highway, the owners wanted something quite distinct from the usual dark-glass boxes. The building was also intended to be a prototype for the entire seven-unit development.

The structure has four floors above grade and one floor of underground parking.

Each 20,000 sq ft floor plate is laid out to accommodate four or more tenants, with reasonable corridor layouts. The depth from exterior to core is 40 ft. The treatment of the building volume as two parallel bars extending into the landscape doubles the number of corner offices to eight on each floor.

The building is more sensitively related to the rolling landscape than the area's typical office building. The structure is not set perpendicular to its access road, but both road and building are oriented to fit the terrain. The siting also takes advantage of

▼ *Chagrin Highlands from approach side. Photo © Björg.*

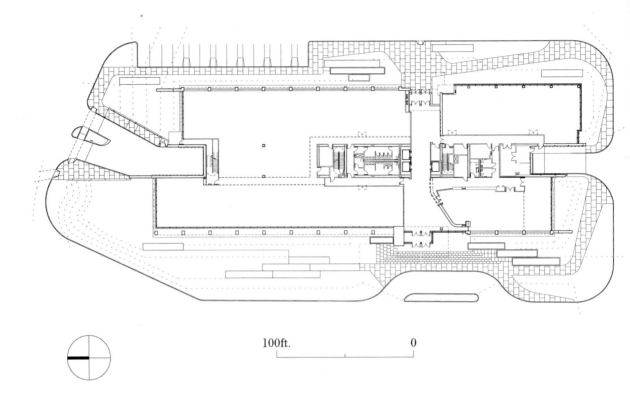

100ft.   0

▲ *First-floor plan. Courtesy KPF.*

Basics

Client: The Richard E. Jacobs Group

Architects: Kohn Pedersen Fox Associates

Principal consultants: Gilsanz Murray Steficek LLP, structural engineers; Cosentini Associates, mechanical and electrical engineers; Opus One, landscape/civil engineer; The Whiting-Turner Contracting Co., general contractor

Building process: conventional design/bid/build; general contractor

Schedule: construction 1998

Site: 11-acre portion of 90-acre development planned to have seven buildings; gently rolling; Interstate 271 along east boundary

Floor areas: typical floor, 20,000 sq ft; total 80,000 sq ft

Height: 4 stories, 70 ft

Occupancy: rental tenants, up to 4–5 per floor, adaptable for more

Workspaces: rental area, 40 ft depth to core

Circulation: three passenger elevators; variable layout of upper-floor corridors

Zoning/codes: local Beechwood, Ohio, codes

Structural system: steel frame

Energy/environment: tinted, coated glass; some set behind frame

Mechanical systems: rooftop cooling towers in central band; more can be added

Envelope/materials: tinted, mirrored glass in aluminum-framed wall; portions of first floor Cambrian black granite

Interiors: lobby with long wall of frosted mirror, metal, textured glass, and tinted plaster, stone floor; remainder of building by tenants

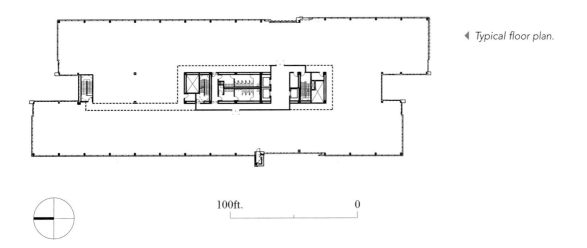

◀ *Typical floor plan.*

100ft.   0

▼ *Building section.*

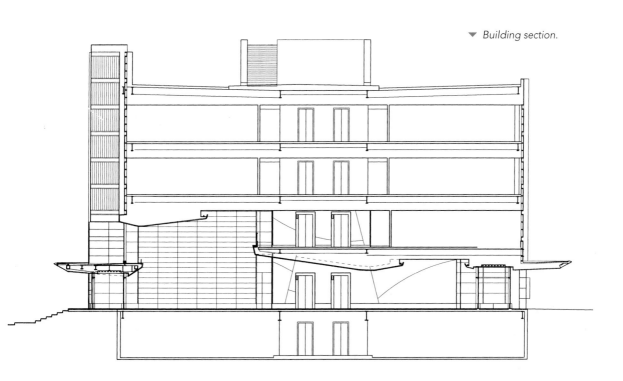

the view over adjoining wetlands, where construction is prohibited. Parking has been removed from the front of the building, allowing the landscape to surround it. The building's geometries and materials are repeated in the landscaping.

In another exception to prevailing suburban office design, entrances from the front and rear are treated as equally important. A tall, thin tower identifies the access drive entrance at pedestrian scale. The parking lot entrance, on the side visible from the interstate, is identified by a simpler but bolder recess between two volumes.

The window and spandrel portions of the curtain wall are treated as equal-sized

▲ Chagrin Highlands from parking lot, showing side seen from highway. Photo © Björg.

◀ Lobby runs through from main entrance to parking lot entrance. Photo © Björg.

▲ Close-up of Chagrin Highlands exterior wall. Photo © Björg.

horizontal bands, masking the building's four-story height and making its scale ambiguous. The bright metal façade components are aluminum shop-coated with a high-performance paint, which can be touched up on the site as necessary. The variety of tenants inside is suggested by breaks in the building volumes and by varied treatment of the first-floor walls: as dark granite walls with punched openings, as pilotis in front of a continuous tinted glass membrane, and as continuations of the upper wall.

THAMES COURT

LONDON, UNITED KINGDOM *Kohn Pedersen Fox Associates (International) PA*

FOCUS POINTS

- Height limit
- Historical setting
- Riverfront site
- Flexible, high-tech workspace
- Atrium
- Trading floor

A narrow riverfront site in the heart of London's City set the program for this 228,000 sq ft investment building. Special qualities of light, air, and view enhanced the value of its central location. On the other hand, the site was subject to severe height limitations because it sits on two strategic view corridors directed toward the dome of

▼ *Thames Court from river, with St. Paul's Cathedral in background. Building height at this location is limited to protect views of dome. Photo © H.G. Esch.*

▲ Street front of Thames Court, with main entrance. Photo © H.G. Esch.

St. Paul's. The height was limited to four floors above grade, with no projections above the roof. (A complex butterfly-type roof, with cut-outs for necessary mechanical plant and window washing equipment, yields a clearance of little more than 2 in. from the view corridors.)

The potential for leasing to a financial tenant prompted a number of design decisions. The building is planned so that the financial trading operation on the

ground and first floors can have secure access directly from the entrance, separate from access to the upper floors. Greater ceiling heights on these two stories allow for raise floors. The insertion of an atrium at the center of the building, with suspended trusses supporting floor areas to either side, permits a column-free trading floor at the second-floor level. An extensive skylight above the atrium and glazing

(continued on page 220)

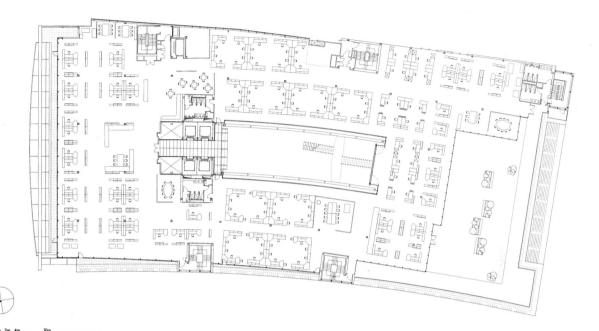

▲▲ Fourth (top) floor plan, Thames Court.

▲ Ground (street) floor plan, Thames Court. Courtesy KPF.

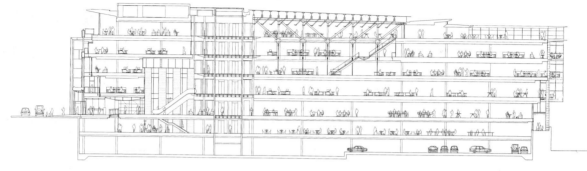

▲ *Thames Court building section, showing progression of stairs from main entrance (at left) to upper-floor atrium, with stairs continuing to top floor. Courtesy KPF.*

▶ *Thames Court lobby, showing stairs and glass-walled elevators. Photo © H.G. Esch.*

Basics

Client: Markborough Properties, Ltd.

Architects: Kohn Pedersen Fox Associates (International) PA

Principal consultants: Waterman Partnership, structural engineering; Flack & Kurtz, mechanical engineering; MACE, Ltd., construction manager

Building process: construction management, fast-track

Schedule: design accepted 1995; construction started 1996; completed 1998

Site: busy street to north; river to south; slope toward river; public walkways around entire perimeter

Floor areas: 228,000 sq ft; offices, 210,300 sq ft; retail, 1,700 sq ft, parking, 24 cars

Height: 4 stories

Occupancy: rental aimed at corporate headquarters and financial institutions

Workspaces: predominantly open plan, with some glass-walled perimeter offices; most of second-floor open dealer area (all by two principal tenants)

Circulation: escalators between ground and first floor; four passenger elevators, first to fourth floor; freight elevator and vehicle lift adjoining service entry

Zoning/codes: height limited because in a designated view corridor to St. Paul's dome; to eliminate penthouses, elevators side-hung; unusual proportion of mechanical plant in basement; retail food outlet required; possible effect on river levels and ecology reviewed; parking limited to one space per 1,500 sq ft

Structural system: steel frame with composite floor slabs; upper floors supported in part by trusses suspended from roof level; provisions for expanding or reducing atrium

Mechanical system: fresh air from river, directed through basement; public spaces act as exhaust plenums; operable windows both on exterior and on atrium walls; various cooling systems, including chilled ceilings on lowest two floors, VAV units on second floor, fan coil units on third and fourth; building is sprinklered throughout; energy conservation is addressed with deep brise-soleil on riverfront areas most exposed to sun; motorized louvers and blinds on other walls with sun exposure; atrium skylight shaded by two layers of motorized shades, plus motorized baffles for intense sunlight

Envelope/materials: custom-designed prefinished aluminum and insulated clear glass curtain wall; glass fire-resistant and exposed structural steel coated with intumescent paint; some limestone on front and sides

Interiors: largely open office, with some perimeter glass-walled offices; exceptional density and communications for trading floor

International concerns: joint financing from Canada and Germany; tenants from the U.S. and the Netherlands; design by London office of KPF, with U.S. and U.K. consultants; one-year archaeological dig required before construction

▲ *Thames Court atrium, showing trading floor extending under suspended top floor. Photo © H.G. Esch.*

(continued from page 216) along the south (river) front admit ample light, which can be controlled by an array of motorized devices. Fresh air from the river is directed through the basement, then up through the atrium to exhaust vents.

The structure has been designed to accommodate possible changes in the atrium configuration: extension southward toward the river frontage or downward as far as the lower ground floor; contraction by installing cantilevers along the sides or by filling in a single bay at any level.

A sequence of escalators and stairs rises in stages from the north entry toward the glazed wall along the river to south.

Glass-walled elevators and shafts adjoin both the lobby and atrium, allowing views into and out of the cabs. Stairwells are dispersed around the perimeter of the building, facilitating further divisions of tenant spaces in the future.

The exterior treatment has been designed to break up the volume of the building from some viewpoints, while giving a unified identity to the street front. Walls are of high-quality prefinished metal and clear insulated glass. On the front, the distraction of the busy street is reduced by a glazed buffer zone that shields offices from traffic noise.

In several ways, the structure illustrates the special circumstances of building in London. The design is by KPF's London office, with U.S. and U.K. consultants. Financing and tenants came from several countries. The site was archaeologically rich and was subject to a one-year dig after demolition of buildings previously on it. View corridor limitations, rather than floor area limitations—are specific to London. The building is hybrid in its mechanical systems—high comfort specs with override for operable windows—and in its floor plates of varying depth.

▲ *Thames Court perimeter office seen through partially transparent corridor partition. Photo © H.G. Esch.*

▶ *Close-up view of Thames Court exterior at cantilevered corner. Photo © H.G. Esch.*

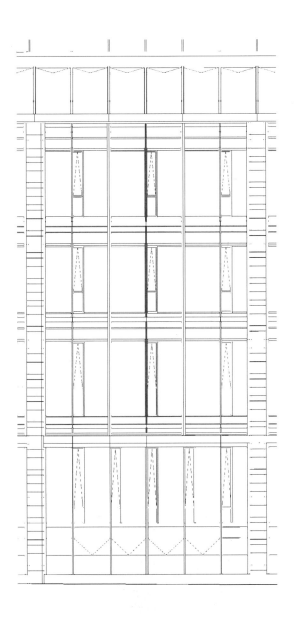

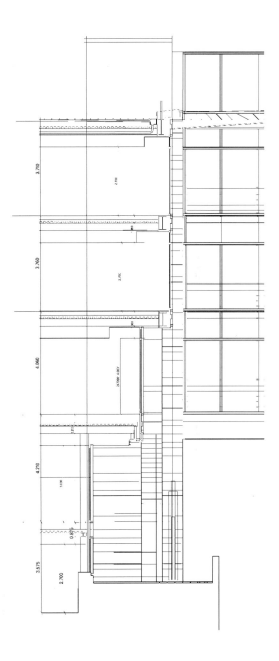

▲ *Elevation and section drawings of curtain wall, south (river) side of Thames Court. Courtesy KPF.*

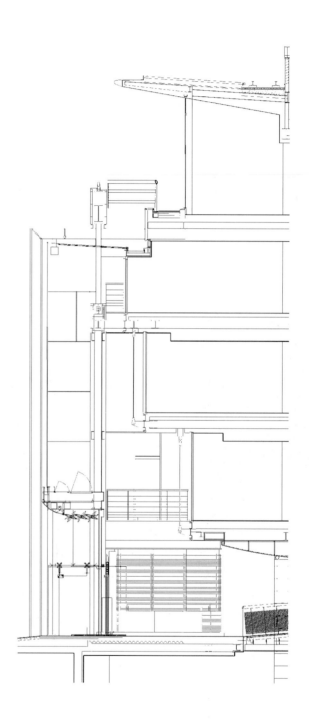

▶ Section drawing of curtain wall,
north (street) side of Thames Court.
Courtesy KPF.

TOUR CBX

PARIS, FRANCE *Kohn Pedersen Fox Associates; Saubot Rouit Associés*

FOCUS POINTS

Unusual shape of buildable area

Required view corridors through site

Complex two-level auto and pedestrian links at base

Underground utility tunnels crossing site

This building will occupy a site that is essentially no site at all. It will stand at a location in Paris's La Defense office district where no building was envisaged in the area's master plan. As a result the design is seriously constrained by existing construction, as well as limitations set by

◀ *Tour CBX model seen from above, with north at top of photo. © Jock Pottle.*

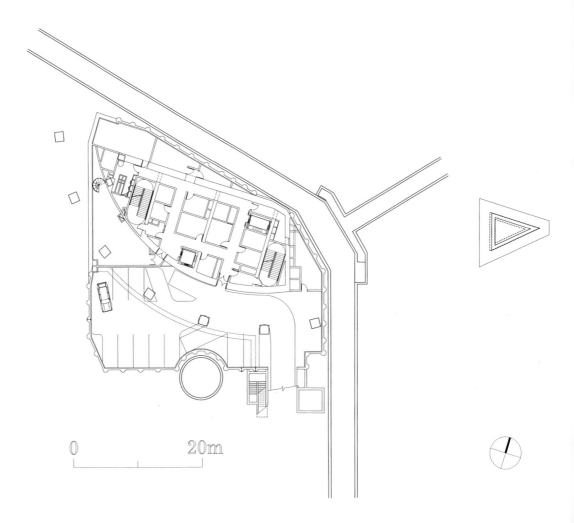

▲ *Tour CBX basement plan, showing extensive utility tunnels limiting construction at this level. Courtesy KPF.*

planning authorities. It will rise from a tangle of subterranean utility tunnels and is penetrated by automobile rights-of-way at street level. At the elevated pedestrian level, walkways and required view corridors cross the site. Mandated view corridors had to be carefully calculated, since nearby owners can sue if requirements are not met.

The tower floors are shaped to leave mandated space around existing buildings and preserve views of (and out of) them.

The resulting tower has an asymmetrical bladelike form, with a glass and metal curtain wall designed to minimize its bulk. Its outer appearance is an especially sensitive issue, since it is in a highly visible location for those approaching La Defense from central Paris.

The building contains 26 office floors totaling 472,000 GSF (43,800 sq m). The 245 ft (75 m) length of the floor is the maximum allowed without a third set of fire stairs. A larger than usual

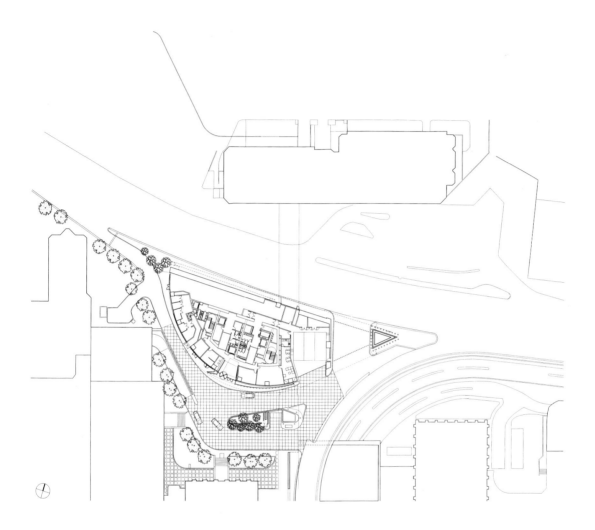

▲ *Tour CBX street-level plan, showing roadways passing under tower.*

perimeter-to-core dimension of 31 ft (9.5 m) was allowed in exchange for greater than normal ceiling heights and the use of floor-to-ceiling glass on north-facing walls. On the south side of the core, where there is less vision glass, the depth is 21 ft (6.5 m), in order to accommodate cellular offices (30 percent of floor area).

The four-story base includes lobbies at two levels, loading facilities, mechanical spaces on the ground floor, and a cafeteria and kitchen on the second level.

The double-height main lobby on the third—pedestrian entrance—floor overlooks the skylit cafeteria below. A street-level automobile drop-off and lobby is an exceptional amenity in the area, where the public enters most buildings only from the pedestrian plaza level.

Of the numerous utility lines under the building (hot and cold water, gas, electric power, communications cables, and sewage) a few were relocated. Footings *(continued on page 230)*

CASE STUDIES

▶ *Tour CBX pedestrian-level plan, showing elevated walkway that connects La Defense buildings passing under tower. Courtesy KPF.*

▶▶ *Tour CBX lobby. Courtesy KPF.*

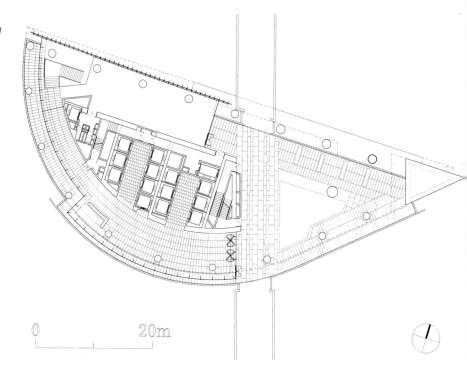

0   20m

▶ *Tour CBX typical floor plan.*

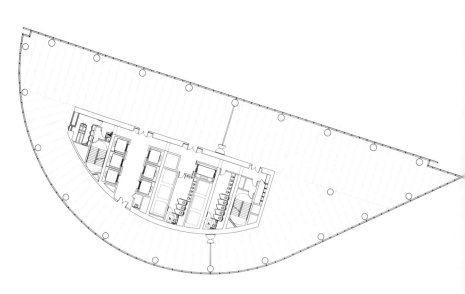

0   20m

Basics

Client: Tishman Speyer Properties LP

Architects: Kohn Pedersen Fox Associates; associated architects, Saubot Rouit Associés (architects of record)

Principal consultants: Setec Travaux Publics et Industriels, civil and structural engineers; Setec Batiment-Climatisation, mechanical engineers; Peltier, curtain wall; Lerch Bates North America, Inc., vertical transportation; Cogedim, client advisor; EPAD, Planning Commission of La Defense; AVLS, acoustical consultants; Socotec, code consultant; Europtima Sarl, cost consultant/estimator; Isometrix, lighting consultant

Building process: fast-track

Schedule: construction start, April 2001; completion, 2003

Site: 30,000 sq ft (2,780 sq m) in La Defense development, along major thoroughfare

Floor areas: 472,000 GSF, office (43,800 sq m), of which 40,000 sq m is offices; 3,800 sq m is cafeteria, snack bar, conference facility, etc.; typical floor: 17,300 sq ft (1,602 sq m); 41,000 sq ft (3,800 sq m) on lower four floors, including lobby, cafeteria, mechanical spaces

Height: 31 stories; 26 office floors; floor-to-floor height: 12'4" (3.75 m)

Occupancy: rental office tenants; cafeteria and snack bar on lower floors

Workspaces: perimeter-to-core depth, 31 ft (9.5 m), north side of core; 21 ft (6.5 m) on south side; layouts by tenants

Circulation: walkways crossing site; two lobbies, at automobile and pedestrian levels; separate elevator, auto lobby to main lobby; six elevators to lower office floors, six to upper

Zoning/codes: specific requirement for site set by EPAD, La Defense zoning commission; required connections to street level roadways and elevated walkways; view corridors through site at pedestrian level

Structural system: concrete

Energy/environment: maximum natural light to office floors; fritted curtain-wall glass modulated to suit orientation

Mechanical systems: central; rooftop cooling towers

Envelope/materials: glass and aluminum

Interiors: lobby, slate floor, veter stone walls, stainless steel, frosted mirror; remainder by tenants

International concerns: allowable perimeter-to-core depth extended for north side of building to 31 ft (9.5 m) in recognition of high ceilings and fully glazed north walls

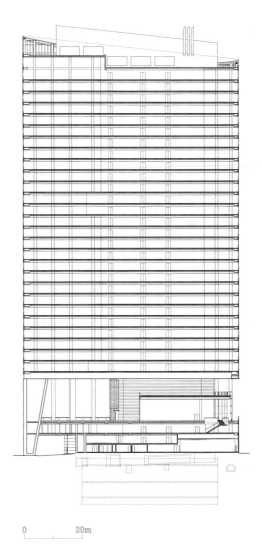

▶ *Tour CBX building section. Courtesy KPF.*

0   20m

(continued from page 227)
and structural columns had to be fitted between remaining obstructions. Since these supports could not be located where needed for tower structural loads, there are several transfer beams and transfer walls to redistribute loads in the lower portions of the building. The concentration of structural loads on a few columns at the lower levels is emphasized in the architectural treatment of these supports.

The pedestrian-level lobby is 46 ft (14 m) high, corresponding to the height of the required view corridor through the building, with clear glass walls largely shaded by cantilevers. Walls of the tower have maximum view glass on the north side, with varying areas of fritted glass toward the south to reduce solar load. The frit pattern changes as it moves across the curving south façade, with its opaque areas increasing as it arcs toward the west.

◀ *Tour CBX model view from east.*
© Jock Pottle.

▼ *Tour CBX pedestrian-level entry.*
Courtesy KPF.

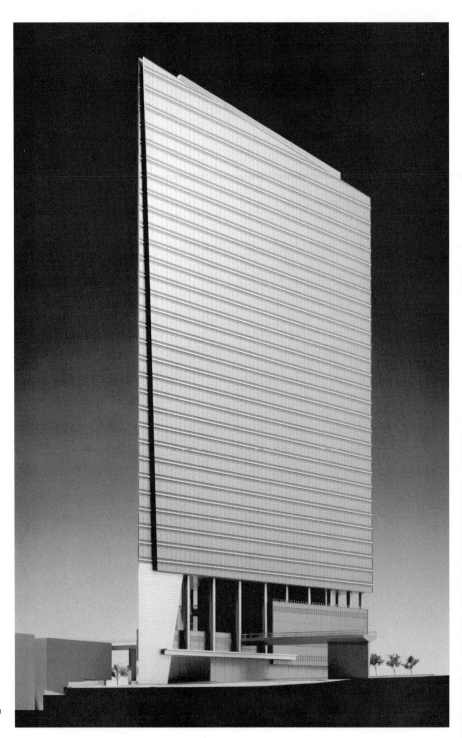

▶ *Tour CBX model view from north. © Jock Pottle.*

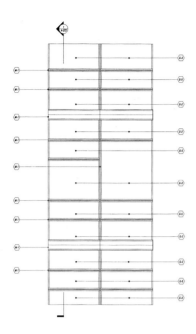

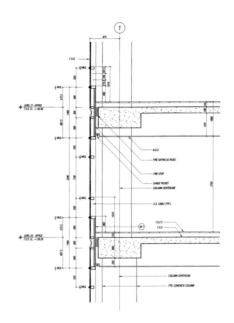

▲ Detail drawings of
Tour CBX south wall.
Courtesy KPF.

▶ Detail drawings of
Tour CBX north wall.

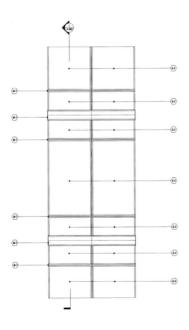

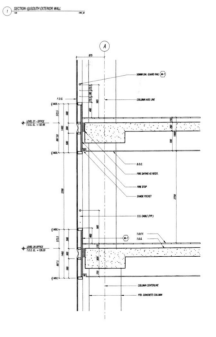

ENDESA HEADQUARTERS

MADRID, SPAIN *Kohn Pedersen Fox Associates; Rafael de la-Hoz Arquitectos*

FOCUS POINTS

- Innovative energy conservation measures
- Identifying owner with sustainable environment
- Proximity to a major highway

Endesa, one of the world's largest private suppliers of electrical power, wanted its new headquarters to project an image of environmental responsibility. The building was designed to demonstrate innovative environmental strategies, while providing exceptional flexibility and employee comfort.

The building is on a highly visible site in the north of Madrid, along a highway, at the gateway to a new business park. The location offers exceptional views of Madrid.

The building will include 378,000 sq ft (35,000 sq m) of net office space on six

▼ *Model of Endesa headquarters, Madrid, showing two linear office blocks flanking central atrium. © Eamonn O'Mahony.*

▲ *Model of Endesa
headquarters, showing
sun baffles on exterior.
© Eamonn O'Mahony.*

Basics

Client: Grupo Endesa s.a.

Architects: Kohn Pedersen Fox
Associates; Rafael de la-Hoz
Arquitectos, associated architects

Principal consultants: Gerens Hill
International s.a., project managers;
Battle McCarthy Consulting Engineers,
mechanical/electrical/plumbing
consultant; Prointec, structural
engineer; Davis Langdon & Everest,
quantity surveyors

Building process: construction
management

Schedule: design accepted 1999;
construction March 2000 to March 2002

Site: 32,000 sq m in a suburban office
park

Floor areas: 80,000 sq m (882,300 sq ft)

gross; 34,200 sq m net offices; 24,000
sq m support facilities; parking for
1,070 cars

Height: 6 stories above grade

Occupancy: corporate headquarters

Workspaces: interior laid out on 8.1 m
grid, subdivided on a 1.35 m module

Circulation: entry at northeast corner
of atrium, with strong indications of
pathways to clarify complex plan; set of
four elevators at either end of atrium

Zoning/codes: atrium was considered
external, unconditioned space for code
purposes

Structural system: concrete frame and
flat slabs; steel framing for atrium roof

Mechanical systems: air distribution and
exhaust through raised floors; fan-coil
units at perimeter zones, night air

cooling of floor slabs through raised
floor; chilled water and heating distributed through floor voids; environmental
strategies include use of "sprayed-
rock" cooled air directed through
underground ducts and induced
exhaust of warmed air through atrium
roof; passive wind towers above atrium
roof increase air flow; night-air cooling
of floor slabs; largest installation of
photovoltaic cells in Europe, mounted
on roof of atrium, also providing
carefully calculated degree of shade for
atrium

Envelope/materials: aluminum and
glass curtain wall; double layer, with
fritted glass on southwest for solar and
sound control; aluminum louvers on
other side adjusted to sun conditions

International concerns: daylighting of
offices, satisfied with 18 m deep wings

levels, plus 25,000 sq m (270,000 sq ft) of support facilities on a partially below-grade ground floor (*semisotano*). This level includes all public areas, exhibition space, restaurant, video-conferencing facilities, retail, training, and archive departments. A basement garage accommodates 1,070 cars. The office floors are configured in two 18 m deep bars, flanking a central atrium.

The atrium, 3,000 sq m (32,000 sq ft) in area and 32 m (105 ft) high, is the core of the project's energy strategies. It functions as the lungs of the building, the space where fresh air is introduced and used air from the offices is expelled. Two underground ducts supply fresh air, which is drawn from the most protected area of

the site (farthest from highway pollution), cooled at intake with a "sprayed rock" evaporative system, and kept cool in its 70 m (230 ft) path below grade. The atrium itself is treated as a transition circulation zone, which will have acceptable, but not closely controlled, comfort levels summer and winter.

In summer, hot air rises through the atrium vents at the top, through glass louvers around the perimeter and through two wind towers or solar chimneys. With clear glass facing approximately south and west, opposite which are two radiation-absorbent surfaces, these towers use solar heat to achieve thermal lift and accelerate the exhausting of air from the atrium. In

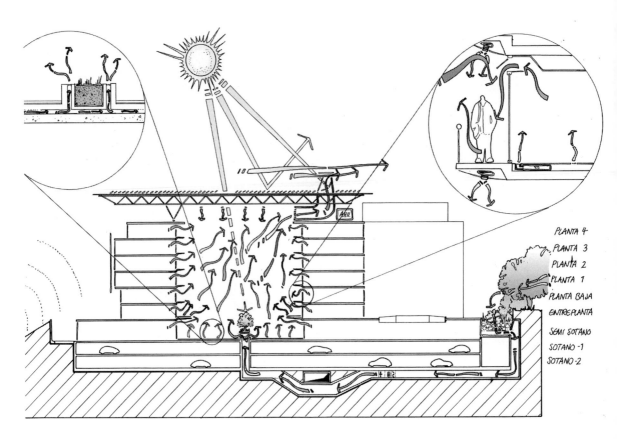

PLANTA 4
PLANTA 3
PLANTA 2
PLANTA 1
PLANTA BAJA
ENTREPLANTA
SEMI SOTANO
SOTANO -1
SOTANO -2

▲ *Section diagram of
Endesa headquarters,
showing movement of air
induced by daytime
warming. Courtesy KPF.*

winter, the wind towers exhaust warmed
air during the day and are closed at night.

The highly engineered atrium roof has a
skin of clear glazing and a shading layer,
calculated to provide 85 percent solar
protection during the summer, while
admitting sufficient daylight for the
atrium itself and surrounding offices. Its
shading devices incorporate one of the
largest installations of photovoltaic (PV)
panels on any commercial building in the
world.

The atrium roof is supported by steel
trusses up to 46 m (150 ft) long. Between
the trusses is a grid of prefabricated
rectangular single-glazed panels, their
frames supporting the photovoltaic
panels. A shading layer, above the structural frame, is composed of laminated

glass PV panels set at a 7-degree angle to
the steel framing, which provide shading
even as they generate energy. Below the
glazing is a series of motorized frameless
glass louvers.

Even though it has a glazed roof, the
atrium is considered an external space
under Spanish code. It contains major
circulation and escape routes, increasing
its statistical efficiency.

The Madrid summer temperatures can
reach 40°C (104°F), with low humidities.
Temperatures typically drop sharply at
night, making circulation of cool night air
an effective device. Winter heating is not a
major issue, since temperatures rarely drop
to 0°C (32°F), except during the night.

Air-conditioning is supplied to the
office floors by an under-floor dis-

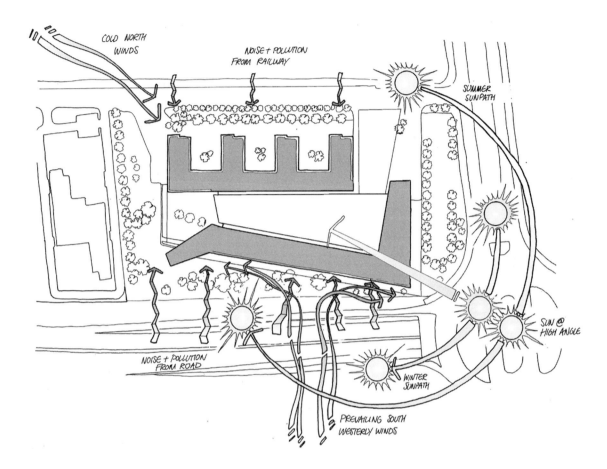

Plan diagram of Endesa headquarters, showing sun angles.

placement system with perimeter fan-coil units. A night cooling system directs outside air through the raised floor when the outdoor temperature drops below 20°C (68°F). In order to benefit from the resulting cooling of the concrete slabs, dropped ceilings had to be made 20–35 percent permeable.

To take advantage of the site's views and bring as much daylight as possible into the interior, the exterior walls have floor-to-ceiling glazing in a consistent wall design, to which a variety of shading devices are applied to suit different orientations. On the southwest side, a double façade of fritted glass protects the interior from both solar gain and the noise of the nearby highway. The company logo is integrated into the glazing, reinforcing the corporate identification of this highly visible façade. On the northeast block of offices, which is laid out with short wings in a "comb" configuration, aluminum louvers shade the walls facing southeast and northwest. Although operable windows were preferred, the hot summers and the need to minimize cooling load dictated sealed windows in the exterior walls.

CASE STUDIES

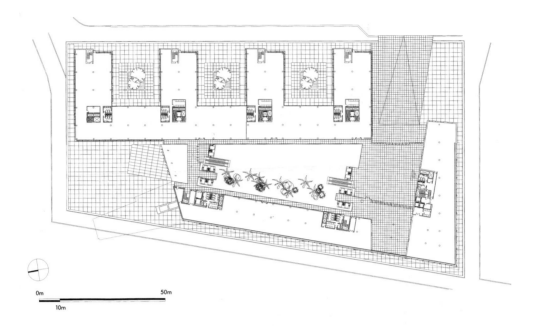

0m   50m

10m

▲ *Ground-floor plan of Endesa headquarters. Courtesy KPF.*

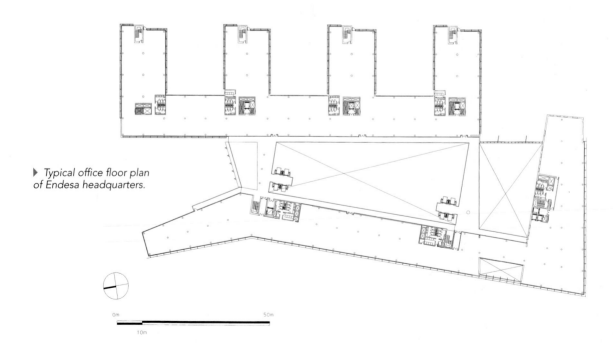

▶ *Typical office floor plan of Endesa headquarters.*

0m   50m

10m

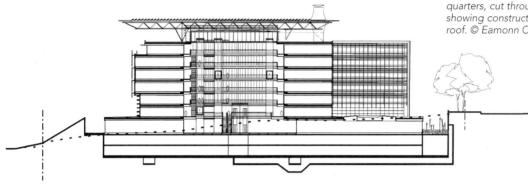

▼ *Section drawing of Endesa headquarters.*

▼▼ *Model of Endesa head-quarters, cut through atrium, showing construction of its roof. © Eamonn O'Mahony.*

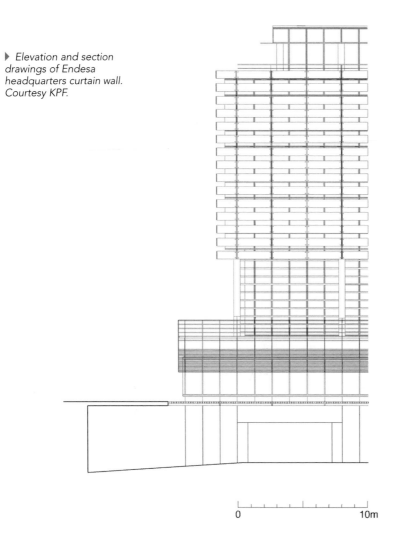
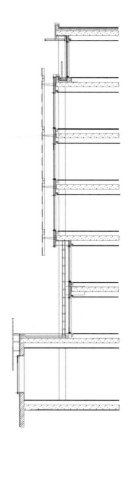

▶ Elevation and section
drawings of Endesa
headquarters curtain wall.
Courtesy KPF.

0   10m

11 CHATER ROAD

HONG KONG *Kohn Pedersen Fox Associates; LPT Architects*

FOCUS POINTS

Multitenant investment building

Prominent retail at base

Pedestrian bridge connections

Sited at the very core of Hong Kong's central district, the building will be at a nexus of elevated walks connecting ferries and the new in-city airport terminal with key office buildings, shops, and hotels. Retail-lined walkway links through the building are expected to accommodate 6,000 people per hour.

The office portion of the 50,600 sq m (546,000 sq ft) structure will rise from a three-story podium comprising: street-level retail; shops along passages at concourse (pedestrian bridge) level; restaurants on a mezzanine above concourse level. Above the 15 m (about 50 ft) height of the podium, the building is allowed to cover only 65 percent of its site; its rectangular volume is set back on three sides and hugs the sidewalk on the fourth.

Office floors are designed to appeal to the local market, particularly to trading companies. The typical 2,200 sq m (23,760 sq ft) floor plate provides a leasing depth of 13.5 m (44 ft) — unusually large for Hong Kong — that can accommodate trading floors for tenants. Floors are also configured to facilitate division among multiple tenants. To meet tenant needs for high technical performance, half of the top floor is reserved for extra cooling towers, backup generators, and "backups for backups." The other half is left unroofed to meet a Hong Kong requirement for a refuge area equal to half a floor for every 25 office floors.

Basics

Client: Hongkong Land Ltd.

Architects: Kohn Pedersen Fox Associates. Associated architect: LPT Architects

Principal consultants: Ove Arup, structural engineers; Flack & Kurtz, mechanical/electrical engineers; ALT Cladding and Design, curtain wall consultant; WTP, quantity surveyors

Building process: construction manager; fast-track; top-down construction; process monitored by client's projects department

Schedule: completion May 2002

Site: 3,448 sq m (37,240 sq ft)

Floor area: 50,600 sq m (546,000 sq ft)

Height: 28 floors plus roof; 23 floors of offices; floor-to-floor height, 4.15 m (13'7")

Occupancy: 4,200 sq m (45,360 sq ft) of retail and restaurants in three-story podium; 950 sq m (10,260 sq ft) of public passages connecting pedestrian bridges one floor above street; three levels of below-grade parking for 123 cars

Workspaces: 2,200 sq m (23,760 sq ft) floors; leasing depth 13.5 m (44 ft)

Ancillary elements: upgrading of four pedestrian bridges entering site.

Circulation: concourse-level retail-lined walkways linking four pedestrian bridges to adjoining blocks with building's vertical core; street-floor lobby

Zoning/codes: building can occupy only 65 percent of site area above 15 m high podium; local zoning measures allow floor area to edge of slab, with curtain wall up to 300 mm (1 ft) beyond, thus encouraging flush curtain wall beyond slab edge

Structural system: composite

Mechanical system: air-cooled chillers; allowance for future tenant mechanical and electrical equipment

Envelope/materials: cladding in several varieties of reflective and fritted glass, with aluminum horizontal and vertical members coated in silver, gray, and white

Interiors: office floors by tenants

International considerations: feng shui

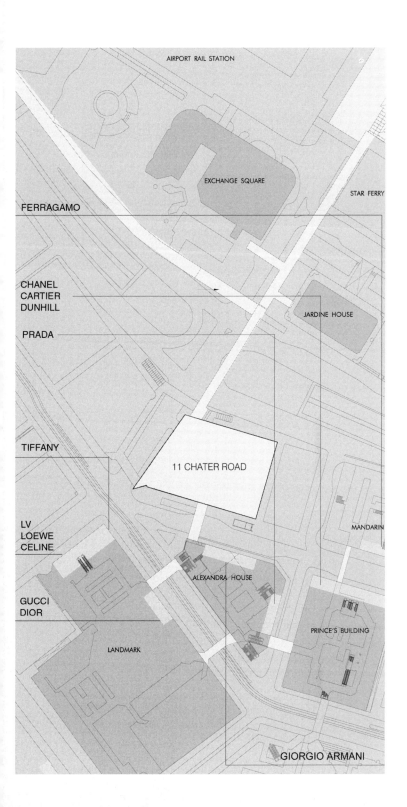

AIRPORT RAIL STATION

EXCHANGE SQUARE

STAR FERRY

FERRAGAMO

CHANEL
CARTIER
DUNHILL

JARDINE HOUSE

PRADA

TIFFANY

11 CHATER ROAD

LV
LOEWE
CELINE

MANDARIN

ALEXANDRA HOUSE

GUCCI
DIOR

PRINCE'S BUILDING

LANDMARK

GIORGIO ARMANI

◀◀ *Rendering of 11 Chater Road, showing surrounding buildings and pedestrian bridges. Courtesy KPF.*

◀ *Plan of 11 Chater Road vicinity, showing pedestrian bridges linking building to key destinations. Courtesy KPF.*

CASE STUDIES

▶ *Plan of 11 Chater Road at street level. Courtesy KPF.*

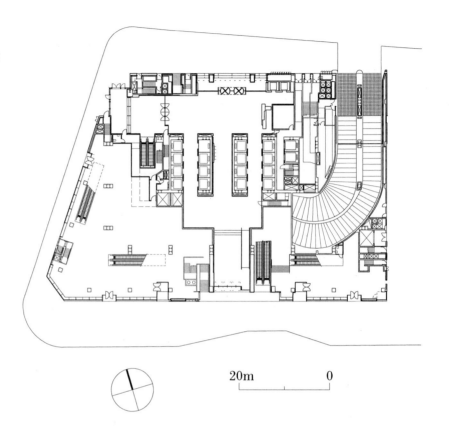

20m 0

On the exterior, the building is conservative in form, with rectangular volumes and relatively consistent cladding. Its apparent bulk is reduced by the visual separation of a corner "tower," which is an identifying element for both the building and its street intersection. The tower is distinguished from the body of the building by its curtain wall framing members, which are all white—with only certain of the white muntins continuing into the typical cladding. Glazing of occupied floors is lightly tinted, with a silver coating that minimizes reflectivity as seen from inside at night. The top portion of the tower is clad in clear glass to act as a lantern.

The greater part of the curtain wall is

designed with a "tartan" of vertical and horizontal members. Distinctions in the width, depth, and color of these members generate the tartan effect. The client required a maximum of glazing on office floors, with no eye-level obstructions. The horizontal members at window head level are ventilating elements, which can be opened to meet a code requirement for 1 percent operable openings. These eliminate the problem of window breakage and interior damage when operable windows are left unlatched in storms—with additional first cost offset by reduced repair costs later.

On the façade facing the harbor, the cladding continues consistently down to the street. On the side facing Chater

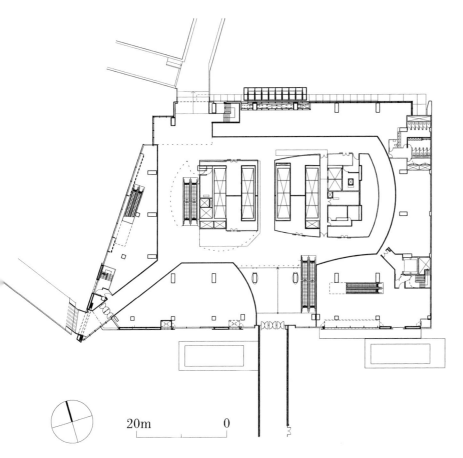

◀ *Plan of 11 Chater Road at second (pedestrian bridge) level, showing retail-lined passages.*

20m   0

Road, which is lined with high-end international shops, the lower three floors are designed for maximum retail exposure and bold identifying graphics. Retail tenants will be able to choose from a palette of cladding materials (stone, glass, metal panels) set in uniform modules. Above the street floor show windows, the structure allows for two-story-high glazed recesses for graphic display.

As part of an agreement with the city, the owner is upgrading the four pedestrian bridges that converge on the site and installing new, consistent signage. The building design team is responsible for the bridge remodeling.

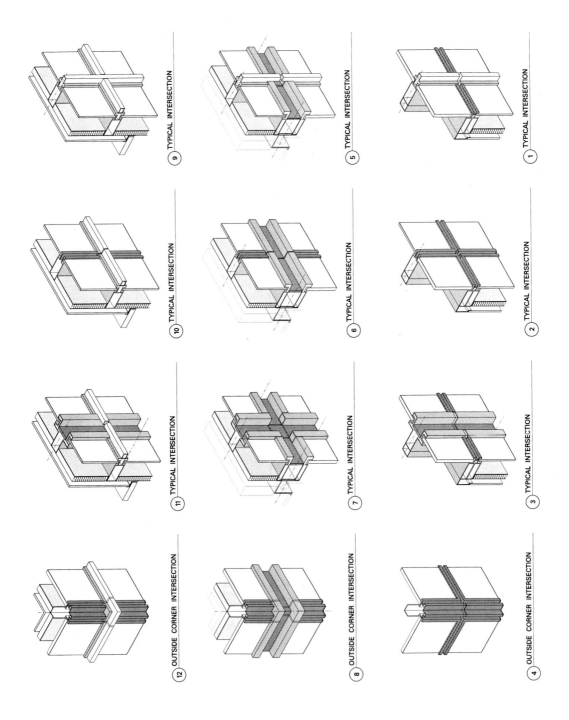

9 TYPICAL INTERSECTION

5 TYPICAL INTERSECTION

1 TYPICAL INTERSECTION

10 TYPICAL INTERSECTION

6 TYPICAL INTERSECTION

2 TYPICAL INTERSECTION

11 TYPICAL INTERSECTION

7 TYPICAL INTERSECTION

3 TYPICAL INTERSECTION

12 OUTSIDE CORNER INTERSECTION

8 OUTSIDE CORNER INTERSECTION

4 OUTSIDE CORNER INTERSECTION

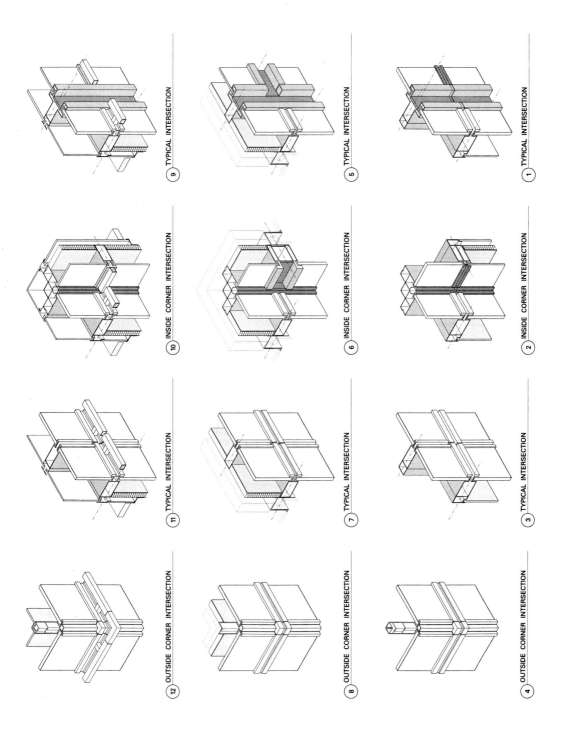

9 TYPICAL INTERSECTION

5 TYPICAL INTERSECTION

1 TYPICAL INTERSECTION

10 INSIDE CORNER INTERSECTION

6 INSIDE CORNER INTERSECTION

2 INSIDE CORNER INTERSECTION

11 TYPICAL INTERSECTION

7 TYPICAL INTERSECTION

3 TYPICAL INTERSECTION

12 OUTSIDE CORNER INTERSECTION

8 OUTSIDE CORNER INTERSECTION

4 OUTSIDE CORNER INTERSECTION

◄ Detail drawings of 11 Chater Road curtain wall.
Courtesy KPF.

249

▶ *Plan of typical office floor, 11 Chater Road. Courtesy KPF.*

20m   0

ONE RAFFLES LINK

SINGAPORE *Kohn Pedersen Fox Associates; LPT Architects Singapore Pte, Ltd.*

FOCUS POINTS

- Ability to house trading floor anywhere in building
- Seven-story height limit
- Location in prominent civic complex
- Street-level arcade required on all sides
- Extensive underground pedestrian links required

The building was shaped in many respects by its prominent location. On its own city block overlooking the historic public open space of the Padang, the War Memorial Park, and the civic landmarks surrounding them, the building required an image of exceptional dignity and restraint. Regulations imposed on the site limited the height to seven stories (to match existing buildings to north and south) and required a covered arcade at street level around the entire structure. At the same time, the new building is the linchpin in a network of climate-controlled subterranean pedestrian passages linking

▼ *West front of One Raffles Link, facing major public park. Photo © John Marshall/Wordsearch.*

▲ *East side of One Raffles Link, which includes automobile drop-off area. Photo © John Marshall/Wordsearch.*

the modern commercial structures of the marina district with the city hall subway station, plus the city's convention center, hotels, retail, and a major theater complex.

In terms of tenants, the building was conceived as a prestigious location for

high-tech financial services companies. Views of the Padang and surrounding civic structures along a 152 m (499 ft) frontage are considered major assets of the office floors. All of the office floors offer column-free spaces with a perimeter-to-core depth of 18 m (about 60 ft), suitable

Basics

Client: Hongkong Land (Singapore) Pte, Ltd.

Architects: Kohn Pedersen Fox Associates; LPT Architects Singapore Pte, Ltd.

Principal consultants: Meinhardt, m/e/p and structural; Isometrix, lighting; Kugler Tilotson, lighting; ACL, landscape, W.T. Partnership, quantity surveyors

Building process: fast-track

Schedule: completed June 2000.

Site: 8,782 sq m (2.2 acres on the Padang, the city's major open space)

Floor areas: 30,740 sq m (332,000 sq ft); typical floors, 4,425 sq m (47,800 sq ft)

Height: 7 stories

Occupancy: rental, primarily to financial services companies; parking for 132 cars in second basement

Workspaces: column-free office areas, 18 m (60 ft) perimeter to core

Circulation: ten passenger elevators; two parking elevators; two freight elevators; five escalators to first basement retail arcade and City Link mall; bridge connection to Marina Square, underground connection to convention center, theater on the bay, and city hall subway station

Zoning/codes: height limited to 40.65 m (133 ft), corresponding to that of existing buildings to north and south

Structural system: long-span steel framing for column-free office spaces

Energy/environment: special pyrolitic-coated heat-reducing glass on west façade, with deep fixed exterior sun screens

Mechanical systems: exceptionally high air-conditioning capacity to permit exceptional density of people and equipment on trading floors at all locations; backup generators to maintain operations if power fails

Envelope/materials: coated insulated glass in aluminum curtain wall; aluminum louvers; Brazilian granite colonnade at street level

Interiors: office, retail, and restaurant interiors by tenants

International concerns: large proportion of access via climate-controlled under-ground passages; feng shui considerations

for trading floors housing up to 400 traders in one space, as well as more conventional open-office and cellular office layouts. Ceiling heights can be 3 m (9'10"), including provisions for 300 mm raised floor for open areas. For cellular offices, ceilings can be dropped to 2.75 m (9'10") to match standard partition heights. The resulting exceptional floor-to-floor height of 5 m (16'5") entails little additional cost, since there are only six office floors. Occupancy by trading floors, with their exceptional population density, required raising the capacity of several systems, including elevators, rest rooms, and mechanical and electrical systems.

The building's form responds to the varied conditions around it by presenting two different faces. On the east side, facing a curved roadway and the diverse, abstract forms of the marina district, the building is fragmented, with angular volumes. The west side, facing the traditionally ordered, classical buildings on the Padang, is unified and repetitive, under a long barrel vault roof. The south and north ends reveal the split character of the design.

Cladding on the west elevation is insulated clear glass, with a high-performance coating that cuts out solar heat gain, yet allows for the greatest visible light transmission with minimal exterior reflection. This glazing is protected by a louvered sunscreen, with fixed blades calibrated to block the afternoon sun. The entire west wall rests on a colonnade of gold Brazilian granite.

The seventh floor includes some extra-height office space, rising into the vaulted roof in the western half. The eastern half houses cooling towers, screened by lattices since the roof is visible from several taller structures. The building's mechanical

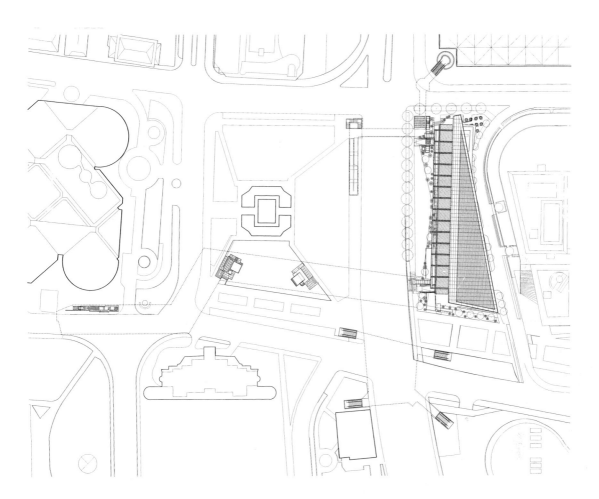

equipment includes a full complement of backup generators to sustain operations under emergency conditions.

A quarter-mile-long underground passage connects the first basement level to City Link, a 60,000 sq ft subterranean shopping mall. Designed by the architects, this link features two courts lighted by monitors rising in the War Memorial Park. Retail spaces in the building's first basement are also linked to the district-wide underground pedestrian passage network.

Influenced in part by the feng shui tradition, the building features several uses of water. One entrance is over a fishpond, a sign of good luck. The waterfall into a subterranean court represents the flow of prosperity.

▲ Map of One Raffles Link district, showing underground and elevated pedestrian links. Courtesy KPF.

◀ Portion of Singapore, with One Raffles Link in foreground. Photo © John Marshall/Wordsearch.

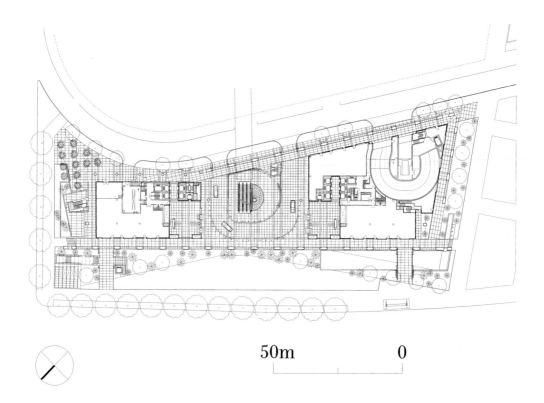

50m   0

▲ *One Raffles Link first-floor plan. Courtesy KPF.*

▶ *One Raffles Link typical floor plan.*

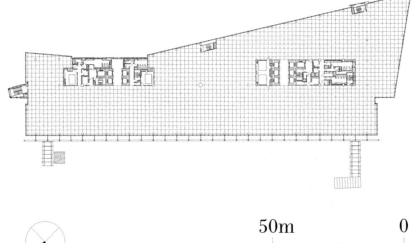

50m   0

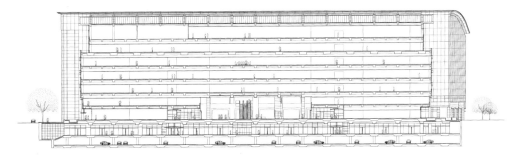

▲ One Raffles Link building section.

▼ One Raffles Link automobile entrance, carved out of street floor. Photo © John Marshall/Wordsearch.

50m   0

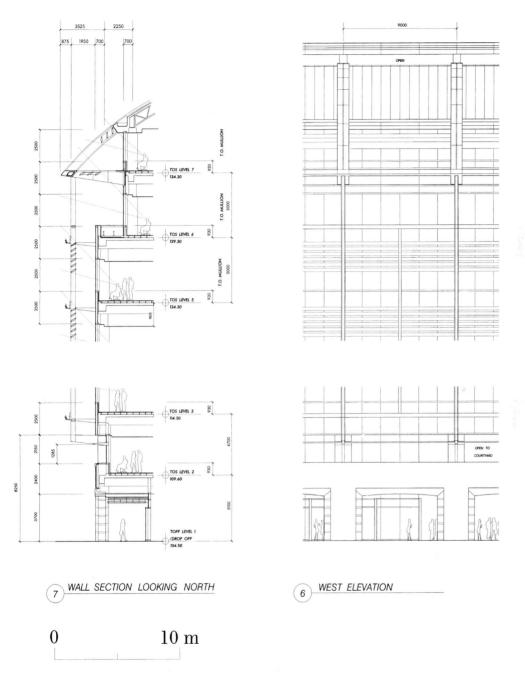

7 WALL SECTION LOOKING NORTH

6 WEST ELEVATION

0   10 m

◀ *Close-up of One Raffles Link west wall. Photo © John Marshall/Wordsearch.*

▲ *Section drawings of One Raffles Link curtain wall. Courtesy KPF.*

259

▲ Underground shopping concourse at One Raffles Link.
Photo © John Marshall/Wordsearch.

▶ Stairway up to public park from underground passage linking One Raffles Link to transit lines and other buildings. Photo © John Marshall/Wordsearch.

▲ Entry pavilion in public park for stairway
down to One Raffles Link's underground
passage. Photo © John Marshall/Wordsearch.

ERNST & YOUNG BUILDING

NEW YORK, NEW YORK *Kohn Pedersen Fox Associates*

FOCUS POINTS

Exterior controlled under special zoning

Required display signage

Prominent street-floor retail

Office floors designed to accommodate "hoteling"

You can't build a sedate office building around Times Square. This building at the key intersection of 42nd Street and Seventh Avenue, under the auspices of the Times Square Subdistrict and the 42nd Street Redevelopment Authority, had to meet the design standards of these public agencies and was subject to review to ensure a generous amount of brightly lit signage to achieve dynamic building volumes, built to look as if they were coalescing or flying apart. Other ground rules for this site included provisions for prominent street-level retail and a high-capacity subway entrance recessed into the building volume (for a station also being designed by KPF).

The challenge for the designers, who won the commission through a design competition, was reconciling the developer's intention to lease the building to a major company with the local requirement for architectural pizzazz. The building was designed during the leasing process and continued after a tenant signed on. It involved constant negotiation with the reviewing authorities. The architects had to balance the tenant's need for a unified exterior appearance against the fragmented, unstable imagery adopted for the district. The result is a composition of angular forms, echoing the geometry of the streets as Broadway crosses the Manhattan grid, unified by consistency in color and detail.

All of the curtain wall glazing is the same color and type, with different degrees of reflectivity. There are metal spandrels and four-inch fins for texture. The variety and reflective quality of the surface added just

Basics

Client: Boston Properties

Architects: Kohn Pedersen Fox Associates

Principal consultants: Thornton-Tomasetti Engineers, structural engineers; Vollmer Associates, site civil/subway consultants; Jaros Baum & Bolles, m/e/p engineers; Jenkins & Huntington, vertical transportation; Gordon H. Smith Corp., curtain wall consultant; Van Wagner, signage consultant; Gensler, tenant architect; Morse Diesel, general contractor

Building process: competitive bidding, general contractor

Schedule: commissioned 1999, to be completed spring 2002

Site: one-acre site at prominent corner of 42nd St. and Seventh Ave.

Floor areas: 950,000 GSF

Height: 38 stories

Occupancy: corporate office building

Workspaces: major portions operated on "hoteling" basis, with staff assigned daily, rather than having own offices (resulting in greater typical floor population)

Circulation: 14 elevators; computer-controlled elevator system, assigning

people entering lobby to elevators and increasing effective elevator capacity

Zoning/codes: controlled by special zoning for Times Square subdistrict and by design regulations of 42nd Street Redevelopment Authority – both promoting angular building forms and extensive lighted signs

Structural system: steel hybrid structure; moment frame

Mechanical systems: rooftop cooling towers; floor-to-floor DX units

Envelope/materials: windows and spandrels all of same tinted glass, with varying degrees of reflectivity

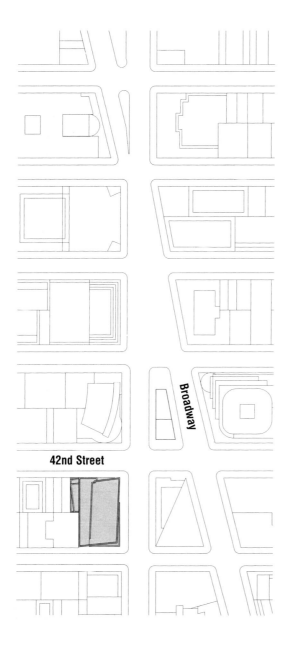

Broadway

42nd Street

◀ *Plan showing location of Ernst & Young in Times Square. Courtesy KPF.*

◀◀ *Ernst & Young Building. © KPF.*

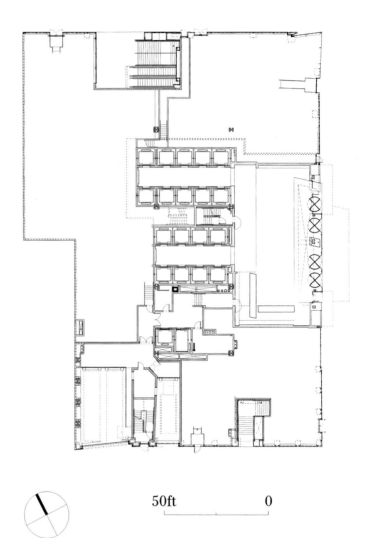

▶ Ground-floor plan,
Ernst & Young Building.
Courtesy KPF.

50ft   0

enough interest to win reviewers' approval, yet left the building consistent and discrete enough to look businesslike.

The tower's irregular shape incorporates varying floor plates as it rises. A portion of almost every floor departs from the rectangular, modular layout.

Signage was a complex issue. The authorities wanted the tenant identified with a sign and corporate logo silhouetted against the sky, but agreed to a large, subtly colored sign running down the façade. To meet the requirement of signs extending to the seventh floor, the architects provided a series of small ones—all within the dimensions of the spandrels— in a vertical line up the 42nd Street façade. The resulting design

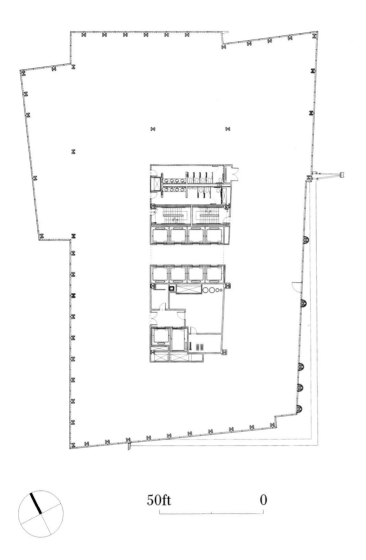

50ft   0

◀ Plan of typical floor
in lower portion of
Ernst & Young Building.

satisfied both sides—apparently—since it won the approval of the district reviewers and was leased to Ernst & Young, one of America's "big five" accounting firms, known for its sobriety and stability.

The building is one of the first to be designed for "hoteling." Many of the projected 4,000 or more employees will be assigned workstations on a day-to-day basis, rather than having permanent places.

With hoteling, the percentage of occupancy can rise from a typical 80 percent of staff to 90 percent. The capacity of the building's elevators, air-conditioning, rest rooms, and other facilities correlated with office population must accommodate that change.

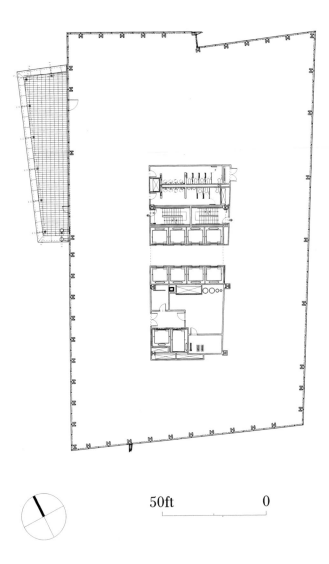

▶ Plan of typical floor in upper portion of Ernst & Young Building. Courtesy KPF.

50ft   0

One measure taken to deal with greater occupancy is the use of Miconic elevatoring (a proprietary system by Schindler) to increase elevator capacity without increasing the number of actual elevators. With this system, the person chooses a floor from a panel near the building entrance door and is directed to an elevator, which has no floor buttons inside the cab. Computer systems assign people to elevators to minimize the number of stops any one will make, and the passengers' perceived waiting time in the lobby is reduced, since much of it is spent walking to the designated elevator. (See chapter on vertical transportation.)

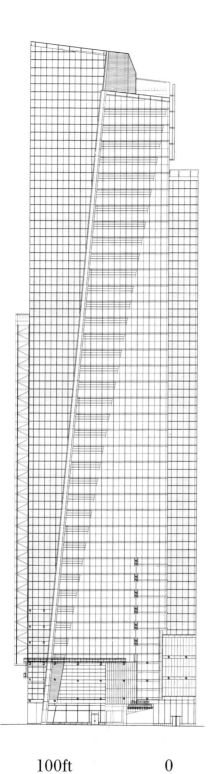

◀ *North elevation of Ernst & Young Building.*

100ft   0

CASE STUDIES

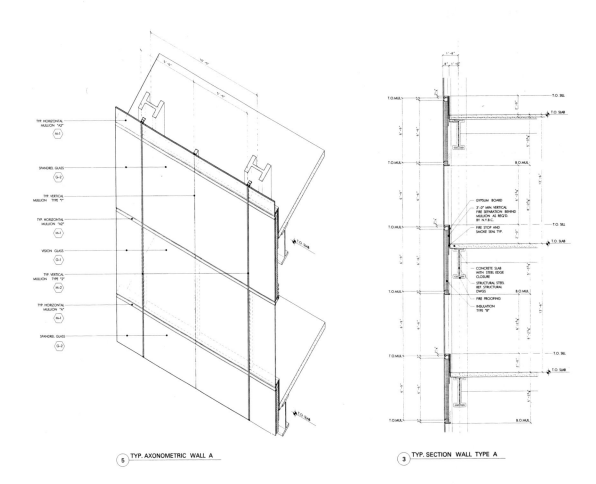

TYP. HORIZONTAL
MULLION "A2"
M-1

SPANDREL GLASS
G-2

TYP. VERTICAL
MULLION TYPE "1"

TYP. HORIZONTAL
MULLION "A2"
M-1

VISION GLASS
G-1

TYP. VERTICAL
MULLION TYPE "2"
M-2

TYP. HORIZONTAL
MULLION "A"
M-1

SPANDREL GLASS
G-2

T.O. SLAB

T.O. SLAB

5 TYP. AXONOMETRIC WALL A

T.O. MUL.

T.O. MUL.

T.O. MUL.

T.O. MUL.

T.O. MUL.

B.O. MUL.

B.O. MUL.

B.O. MUL.

T.O. SILL
T.O. SLAB

T.O. SILL
T.O. SLAB

T.O. SILL
T.O. SLAB

GYPSUM BOARD
3'-0" MIN. VERTICAL
FIRE SEPARATION BEHIND
MULLION AS REQ'D.
BY N.Y.B.C.

FIRE STOP AND
SMOKE SEAL TYP.

CONCRETE SLAB
WITH STEEL EDGE
CLOSURE

STRUCTURAL STEEL
REF. STRUCTURAL
DWGS

FIRE PROOFING

INSULATION
TYPE "B"

3 TYP. SECTION WALL TYPE A

▲ *Details of Ernst & Young
Building curtain walls.
Courtesy KPF.*

ESPIRITO SANTO PLAZA

MIAMI, FLORIDA *Kohn Pedersen Fox Associates; Plunkett & Associates*

FOCUS POINTS

Mixed office/condominium/hotel use

Atrium

Flood protection measures

The mix of uses in this project underwent a change while it was in design. When the architects won a three-firm, invited design competition for a new tower to house the headquarters for Banco Espirito Santo of Portugal (on a site partly occupied by its earlier offices), the owners included a mix of uses in the project to earn a floor-area-ratio bonus.

Initially, the mix was to include 20,000 sq ft of retail space, 330,000 sq ft of offices, and 85,000 sq ft of condominiums, intended for sale mainly to foreign buyers who could occupy the units while in Miami and put them into rental pools for the rest of the year. In 1999, however, the client made an agreement with a hotel group looking for a prime Miami location. The final scheme calls for seven floors of hotel above 14 floors of offices. Above that will be 11 floors of condominiums, to be managed by the hotel operators. Roughly half the condominium units will serve as the hotel's executive guest rooms.

Entry to both hotel and condominium units will be via an expansive 25th-floor lobby, with a broad view toward Biscayne

Basics

Client: Estoril Inc.

Development manager: Euroatlantic Development, Inc.

Architects: Kohn Pedersen Fox Associates (design architects); Plunkett & Associates (client architects)

Principal consultants: Architectural Alliance, landscape/land planning; Leslie Robertson Associates, structural engineering; Flack & Kurtz, MEP engineering; R.A. Heintges, curtain wall consultant; Van Deusen & Associates, vertical circulation consultant

Building process: competitive bidding and general contractor; construction oversight provided by CM hired independently by owner

Schedule: commission awarded by design competition, 1998; construction began 2000; completion, spring 2003

Site: 138,500 GSF, flat, fronting on Brickell Avenue, major thoroughfare

Floor area: 610,000 GSF; 65,000 sq ft bank; 200,000 sq ft office; 10,000 sq ft retail; 140,000 sq ft residential (144 condominiums); 195,000 sq ft hotel (including 200 guest units, meeting rooms, and ballroom); 1000-car parking garage (not included in 610,000 GSF)

Height: 37 stories (35 occupied); about 492 ft; parking garage, 12 levels

Occupancy: bank headquarters and banking hall; commercial office space; hotel; condominiums managed for rental by hotel

Workspaces: floor areas 30 or more ft deep around central core; fit-out by tenants

Circulation: escalators from street floor to first floor office elevator lobby; six elevators for 14 office floors; three shuttle elevators from street floor to sky lobby; three additional elevators serving upper 18 floors

Zoning/codes: floor area ratio increased from 3.25 to 4.25 as bonus for including mix of uses; FEMA rules (see Energy and Envelope listings below)

Structural system: conventional reinforced concrete frame with post-tensioned floor slabs
Energy/environment: Under FEMA code for area subject to flooding, wave trip wall to east, permitting use of street floor if constructed to hold back 6 ft of standing water

Mechanical system: centrally provided chilled water feeds fan rooms on office floors and overhead fan units in the hotel and residential units

Envelope/materials: curtain wall with horizontal mullions at 3'4" intervals; storm codes requiring walls to remain watertight after being struck by debris (type varying with height above ground) at 35 mph

Interiors: By occupants

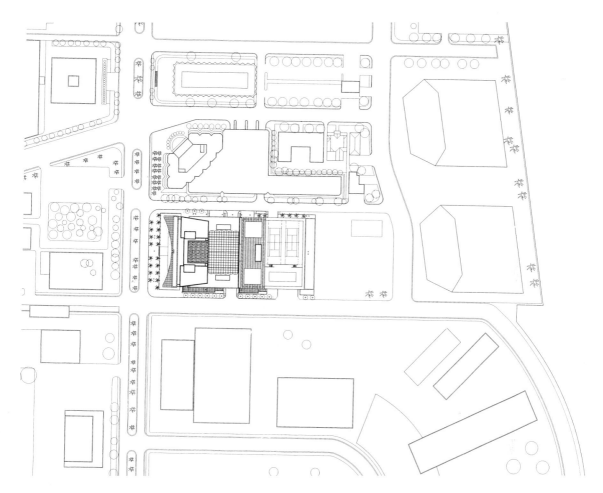

Bay, which will be the base of a ten-story
atrium. Guests staying in the regular hotel
rooms will take elevators down from the
atrium/lobby level to their rooms.

Bay, which will be the base of a ten-story
atrium. Guests staying in the regular hotel
rooms will take elevators down from the
atrium/lobby level to their rooms.

The 37-story tower, flanked by 27- and
14-story structures along Brickell Avenue,
was placed forward to maximize its
presence. The concave curve cut into the
slightly sloping front wall provides a
welcoming forecourt at street level, with a
symbolic arch above connoting both
stability and entry. The geometry of the
front—simpler than it looks—is
generated by the intersection of a vertical
cylinder with a slanted plane.

From outside, the tower was meant to
present a unified image, despite the very
different requirements of office and hotel
portions in terms of floor-to-floor height
and core-to-exterior-wall dimension.
These conflicting demands were rec-
onciled by adopting a 3'4" vertical
module for the exterior walls, equally
applicable to 10'0" floor heights for
residential uses and 13'4" heights for
office floors. On the hotel floors, the
dimensions of the tower are appropriate
for hotel rooms, and on the condo-
minium/executive unit floors, wrapping

(continued on page 277)

▲ *Plan of area showing
location of Espirito Santo
Plaza. Courtesy KPF.*

◀ *View of Espirito Santo
Plaza looking south along
Miami's Biscayne Boulevard.
© KPF.*

273

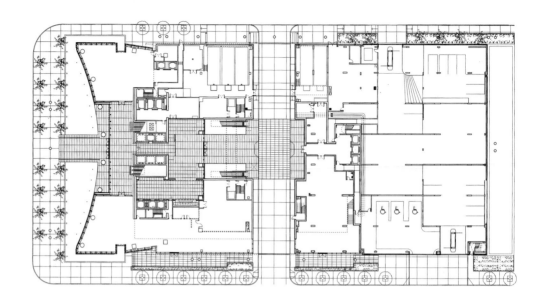

100ft.   0

▲ Street-level plan of   ▼ Second-floor plan of
Espirito Santo Plaza.   Espirito Santo Plaza.
Courtesy KPF.

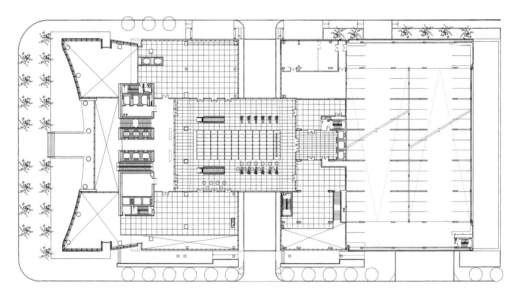

100ft.   0

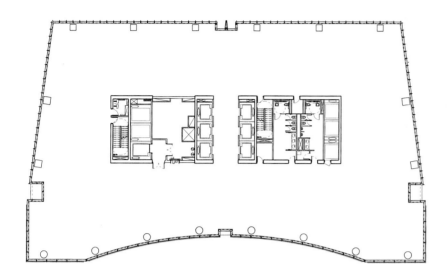

◀ *Typical office floor plan of Espirito Santo Plaza.*

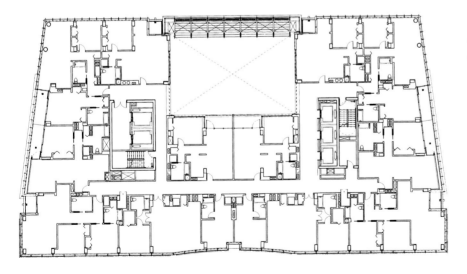

◀ *Typical apartment floor plan of Espirito Santo Plaza.*

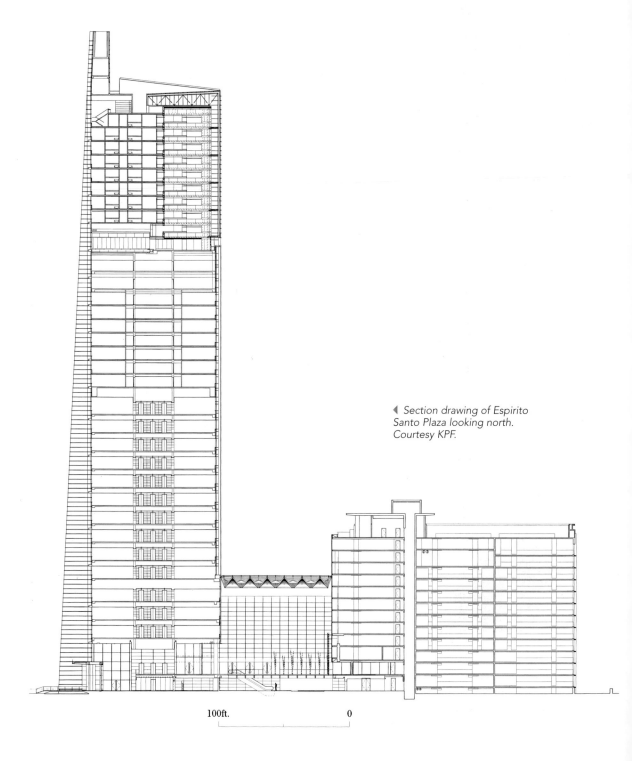

◀ *Section drawing of Espirito Santo Plaza looking north. Courtesy KPF.*

100ft.   0

◀ *Rendering of hotel/ apartment atrium rising from 25th floor of Espirito Santo Plaza. © Vladislav Yeliseyev.*

(continued from page 273)
the suites around three sides of the atrium provides a good ratio of perimeter, with some units having views across the atrium toward the bay.

Choosing a consistent glazing for the entire tower also required reconciling different needs. Most high-performance glass used for offices would be too reflective for residential or hotel interiors at night. The low-e glass that was selected has a lower reflectivity seen from the

▲ Second-level east entry to Espirito Santo Plaza from parking garage. © KPF.

interior than from the exterior, permitting residents and guests to view the moon over Miami from a lighted interior, while still providing enough reflectivity to mask the varying interior conditions from the exterior. Balconies provided for most condominium units (expected in this market) are variously tucked into notches or masked by vertical mullions, except for a few boldly recessed ones on upper floors.

The main pedestrian entry from Brickell Avenue is an axial bridge over a reflecting pool. Acknowledging that most building users will approach from the automobile court or parking garage to the east, the approach here is also along the main axis, through a two-level symmetrical courtyard lined with shops. Entrances from the courtyard are on two levels, with the hotel/residential entrance on the street floor and the office entrance on the first floor (one story above). The roof of the

11-story parking garage serves as the hotel garden, with health club, tennis courts, and swimming pool, all connected by a dedicated bridge to the hotel elevators.

Because of its low elevation (9'0" above sea level) and its proximity to Biscayne Bay, the site was subjected to Federal Emergency Management Administration (FEMA) flood codes. To allow for street-level lobby, banking hall, and retail uses—desired by the city—a wave

trip wall had to be built at the eastern edge of the site. With the wall reducing wave action, public and retail areas at the building's base must be designed to hold back 6'0" of standing water—in effect making the street floor a reverse fish tank under flood conditions.

Aside from flood control requirements, the project was subject to review by all 17 of the city's agencies, plus a public review process.

▲ *Main (west) entry to Espirito Santo Plaza from Biscayne Boulevard. © KPF.*

CASE STUDIES

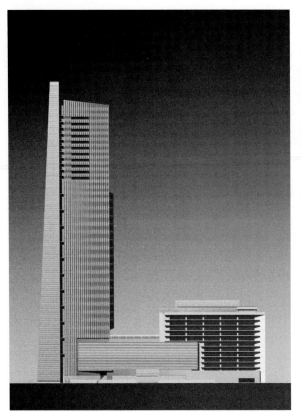

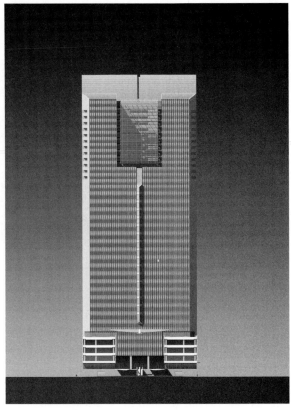

▲ South elevation of
Espirito Santo Plaza. © KPF.

◥ East elevation of Espirito
Santo Plaza. © KPF.

▶ Elevation of Espirito
Santo Plaza curtain wall
for residential floors.
Courtesy KPF.

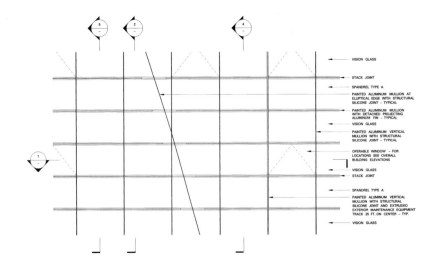

③ PARTIAL ELEVATION AT WALL TYPE A – TYPICAL RESIDENTIAL FLOOR

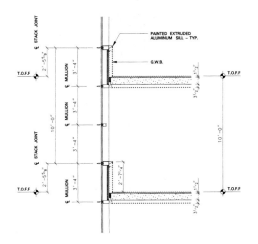

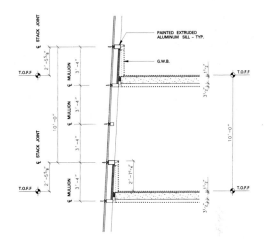

PARTIAL SECTION THROUGH
WALL TYPE A – TYPICAL RESIDENTIAL FLOOR
5

PARTIAL SECTION THROUGH
WALL TYPE A – TYPICAL RESIDENTIAL FLOOR
4

▲ *Section drawing of Espirito Santo Plaza curtain walls for residential floors.*

◀ *Elevation of Espirito Santo Plaza curtain wall for office floors.*

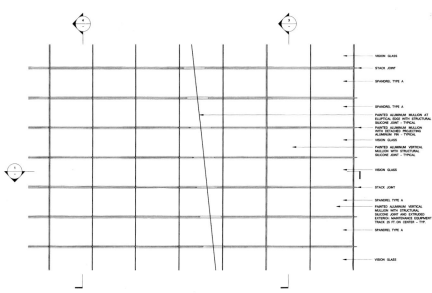

PARTIAL ELEVATION AT WALL TYPE A – TYPICAL OFFICE FLOOR
2

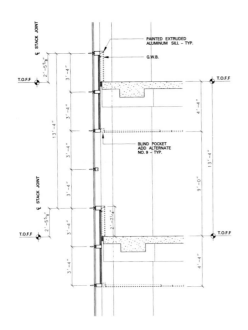

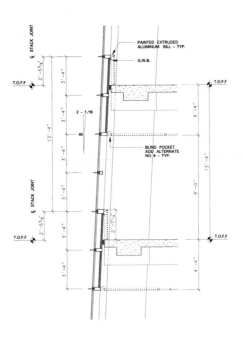

PARTIAL SECTION THROUGH
(4) WALL TYPE A – TYPICAL OFFICE FLOOR

PARTIAL SECTION THROUGH
(3) WALL TYPE A – TYPICAL OFFICE FLOOR

▲ *Section drawing of*
Espirito Santo Plaza curtain
walls for office floors.
Courtesy KPF.

BIBLIOGRAPHY

Albrecht, Donald, and Chrysanthe B. Broikos, eds. 2000. *On the Job: Design and the American Office.* New York: Princeton Architectural Press and National Building Museum.

Antonelli, Paola, ed. 2002. *Workspheres: Design and Contemporary Work Styles.* New York: Museum of Modern Art.

Becker, Franklin, K. L. Quinn, A. J. Rappaport, and W. Sims. 1994. *Implementing Innovative Workplaces: Organizational Implications of Different Strategies.* Ithaca, N.Y.: Cornell University International Workplace Studies Program.

Becker, Franklin, and W. Sims. 2000. *Managing Uncertainty: Integrated Portfolio Strategies for Dynamic Organizations.* Ithaca, N.Y.: Cornell University International Workplace Studies Program.

Becker, Franklin, and F. Steele. 1995. *Workplace by Design: Mapping the High-Performance Workscape.* New York: John Wiley & Sons/Jossey-Bass.

Becker, Franklin, and C. M. Tennessen. 1995. *The Hotel as Office.* Ithaca, N.Y.: Cornell University International Workplace Studies Program.

Beinhocker, E.D. 1999. "Robust Adaptive Strategies." *Sloan Management Review* 40 (no. 3): 95–106.

Betsky, A. 1993. "Under the Big Top." *Architectural Record*, March, pp. 94–100.

Champy, J. 1998. "Goodbye, Info Age; Hello, Age of Logistics." *Computer World* 32 (no. 34): 54.

Dove, R. 1999. "Agility = Knowledge Management + Response Ability." *Automotive Manufacturing and Production* 111 (no. 3): 16–20.

Duffy, Francis. 1997. *The New Office.* London: Conran Octopus.

Eisenhardt, K.M., and J.C. Brown. 1998. "Time Pacing: Competing in Markets That Won't Stand Still." *Harvard Business Review* 76 (no. 2): 59–69.

Eley, Joanna, and Alexi Marmot. 1995. *Understanding Offices: What Every Manager Needs to Know About Office Buildings.* New York: Penguin.

Fradette, M., and S. Michaud. 1998. *The Power of Corporate Kinetics.* New York: Simon and Schuster.

Hartkopf, Volker, et al. 1993. *Designing the Office of the Future.* New York: John Wiley & Sons.

Laing, Andrew, Francis Duffy, Denice Jaunzens, and Stephen Willis. 1998. *New Environments for Working: The Redesign of Offices and Environmental Systems for New Ways of Working.* London: Building Research Establishment, Ltd., and DEGW.

Lewis, Michael D. 1995. *Modern Stone Cladding.* Philadelphia: American Society for Testing and Materials, ASTM Manual 210.

Marmot, Alexi, and Joanne Eley. 2000. *Office Space Planning: Design for Tomorrow's Workplace.* New York: McGraw-Hill.

Mitchell, William J. 1995. *City Bits: Space Place and the Infobahn.* Cambridge, Mass.: MIT Press.

Munro, N. 1998. "The New Deal." *National Journal,* November 21, p. 27.

Pevsner, Nikolaus. 1976. *A History of Building Types.* Princeton, N.J.: Princeton University Press.

Sassen, Saskia. 1992. *Global City.* Princeton, N.J.: Princeton University Press.

Willis, Carol. 1995. *Form Follows Finance: Skyscrapers and Skylines in New York and Chicago.* New York: Princeton Architectural Press.

Worthington, J., ed. 1997. *Reinventing the Workplace.* York, U. K.: Oxford and Institute of Advanced Studies, University of York.

REFERENCES AND STANDARDS

The following standards govern the design and fabrication of curtain walls and their components.

AAMA Standards in Full. AAMA provides four bound volumes including specifications, test descriptions of curtain walls, glass and windows, storefronts, hardware, finishes, fasteners, and so forth. This resource covers most of the aluminum-associated products, from testing to methods of application to specification.

ASTM Standards. ASTM standards issues a large number of reference books for industry. For building construction, however, ASTM issues four volumes of condensed standards, specifically geared to the subject.

AISC Manual of Steel Construction Allowable Steel Design. American Institute of Steel Construction.

FGMA Glazing Manual. Flat Glass Marketing Association. There are also a number of other organizations that issue glass standards and manuals:

- SSPC Steel Structures Painting Council
- IGCC Insulation Glass Certification Council
- GANA Glass Association of North America

Aluminum Design Manual of the Aluminum Association.

NAAMM Metal Finishes Manual. National Association of Architectural Metal Manufacturers. For recommendations on applying and designating finishes.

Architects' Guide to Stainless Steel. Steel Construction Institute, Silkwood Park, Ascot, U. K.

Stone organizations issuing standards and manuals:

- National Building Granite Quarries Association, Inc.
- Marble Institute of America

INDEX

BUILDING TYPE BASICS FOR OFFICE BUILDINGS:

1. Program (predesign)
What are the principal programming requirements (space types and areas)?
Any special regulatory or jurisdictional concerns?
3, 15–17, 29–31, 47, 52–53, 64–66, 114–15, 125–29

2. Project process and management
What are the key components of the design and construction process?
Who is to be included on the project team?
42, 58–59, 62–63, 189

3. Unique design concerns
What distinctive design determinants must be met? Any special circulation
requirements?
41, 43, 73, 96, 188, 190–93, 204, 225–27, 235, 237–39, 245–47, 255, 257, 262, 273

4. Site planning/parking/landscaping
What considerations determine external access and parking? Landscaping?
3–4, 6, 11–14, 18–19, 23–28, 32–40, 42, 49–50, 52–53, 57, 60–61, 67–71, 77–78,
96–97, 114–15, 125–29, 139–58, 159–67, 185–87, 192–94, 200–203, 209–24, 225–30,
233, 235–38, 240–62, 271–82

5. Codes/ADA/security
Which building codes and regulations apply, and what are the main applicable provisions?
(Examples: egress; electrical; plumbing; ADA; seismic; asbestos; terrorism and other
hazards)
41, 157–58, 169–81

6. Energy/environmental challenges
What techniques in service of energy conservation and environmental sustainability
can be employed?
48–49, 75–76, 117–19

7. Structure system
What classes of structural systems are appropriate?
36–37, 39–40, 45, 71, 83–101, 162–64, 172, 178–80, 199, 230, 233

8. Mechanical systems
What are appropriate systems for heating, ventilating, and air-conditioning (hvac) and
plumbing? Vertical transportation? Fire and smoke protection? What factors affect
preliminary selection?
38, 44, 71–72, 103–20, 169, 175–76, 195–97

9. Electrical/communications
What are appropriate systems for electrical service and voice and data communications?
What factors affect preliminary selection?
46–47, 65, 72–73, 103–20, 197–98

CALLISON
LONDON RESEARCH CENTER
T 44-0-203-008-4985   www.callison.com